MW01092263

Fingerprintz

*One Woman's Journey
Through Loss, Love,
and Very Little Babies*

Lisa Printz Roday

GREEN HEART
LIVING
—PRESS—

Copyright @ 2024 by Lisa Printz Roday

All rights reserved. No part of this book may be used or reproduced by any means, graphic, electronic, or mechanical, including photocopying, recording, taping, or by any information storage retrieval system without the written permission of the publisher, except in the case of brief quotations embodied in critical articles and reviews.

ISBN Paperback: 978-1-954493-76-6

ISBN Hardcover: 978-1-954493-77-3

Published by Green Heart Living Press

Cover Photo iStock™ by Manonallard

Cover Design by Karen Viola

Author Photo by All About Presentation

This is a work of creative nonfiction. The events are portrayed to the best of the author's memory. While all the stories in this book are true, some names and identifying details have been changed to protect the privacy of the people involved.

"Candy's Room"

Words and Music by Bruce Springsteen

Copyright © 1978 Sony Music Publishing (US) LLC and Eldridge Publishing Co.

Copyright Renewed

All Rights Administered by Sony Music Publishing (US) LLC, 424 Church Street, Suite 1200, Nashville, TN 37219

International Copyright Secured All Rights Reserved

Reprinted by Permission of Hal Leonard LLC

Contents

"You can't always get what you want.
You can't always get what you want.
You can't always get what you want.
But if you try sometimes, well,
you just might find,
you get what you need."

"You Can't Always Get What You Want"
Words and Music by Mick Jagger and Keith Richards
© *1969 Copyright Renewed*

Author's Note

I know better than to claim that this book is "true." It is as true as I can make it, with as much honesty and context as I can provide, with heartbreak, failure, guilt, perspective, and reflected wisdom shaping my recollections. I also know how lucky I am to have the advantages that education, access, and financial resources provided to me and how those advantages shaped my experiences and my telling of them. While people and events will be familiar to some readers, I have elected to share these recollections in all their messiness, resorting to pseudonyms only to protect someone who would otherwise be embarrassed, disowned, fired, divorced, arrested, or murdered. Even then, every word here is inextricably intertwined with the facts as I recall them.

Of this I am certain: knowing despair gave me my appreciation for hope, experiencing failure enabled me to relish the fullest joy of success, living through tragedy helped me develop grit, and being broken forced me to summon the strength and determination to fix myself. I continue to marvel that in every way that matters, the worst thing that ever happened to me paved my way too.

The combination of heartbreaks that litter my path may be uniquely mine, but I don't claim to have cornered the market. We all face adversity. Wherever you are on your journey, I hope that reading about my challenges will help you more easily shoulder yours. At the very least, I hope to reach back and give you a hand as we both try to climb up.

Prologue
DEATH 101

The first rule of grieving: there are no rules.

My forty-seven-year-old father, so alive, suddenly became very dead, beneath my interlocked and pumping hands, under my frantic lips, in front of my disbelieving eyes. His untimely loss turned out to be painful but necessary preparation for the messiness that happened to me later.

As distressing as it is for me to remember the details, I fear the anguish this retelling will cause those nearest to me when they read it. Unspooling these particulars feels necessary. It also feels like the gratuitous violence of a Quentin Tarantino movie. The "plot" advances without them, but dear friend, you would miss what is crucial in their absence.

Forty-five years doesn't provide an emotional buffer. If anything, the drama unfolds so clearly that I recoil from the keyboard. As the grim details collide to be first to make the journey from my deep brain to my consciousness to my fingers, my fingertips jump in surprise, each letter scalding my flesh.

The collage of colors, smells, and sounds, the rush of adrenaline, and the hyperawareness and superhuman strength of that night come elbowing out, jockeying for position on the page.

And none of it matters, really.

Because at the end of this barrage, Dad will still die and I will still fail to save him.

Yet it did matter. My crash course in premature death changed everything. And when forced to confront premature birth, the first rule was already part of my DNA. There are no rules.

BOOK ONE
LOVE AND DEATH

1

A Beginning

November 29, 1979

The headlamps of the #2 train came into view as it rounded the last curve heading into the Borough Hall subway station. The rain above ground enveloped the subterranean platform with a chilling dampness. The wind that presaged the arrival of the train took hold of my dirty blonde hair and sent a lock flying into the eye of my handsome companion.

Six foot one to my five foot six, the Rogue Prince stood close, his mustached face bending toward me, his usually blue eyes now tinted green, matching the hue of his velour sweater. Even in the dingy light, his flaxen hair shone with flecks of sun-bleached gold.

Flirting for weeks across the lecture halls we shared as first-year law students at Brooklyn Law School, today we continued our post-class conversation out of the building, bisecting the broad, rain-slicked brick plaza, and down the steep stairs to the subway.

Surely he will leave me here, I thought, never expecting him to pull out a subway token and pass through the turnstile beside me. Months later, reflecting on that afternoon, it seemed safe to assume he must have been on his way somewhere else—to meet *someone* else.

But that day, as I was standing with him on the cold platform, the destiny the dean had foretold on the first day of law school leapt to mind. In a cornball request, Dean Glasser had first asked us to look left and right, then prophesized that we were gazing into the faces of future lifelong friends, and for some, into the faces of our future spouses.

Too much for the cynics in the audience—which turned out to be most of us—the comment met with a boisterous collective groan. Yet, as I looked to my right, the Rogue Prince caught my eye for the first time, his hair shining in the brightly lit auditorium. Maybe not love at first sight, but lust, for sure. And something else. A perceptible flutter hinted at more.

The suggestive looks began almost at once. The provocative comments soon followed. Months of a prolonged and, so far, chaste seduction brought us to the subway platform that afternoon.

He leaned in, wiped my stray lock of hair away from his face, and kissed me. It felt electric. The wind of the arriving train mixed with the thrumming in my ears generated a cacophony of sound.

His body pinned against mine, his taste like chocolate and almonds and raspberries, his words barely registered when he put his lips to my ear and shouted over the noise, "C'mon. You'll miss your train." With a swat on my butt, the Rogue Prince pushed me through the closing train doors.

My usually monotonous commute from Brooklyn flew by, the surprising desire that kiss unleashed distracting me from the panhandlers on the subway, the gin rummy players on the Long Island Railroad, and the Contracts Law casebook dutifully removed from my backpack at Atlantic Avenue. As the Far Rockaway line wended its way to my stop in Cedarhurst, I was staring out the window at the red-and-white crossing gates and the waiting cars at the station, then at the ever-increasing blur of shapes and colors as the train accelerated toward the next station.

The scene returned to focus as the train slowed again. When it finally pulled into Cedarhurst, I repacked the untouched casebook in my backpack, reliving in my mind those breathtaking few minutes on the Borough Hall subway platform.

As I was stepping off the train, the sight of the white Lincoln Continental, driver's side window opened a crack to keep the chill of the November night at bay, made me smile. The plume of cigarette smoke drifting out signaled that my father was waiting for me behind the wheel.

In the damp and misty thirty-yard walk from the train to the warm front seat of Dad's car, keeping the Rogue Prince to myself for the moment seemed like the right choice.

Dad, usually my Confidant in Chief, greeted me with an arm hug around my shoulders, glowing Kent 100 hanging from his lips. He pulled me closer to him across the hunter green Corinthian leather front seat, as close as the seat belt would allow, and started peppering me with questions, as he did every day. He nosed the car out of the packed parking lot, passing commuters, their collars up against the cold as they were criss-crossing the asphalt to waiting cars.

He asked about my day, what my study group was working on, how things were coming at the law school newspaper ... and made me momentarily regret keeping a secret from him.

He wore tennis whites, already dressed for his regular Thursday night game.

"You didn't need to pick me up, Dad. I would have walked home," I said as he pulled into our driveway. He reached for the pack beside him and lit a new cigarette with the dying embers of the one still in his mouth.

"I wasn't sure you'd still be up when I got back from tennis. Gotta stay up to date on all the latest news from my star law school student," he said, grinning ear to ear. At that last bit, the only actual *news* nearly slipped out. He leaned over to kiss the top of my head and said, "Run on in. Mom has dinner waiting for you. I'll come say good night later if I see your light on."

When Dad got home, I smelled the cigarette smoke wafting up the stairs an instant before I heard his footsteps. He was jubilant, but exhausted. His opponent hadn't won a single game in their match, he reported with satisfaction.

Although drowning in contracts law, and still a bit distracted by the lustful subway kiss, I was grateful when Dad rewarded my quick glance at him with the flash of his gap-toothed smile before he pulled my bedroom door partway shut.

2

An End

November 30, 1979

The flushing toilet wakes me from a light sleep. Contracts I kicked my butt all fall, and staying up late to try to understand an ancient case about the acceptance of an offer hadn't been helpful.

Squinting at the bedside clock, I see 2:00 a.m. peer back at me. There's light under my door—too dull to be the hall light right outside my door, too bright to be my brother's light on the other side of the hallway. No, this light comes from my parents' bedroom next door to mine.

I pull myself out of bed and cross the few yards to the next bedroom. My eyes land on my mother.

Visibly agitated, she is fidgeting beside her night table. The telephone sits atop a pile of *Architectural Digest* magazines. My father lies propped up on several pillows, shirtless, his face flushed, his thin lips set in a straight line, thinning hair askew. When he sees me, he smiles and waves me over. At twenty-one, crawling up under his left arm and laying my head on his shoulder feels natural. We've rested like this thousands of times. The crack between the twin mattresses is unavoidable no matter how thick the mattress pad or how fitted the king-size sheet is.

"What's up?" I ask.

They answer simultaneously.

He says, "I'm fine. Your mother thinks I'm having a heart attack."

She says, "He's sick. I think he's having a heart attack."

"Are you?"

Before he can answer, I chide my mother, "Did you call 911?"

"No," they answer.

My mother wanders around the bed to Dad's side and now leans against the wall in her long flannel nightgown. She is as far as she can be from the telephone.

It's Dad's turn to hear a lecture. I lay my head back down on his shoulder and say, "You know, you shouldn't be a moron. If you don't feel well, we should go to the hospital." This will not be the first time in my life that I have wondered how such a smart person can be such a stubborn idiot.

"I feel fine," he says. "Just tired from tennis. And a little stomachache, that's all." My left ear hears his words in the air. My right ear, resting on his shoulder, hears them reverberate in his body. He squeezes his left arm around me even tighter.

Calmed by the hug and his reassurance, I am caught off guard when his body tenses. My mother starts screaming. His arm has me pinned to his side. Dad is *not* fine. My mother nailed it. He *is* having a heart attack.

I yell to my mother to call 911, but she stands frozen in place, open-mouthed, shrieking his name.

Shimmying down toward the foot of the bed, I have only one thought—to get to the phone. My mother is still screaming. Sliding far enough from under his vise grip to get up, I meet my father's eyes. His face contorts with pain, his pallor is gray, and he's sweating.

I grab the phone and dial 911. The script we've all rehearsed since shelter drills in first grade comes rushing out of my mouth.

"This is an emergency. My father is having a heart attack. We're at 422 Cedarhurst Avenue, three houses from the intersection of West Broadway toward Maple Avenue."

The operator assures me she will send help right away.

One look at Dad tells me that "right away" will be "too late." My mother stops screaming my father's name and starts screaming in the direction of the bedroom door, where my brother, Rob, is now standing: "Don't come in here! Don't come in here!"

There's no time to worry about my seventeen-year-old brother, or my hysterical mother.

My heart races. My mind speeds through the steps for mouth-to-mouth resuscitation and CPR learned years before as a camp counselor. My mind screams at my mother for not calling for help hours sooner, and then it yells at my father for not letting her call. The sirens are blaring at the volunteer firehouse less than a mile away. Three minutes if they drive fast.

Flinging away the pillows from behind Dad's head, and tilting his head back, I use my left hand to hold his chin and my left thumb to try to open his mouth. Well, that worked on the CPR dummy. On someone having a heart attack, not so much. It takes two hands to pry open his jaw. I forgot to do the chest compressions first.

Time passes, my mind races.

In position, finally, my right hand pinches his nose. Trying to take a normal breath like they taught me in first aid class seems impossible. My breaths feel shallow. Covering his mouth with mine, I hear my instructor's voice recite the sequence in my head. A blow into his mouth. His chest rises. His mouth feels rigid underneath mine. Our lips can't make a good seal. Another breath. His chest rises again.

Straddling him, with my back to the bedroom door, my fingers interlocked, my hands centered between his nipples, I start compressions, counting aloud. Soon there's lots of noise behind me. The paramedics. Suddenly the room feels crowded.

"Miss, Miss, you can stop now. We'll take it from here," says a deep voice. An arm on my shoulder, gentle at first, now pulling me off my father's body.

"On three. Let's get him off the bed. One, two, three ... " The medics aren't talking to me, but my instinct is to grab Dad's right leg and pull hard. Dad soiled himself and the stool streaks up the sheet as we pull him off the mattress and onto the gurney. "Step away, Miss. You did great. Now step back," comes the deep voice again.

"Oh my God, Harvey, oh my God," my mother repeats from her spot against the wall. Leaning against the chest of drawers, my arms trembling from adrenaline and exertion, it feels sur-real to watch six practiced hands try to save my father. He lies still.

Footsteps on the stairs. Dr. M, a well-known cardiologist, and the father of one of my brother's best friends, appears at the door. My body floods with relief. Dr. M will "fix" this.

The deep voice says, "Well, that's it, men. He's gone." My throat starts to close.

Then the quiet, commanding voice: "I'm Dr. M. I'm a cardi-ologist." He uncurls the snake of a stethoscope from around his neck, bends toward my father. He touches the stethoscope to Dad's neck and says, "I hear a faint pulse. Let's move."

My heart flutters with hope. My mother grabs a sweater off the chair and runs from the room yelling for my brother.

And then the deep baritone protests, "But, Doc, he's gone."

As he stands, I see Dr. M wink at the paramedics. I know I'm not supposed to see this. My father is dead; there's nothing to be done to save him, but Dr. M clearly wants them to take him out of this bedroom, out of this house. No one else occupies the room where it happened. Just the paramedics, Dr. M, my dead father, and me. It won't occur to me until much later that Dr. M's great kindness spared our family the required autopsy if Dad died at home, an autopsy that violates our religion.

The paramedics make a grand show of maneuvering the gurney around the corner of the bedroom and line it up to head down the staircase, with one paramedic holding up a bottle of whatever they've got dripping through an IV in Dad's arm. Through the living room and out the front door and screen door they go, down the three front steps and across the front walk—serenaded the whole way by Coco, our aggressively unfriendly, windowsill-eating, mail-slot-gouging German shepherd/Labrador retriever mix, who barks ceaselessly from wherever she and my brother are hiding out. The medics carefully place the gurney into the waiting ambulance and Dr. M's small frame is silhouetted in the open doors as he nimbly hops inside.

At the hospital, the on-call doctor appears too quickly in the ER's family lounge, his swift appearance telling me what I already know, what the death certificate later confirms—DOA—dead on arrival.

A nurse sends us home.

The neat white house on Cedarhurst Avenue looks gray in the early dawn light as Uncle Julie pulls the car carefully into the driveway. We each stumble out of it, weighed down now with the heaviness of grief. There is a momentary pause as we awkwardly collect on the front porch, each of us assessing the "right" way to head back inside.

The massive black front door looks the same as always, but the portal back to my former life has irrevocably closed. Walking into the foyer, and through the living room with its 1970s fashionably mirrored wall, it barely registers that sheets hang from painter's tape, covering the mirrors.

In the Jewish tradition, the house is already dressed for mourning.

We gravitate toward the den, a room that usually beckons warmly with its yellow-and-orange shag carpet, needle-pointed, flame-stitched throw pillows, and cozy rust-colored crushed velvet tub chairs arranged in front of a massive brick fireplace. This morning, the room looks the same, but the air feels different. Stale and claustrophobic.

Coco barks fiercely from the confines of the basement. When I open the bifold door to let her out, she muscles past me—ninety pounds of raw power. She makes a beeline for my mother, her favorite family member. But instead of giving Coco the cooing and cuddling she's used to getting, my mother manages to only touch her head, staring into space and softly murmuring, "Harvey."

Coco senses that something has changed. She nervously trots from my mother's chair to mine, to Rob's, to Uncle Julie's, to Cousin Bruce's, and heads back toward my mother. Her thick, black tail is down now, her head lowered as she approaches.

I feel a frigid wind caress my face. *Too trite*, I think, *to feel the chill reminder that Death visited tonight.* But I look at Coco. Her hackles are up from the back of her neck all the way to her tail, and I know she feels it too. I shiver.

Coco patrols the room, panting, making wide circles around us and then tight turns between us. She is on high alert, her body taut with the same coiled energy typically reserved for the UPS driver, for whom she has a particular antipathy.

She can't quiet herself, and none of us try to calm her as we each adjust to the epic shift in our world order. With Dad, the unassailable alpha in the family pack, gone, I wonder if Coco will take his place.

It doesn't strike me as absurd or insane to consider this. Among those of us who are left in this broken group, Coco currently seems the only one willing to take control.

Momentarily, I consider the Orwellian possibility that we will reorganize our family under the leadership of a vicious dog. (She is in fact under house arrest, having broken the Village of Cedarhurst's "three-bite" rule. She was spared euthanizing because my father promised the mayor, Mr. Farina, that she would never leave the premises.)

I shift in my chair, first eyeing Coco as she makes her twelfth sweep of the room, then my broken mother, who gazes mournfully at something only she can see, and finally the tousled mop of hair that tops my younger brother's crumpled face. Despite the suffocating void choking my breath, with Dad gone, I realize the only one of us remotely capable of taking charge is me.

The idea of stepping onto the path my father forged during his too-brief forty-seven years threatens to cripple me. But even as that thought momentarily distracts me, I feel a glimmer of confidence. In that extraordinary way that certain people leave permanent footprints, Dad blazed that trail for me, and I know I will find myself walking beside him for the rest of my days.

He crammed so much wisdom into our twenty-one years together. I know there will be many stumbles and false starts, but I think I can be the person he knew I could be. This buoys me for an instant. The idea that I can be the leader, the one who will shoulder the burdens and keep the whole crazy circus act moving along, seems at once implausible and undeniable.

For the moment, though, I allow the wreckage of the last few hours to beach me. My entire world seems confined to this swiveling tub chair, rolling from side to side as the dawn melts into the first day without Dad. I let myself fill with regret for the life I wouldn't have without him.

The Rogue Prince forgotten in the maelstrom of tears and regret, I swirl down into a cesspool of darkness and grief.

3

The Most Awful Sound

December 2, 1979

The bone-chilling dirt clods thudding on the coffin by the shovelful gutted me. My resolve to stand tall for my mother and brother seemed much easier in the abstract than it did in the cruel reality of the cemetery on that damp and windy December day.

Among the hundred or so people gathered around the open gravesite stood Dad's three siblings, each one older than the brother they had come to bury. The three huddled together, two sisters and a brother, supporting one another in the silent grief that often accompanies sudden, unexpected, and premature death. Although others gathered around the casket were crying, weeping, keening, the three siblings stood stoically and solidly together, pained expressions on their faces.

Looking across the few feet of open earth that separated us, I felt comforted by the strength they exuded. I locked eyes with the tallest of the three, Aunt Vi, an elegantly dressed woman whose long, thin face drew down in the characteristically pointed "family chin." She was fifty-nine years old, but looking decades older that day, the natural order of her universe interrupted. Yet there she stood, dignified, almost regal. Although I was numb with shock, the sight of her gave me the strength to endure the twenty-minute ordeal of burying her baby brother, my father.

On a similar cold and misty morning in late February 1979, about nine months earlier, some of us had gathered around a plot only six feet away from where we now stood. That morning we had buried my grandmother, Rose, the family matriarch, beside her husband, Sam. Rose would spend eternity with her husband and youngest child beside her. I felt sad imagining my grandparents' sorrow when my father showed up in Heaven decades ahead of his older sisters and brother. The thought of their premature reunion sucked the air from my lungs and sent my mind spinning into the alternate reality that this imagined meeting entailed. Frantically glancing from face to face, my eyes found Aunt Vi, who looked back at me with a preternatural calm. My breath slowed. I could hear the rabbi's words, feel the cold, damp earth through my shoes, and smell the loamy scent of freshly turned dirt. I stood taller beside my sagging mother. I didn't cry, not even when the mournful notes of "Taps" filled my ears to honor Dad's service in the Army.

Once home from the cemetery, we found the house packed with people there for the *seudat havra'ah*, the meal of condolence, their voices a constant hum punctuated by a sound so very painful to me—laughter.

"How can people be so insensitive? How can they be laughing when my father just died?" I yelled to Aunt Vi over the din.

"*Ozmer lebt, derle'bt*," she said to me in Yiddish. "If you live, you live to see."

What does that even mean? I thought. "It must lose something in translation," I said to her, with more sass than respect.

Sitting on the traditional wooden bench of mourning, wearing a torn black ribbon to symbolize the rending of my clothing, I didn't find my aunt's words particularly comforting, let alone inspirational or earth-shattering. It seemed obvious that if I woke up in the morning, I would see what happened that day.

If she was frustrated by my lack of understanding, she didn't show it. "It's not enough to wake up, to breathe, to exist, although you should thank God every day that you do. You have to *live*," she stated emphatically. "The only way to see what happens next is to be part of what happens now. If you live, you live to see." She gestured toward the rooms packed with relatives and friends who were eating, drinking, smiling. "These people here... of course they are sad that our 'Harvela' died," she continued, using the Yiddish diminutive of Dad's name. "But what choice do they have? What choice do any of us have? We go on. We live so we can see what's coming."

That her words held wisdom—and that they would forever change me—wasn't entirely clear to me that day. I couldn't imagine being on Earth without Daddy, let alone live, love, or laugh ever again. But Aunt Vi's fortitude gave me exactly the stability I needed to get through that day.

It took years for me to get comfortable taking care of the people around me, and the early days showed no signs of either my aptitude or my desire to be the "go-to" person in our family.

Aunt Vi's philosophy, enigmatic to me at the time, began to make more sense only when I started to fumble through my newly fatherless life. Like many things, my real learning came from the mistakes. Not just mine, but Dad's too. Understanding how *not* to do something gave me an even deeper understanding of how to do it right. Even then, success didn't always come to me right away. The most valuable course corrections helped make me more persistent, some might say more stubborn. Over time, though, that doggedness led to an important realization. Sometimes the only reason I succeeded was that I refused to quit.

4

A Still Missing Peace

January 16, 2020

Seated in a vast church-in-the-round, a modern rotunda suffused with light from the dozens of windows of varying sizes, I read the four-page "Celebration of Life" program. Glancing up from it, just moments before the scheduled start of the funeral service, I marvel at the size of the sanctuary—so gigantic that the several hundred mourners barely fill a quarter of it.

Although I'm a lifelong practicing Jew, I'm comfortable in this space, taking in the faces gathered here, appreciating the elegant adornments of the readers' table, the workmanship in the highly polished wood carving of Jesus. The unease I first felt as a young girl attending church with my childhood best friend quickly evaporated by going to Midnight Mass, attending baptisms, First Communions and confirmations, weddings, and other joyful Sunday services over the years. These have made the initially mysterious practices feel less bizarre to me. I no longer feel awkward when everyone else sings from the hymnal to their Lord Jesus Christ. I never feel conspicuous when everyone else is kneeling on their bench and I'm seated in my spot in the pew. And when the faithful line up to receive Holy Communion, I reverently sit still and let the beauty and power of the collective energy fill me up.

For me, the reasons to go to a funeral are some combination of my love for the deceased, my love for a member of the deceased's family, and my respect for the deceased and his or her family—or because it's simply the right thing to do. Being a good friend, colleague, or neighbor includes showing up for them at the funerals of their loved ones. This didn't come easily to me. The hard-fought internal battle to overcome my funeral demons took me years to win. But life intervened, quickly, and the business of dying went on unabated, without regard for whether I felt emotionally prepared for it. In short order after my father's funeral, I got plenty of practice at keeping my emotional lid on tight.

The repeated devotion to following my Aunt Vi's advice, "If you live, you live to see," helped me stay stoic and strong. Like everything else in life, the more funerals I attended, the better I got at it.

By 2020, I had buried all four grandparents, five uncles, four aunts, several in-laws, three first cousins, dozens of parents of friends and colleagues, too many actual friends and colleagues, treasured mentors, and an overwhelming number of infants, the latter being the collateral damage that came with being the March of Dimes NICU Family Support Specialist for over five years.

The funerals weren't any easier. What improved was my ability to separate myself from my feelings, to be physically present while carefully arranging my facial expression to match the necessary decorum and letting my feelings pool into my ankles like so much extra water weight.

This tactic allowed me to be a supportive rock for all those who needed to lean on me, but it came with a heavy price.

Although I figured out how to bottle up my feelings at a funeral, I am incapable of sitting through a wedding, whether it's happening in front of me, on television, in the movies, or in a book, without collapsing into a puddle of all-consuming grief that this particular guy or gal got to have their father give them away and I didn't.

It's a bizarre dichotomy: I possess incredible strength during people's darkest times and become a blubbering fool during their most wonderful ones.

This January afternoon, I find myself in church to support a colleague who lost her husband in a devastating battle with a cruel illness. Although not among her inner circle, I want to alleviate her suffering in any way I can. Perhaps I'm being foolish to think that by being here I can bring her some strength to get through this terrible day.

As I often do, I picture Aunt Vi across the chasm of my father's open grave, see her resolve, feel her solid presence. I rarely cry at funerals. Today is no exception. A small sniffle at the cute story about how the deceased met my friend, a silent tear when a mutual friend gives a moving eulogy, and a stifled sob when the daughter, overcome by emotion, punctuates her reflections on her father with tearful gasps momentarily threaten my poise.

Already more than an hour long, the program shows only one item left before the recessional: the military presentation of the flag.

The ossuary, a truly lovely mini wooden ark adorned with carved crosses and scrollwork, rests atop a platform. Beneath it a shelf holds a simple black trestle holding a tricorn-folded American flag honoring the deceased's service to his country as a former Navy pilot.

Just then, two airmen march in lockstep up the center aisle directly toward the flag. They bow. They salute. They reverently pick it up and with synchronistic perfection turn and face the gathered mourners. "Taps" fills the room, the bugle signaling to something deep inside me. As each mournful note honors the service of this dead pilot, one lone tear quickly becomes a torrent.

The airmen face each other. With care and exactitude, they begin to unfold the meticulously folded flag. With a flourish and a sharp snap, the Stars and Stripes unfurl, opening before us in red, white, and blue splendor. The colors blur through the unbidden tears streaming down my cheeks, so copious that blotting them with my fingers fails completely.

Where are they coming from? My mind races to find the answer, my heart beating way too fast. I'm mortified at the spectacle I feel sure I must be making.

The airmen begin to fold the flag. Thirteen precise folds, one neat crease for each of the original colonies. The procession, the bowing, the saluting, the unfolding, the unfurling, the folding, the bowing, the saluting—many minutes have passed. I'm still ceaselessly and inexplicably crying.

One airman passes the flag to the other. Another bow. Another salute. An about-face. Forward march, bearing the folded flag. Kneeling now, on one bent knee, like a lover offering a ring. He is speaking to my friend. I'm dozens of yards away from them.

How can it be that I hear the words? They fill my ears with a gentle roar, and sound fills my head like wind over a canyon whispering into my ears in a rush. I hear them as a single thought, yet I know each one: *On behalf of the President of the United States, the United States Army, and a grateful Nation, please accept this flag as a symbol of our appreciation for your loved one's honorable and faithful service.*

Forty years melt away. A memory floods back with vivid clarity. I'm twenty-one years old and I'm accepting the proffered triangle from the white-gloved hands of a young, clean-shaven member of the United States Army. He brings me the gratitude of a nation for my father's service. Although protocol dictates that the flag be presented to the next of kin, beside me my mother is paralyzed with grief; she cannot move or speak or acknowledge the presence of the young man kneeling in front of us. He offers the flag to her, but she cannot lift her arms to accept it. I lean against her, loop my arm through hers, and pull the flag to her chest, feeling the solid serge against my hand, cold from the raw December day. In that instant, when I stood with my mother because she could not stand alone, I took my grief and pressed it far, far down. I knew that this tiny corner of turned earth couldn't bear the weight of her grief *and* mine. That if I didn't absorb her sorrow, we would both tumble into the hole containing the dead remains of my father.

As the airman in the church stands and salutes, as my friend, wearing her grief with dignified grace, hugs the flag to her chest, I see *me* through my distorted, liquid eyes looking back at myself.

I'm willing my thoughts to reach the three of us—my friend, my twenty-one-year-old self, and my present-day self—thoughts that I feel capture the essence of grief as I have come to understand it. *The hole in your heart will never go away, but with time, it becomes easier to bear.*

This afternoon, the hole in my heart feels as bottomless as it did on the chilly December day we buried Dad. The enormous sanctuary suddenly feels claustrophobic as I stare at the backs of the honor guard now marching in lockstep down the long center aisle toward the church doors.

Too exhausted to politely wait for the well-prescribed practice of exiting row by row, I scramble out of my seat in the second row and mumble "Excuse me" as I quickly weave through the departing crowd of mourners and make a run for the safety of my car.

I shut my eyes tightly, but the tears come again, along with a kaleidoscope of colors dancing behind my lids. The memories tucked neatly away for all these years, now unleashed, swirl through my head.

The painted turmoil slows. The colors begin to separate and become clear, some bright and cheerful, some dark and foreboding. I know what they want. They demand that I name each of them.

Taking a deep breath before starting the car, vision still blurred, I think of Dorothy Gale waking up back at home in Kansas, telling Auntie Em about her trip to Oz. "I remember some of it wasn't very nice," she says. "But most of it was beautiful."

BOOK TWO
NAMING MEMORIES

5

T-Minus Not Counting

EXHIBIT A—A SPECIAL DELIVERY

August 15, 1991

Few things in life run with the precision of a NASA space launch. Human lives depend on the accuracy of the countdown, the synchronous choreography between people and machines that results in a picture-perfect takeoff at the exact instant a voice declares, "Liftoff, we have liftoff!"

Most of life not only runs on its own imperfect schedule but is also filled with all sorts of failures, from small missteps to colossal collapses.

Sure, it would be handy to know the exact time your future fiancé planned to propose so you could be sure you hadn't just eaten peppers and onions, or the moment the postal worker dropped off your college acceptance letter (if they still mailed acceptance letters) so you didn't waste a week standing next to the mailbox waiting for it, or the five minutes before you got your first period so you could change out of the tight, white Danskin shorts you were wearing.

But would we really *want* that? What if nothing happened spontaneously? Where would the fun be if we knew we could count down with precision to the moment our first tooth would fall out, or the exact instant we would catch our first snowflake on our tongues, or the heartbeat that would skip when we first fell in love?

Most of life passes at "T-minus *not* counting." There lies the mystery that comes with the journey—the *not* knowing that it's T-minus six hours before your father is going to die, or T-minus five minutes before you're going to fly over your handlebars and knock out your front tooth, or T-minus a few seconds before some other random event that will catch you by surprise and change your life forever.

Being squarely of the mindset that *my* life should run with the accuracy of a Swiss watch, my memorable "T-minus *not* counting" moments certainly changed my trajectory, but also shaped my compulsion for being in control. Although there might have been other formative experiences to explain my uncompromising expectations for perfection, I attribute them to NASA! The Space Race eclipsed everything on my childhood world stage. As I watched the professionals at Mission Control precisely calibrate each movement, I became obsessed with a need for perfect planning in my own life.

On July 16, 1969, three days after my eleventh birthday, Apollo 11 stood majestically on the launchpad at Cape Kennedy. It felt like the culmination of my entire sentient life up to that moment: the goal set by President Kennedy in 1961 to put people on the moon had been fulfilled. Or, as Dad once told me years before, the book *Goodnight Moon* opened on his lap, the president wanted to send people "to meet the cow jumping over the moon."

My father and I watched countless launches before and after Apollo 11. We tried to watch them all. The backward countdown from "T-minus ten seconds and counting" gives me goosebumps even now.

We would sit close, clasping our hands, counting those last ten seconds out loud with Mission Control until "Liftoff. Houston, we have liftoff."

Even in an age of 3D-printed prosthetics and bio-printed body organs, when the world's largest particle accelerator, buried deep under France and Switzerland, facilitates the discovery of the Higgs-Boson (a new particle), and when a novel

virus encircles the globe in a matter of weeks, a rocket launch-
ing into space still makes my heart race.

But growing up in the '60s, going to the moon defied what
little I understood about space and made the science fiction
I watched (*Star Trek*—the original series, of course) seem less
fantastical and entirely more achievable.

It seemed that every six months or so, our eyes would be
glued to the television and the events at Kennedy Space Center
in Cape Canaveral, Florida, or the Johnson Space Center in
Houston, Texas. My father and I would hold hands and gleeful-
ly count backward until that sliver of a second between "one"
and "liftoff"—the instant when the impossible feat of shooting
tons of metal upward toward the stars became real, that tiny
portion of time when maybe it won't make it off the launchpad.
We would lean forward together, closer to the spacecraft on the
television set, urging it on, thrilled by the plume of smoke it
left behind as it took off on its journey.

By the time Apollo 11 launched, I was old enough to understand the race to the moon and the awful racial and political
climate in the country, including the unrest caused by the
Vietnam War.

I recall the live footage of the wives standing nervously at
Mission Control in Houston as Dad and I sat nervously watching the takeoff that would carry Neil Armstrong, Buzz Aldrin,
and Mike Collins to the moon—if it worked.

On the afternoon of July 20, 1969, it did work! Seeing the
American flag on the moon, with Neil Armstrong's famous
words coming to us live FROM THE MOON, Dad didn't try
to hide his tears of joy. Although we shared that moment with
millions around the world—and even a crowd in our own
house—it felt as if the two of us had somehow helped. Crazy,
I know, to have so much emotional energy invested in this
adventure to the moon, but we did.

The moon landing felt to me like the culmination of years
of effort by Dad and me to urge those crazy tin cans off the
launchpad and into the sky. It also taught me two invaluable
lessons that stuck with me throughout my life.

First, whether you are the president of the United States, a buck-toothed preteen, or a seasoned lawyer, if you make a promise, you need to keep it.

Second, the moon landing was so bold, that my own potential felt limitless. I set my sights on overachieving. "Less than my best" had no place in my world.

The certitude of the many shared countdowns I'd watched with Dad and the reliable cadence of those many "T-minus ten seconds and counting" launches stand in sharp relief to some of the more memorable "T-minus *not* counting" moments in my life. Logic might dictate starting sequentially with those moments, but for sheer knockout value, August 15, 1991, seems the exact right place to start.

The weather that day could not have been more perfect for an outdoor concert in Central Park.

A light breeze cooled the 82-degree afternoon, the humidity hovered at a comfortable 60 percent, and not a drop of precipitation threatened to fall on Paul Simon's triumphant return to New York City's greatest outdoor stage.

My husband, Leon, and I had long planned to go. Before we left home that morning, we packed the trunk of the car with a blanket, lawn chairs, some picnic supplies, and a strategy of where to buy the rest in Manhattan on the way to Central Park after work.

I had a full day of appointments, which included a lunch meeting with one of my favorite clients. She had achieved tremendous success in a male-dominated industry while her stay-at-home husband took care of their beautiful children. As she described it, she "outgrew him" and wanted out. He wanted half of everything and sole custody of the kids. She had a well-deserved reputation as a workaholic, and despite the prevailing "maternal presumption" favored by New York judges at the time that children do best when placed in the care of their mother, my client's hundred-hour workweeks and frequent business travel made for long odds of her getting custody.

Ten minutes into our courtesy consultation, she had hired me to represent her in her divorce/custody case. I felt flattered when she shared that she had done a great deal of homework to find me, concluding that she wanted to be represented by "another highly accomplished woman."

As we sat eating chicken paillard, her favorite, and my lazy "I'll have what she's having" choice, something felt odd. Nothing specific, but my face must have betrayed me, because my client looked concerned and asked if I was okay.

Lucky to be twenty-seven weeks pregnant at a time when linen swing dresses graced the windows of department stores throughout Manhattan, I wore a lovely powder blue version that did an excellent job of hiding my baby bump.

It had been a tumultuous several years for me and my cervix, and my checkered gynecological past caused me to be incredibly cautious. Self-protectively, I chose not to share the news of my pregnancy with very many people.

In fact, I didn't tell *anyone* except Leon and my mother for the first four months. By the time my amniocentesis results arrived, so had summer in all its glory. Midtown Manhattan became a sensory assault of smelly garbage, sticky tar, and randomly dripping air conditioners.

Out came all those fabulous swing dresses that my mother had thoughtfully gotten for me. I could conceal my growing belly in all but the most stubborn headwinds, when the billowing fabric flared out behind me like a sail, outlining my front profile in full relief.

When my client repeated her concerned question about whether I felt all right, I simply said I felt fine, "just tired," and left it at that. We spent the rest of our lunch together discussing when she had last taken one of her kids to the doctor, if she knew the names of either of their teachers, or if she recalled the name of the girl with whom her youngest child had most recently had a playdate.

I left her on Madison Avenue with a firm handshake and a stern homework assignment designed to ensure that the judge could only conclude that she successfully juggled her impressive career while also being an involved mother.

I headed up the elevator, got back to my desk, and dutifully called Leon to report the momentary pain in my lower back during lunch. He decided on the spot that we should skip the expected hordes of people in Central Park that night and go home instead.

We had a picnic dinner on our lawn, played Simon & Garfunkel records while we ate, and waited patiently for the live broadcast on HBO. Looking at the crowds on television, I knew Leon had made the right call to watch from home.

Partway through the concert, my low back pain became more intense and more frequent. When the concert ended and Leon turned on the lights—we had been watching in the dark to pretend we were really in Central Park—his first words were, "What's the matter with you? You look terrible."

"Wow," I deadpanned, "you really know how to make a girl feel special. Fine, just a little low back pain. No big deal."

By 3 a.m., something felt very wrong. I called my OB-GYN, the much loved and aptly named Sheldon Cherry. His on-call doctor got back to me in seconds. She asked me several questions, but did not like the answers, and told me to get to the hospital immediately.

Between our house in Lawrence, on Long Island, and Mt. Sinai Hospital in Manhattan, lay twenty-five miles of some of the most heavily trafficked roads in the country. Even at 3 a.m., an overturned tractor trailer, middle-of-the-night construction, or trash that fell off the back of a truck could bring the traffic on the Van Wyck Expressway, the Grand Central Parkway, and the Triborough Bridge (or worse, the Long Island Expressway to the Queens Midtown Tunnel) to a maddening crawl.

The only other person who might have gotten me to the hospital quicker would have been race car legend Mario Andretti. Leon got us there in eighteen minutes.

"There" means the general area where we both knew Mt. Sinai stood. We had not accounted for the fact that the hospital stretches the width between Madison Avenue and Fifth Avenue and runs the length of three city blocks. That's a whole lot of New York real estate to cover while doubled over in pain.

Since the clock had not yet seen the right side of 4 a.m., parking was an easy problem to solve. Finding the right door to enter that massive complex of buildings—now THAT turned out to be a big problem.

So here we are. The first unlocked door we find is on Madison between Ninety-Eighth and Ninety-Ninth. As soon as we get inside, we know we are *not* in the right place. A maze of pipes and a cacophonous din greet us—clearly a utility room of some kind—but at least we're in the building.

We begin to wander around the bowels of the hospital. There's no signage, no people. Just my husband and me—breathing hard. That's Leon doing the heavy breathing. Me? I'm barely able to put one foot in front of the other, not because it hurts so much (which it does), but because I don't want to jostle anybody loose in my uterus.

We aimlessly walk up and down random corridors for about ten minutes when a custodian spots us.

"Hey," he calls, "you can't be in here. This area is closed to the public."

He's walking toward us as he's saying it, and as he gets closer, our predicament becomes obvious. He grabs a walkie-talkie off his hip clip and starts barking orders into it as he runs off in the opposite direction. A minute later he's running behind a wheelchair, heading straight for us.

"Ma'am, your chariot," he says gallantly, and I gratefully collapse into the seat.

I'm positive that we wandered around inside the hospital for far longer than the eighteen minutes it took us to drive there. And then it took another hundred years to get to the Labor and Delivery floor.

Truth be told, exactly sixty minutes elapsed from the time the on-call doctor told me to get to the hospital until I lay on a gurney in front of her—whoever this on-call doctor might be.

In New York City it was common in large OB-GYN practices to meet all the doctors as you attended your checkups during your forty-week pregnancy. It's supposed to alleviate the worry about having some doctor you've never laid eyes on delivering your baby.

Perhaps if I had been pregnant for forty weeks, I might have met the woman who was greeting me now. But I'd only been pregnant for twenty-seven weeks, so I am now in the care of a total stranger for this emergency.

"What's happening?" I ask.

"You're in labor," she answers without warmth or reassurance.

There's some hushed conversation among the doctor and a group of other medical personnel—they all look alike in their ocean-blue scrubs. A nurse comes to take my temperature. I have a high fever. The conversation now becomes more animated, but still hushed.

A minute later a nurse wheels over a trolley with a tray. All I see is the gigantic needle right in the middle of the tray.

I KNOW that needle. It's the amniocentesis needle. I have no earthly idea how big it really is, but the needle-and-syringe combo looks about a foot long.

"What's the plan?" I ask, trying for nonchalance.

"The plan is to draw a bit of amniotic fluid, check it for any infection, and take it from there. Ready?" she says, already gloved and gowned.

Leon stands on my left as I clutch his hand in mine.

Twenty-seven weeks—can a baby even live at twenty-seven weeks? I'm thinking this as she inserts the needle and begins to draw what to my untrained eye is clearly abnormal—a putrid, yellowy, cloudy fluid. The sight barely registers before I feel my water break.

"Her water just broke. Get her to a delivery room. STAT."

Dr. Cherry arrives, looking really, really concerned. I am not reassured. Leon has on a gown and booties.

Out of the corner of my eye I see a clear plexiglass box that looks like a zoo exhibit. "That is an incubator," says a member of the staff helpfully. "It will keep the baby in a temperature-controlled environment for safe transport to the Neonatal Intensive Care Unit."

There's a hubbub of activity. I've got a drape across my abdomen so I can't see what's going on. But I can certainly feel it. And I can certainly hear it.

"Push," comes the directive from Dr. Cherry.

I push.

"Almost here. Your baby is almost here. One more push."

I push.

Then nothing.

For one unbearably long heartbeat, there's just silence.

It's like a music box winding down. One second there's sound and the next second there's none.

And then, as if someone had wound the key, everyone springs into action.

"Bag him," I hear.

I see a doctor holding aloft a tiny form that she carefully places in the incubator. Someone else is squeezing what from my vantage point looks like a mini turkey baster.

"We'll need to intubate," I hear, having no idea what that even means. Whatever they have done has stabilized our baby enough to move the incubator. Along with two nurses and my husband running behind the wheeled box, they all disappear out of sight.

"What is it?" I ask. "A boy or a girl?"

"A boy," says a voice.

"Why didn't he cry?" I ask.

"His little lungs aren't quite ready for crying," comes the answer.

I'm exhausted. I can't process the whole "no crying, little lungs" connection, and I drift off to sleep.

Harrison Nathaniel arrived on Friday, August 16, 1991, at 8:37 a.m., weighing 1,040 grams. Two pounds, two ounces. When Leon brings me to the NICU to see him for the first time a few hours later, the sight of Harrison shocks me. His hairless body covered in nearly translucent skin, his veins visible, his eyes fused shut, his breathing only possible with the assistance of a ventilator that covers much of his face, my son looks like a tiny, grizzled old man.

Gripping Leon's hand in mine, I want to be brave, to summon my usually reliable inner strength. Instead, my neurons stage a revolt. As I start to quiver all over, I look at our son and wonder if something this tiny can survive. Willing him to live, I let Aunt Vi's words swim through my brain. *Ozmer lebt, derle'bt,* dear baby. If you live, you live to see.

6

Empty-Handed

By the morning after Harrison's harrowing arrival into the world, his lungs so unready to be outside instead of inside, he lost several ounces just trying to stay alive.

On August 17, he weighed one pound, fourteen ounces.

The number 1.14 became a talisman that follows me to this day.

I don't know how many times I have stood in the meat section at the supermarket and randomly selected a package of chicken breast or chopped meat that weighs 1.14.

Or shipped a package at the post office, put it on the self-service scale, and it weighs 1.14.

Or ordered a pound of fresh coffee beans that the young lady behind the counter tells me is "a little over," and it turns out to weigh 1.14.

Or filled a bag at the bulk food aisle with nuts or rice or red lentils, put the little twist tie on it, picked up the pen (that always has the fake flower attached to it) to record the SKU number, made my way to the checkout counter, and when the bag is put on the scale, it weighs ... 1.14.

And each time, I take the meat, the package, the coffee, the bulk food, and I put it in my left hand and just feel its weight—really concentrate on what it feels like—1.14. It's crazy how light it feels, how impossible that a human being can weigh that little and survive.

On the morning of August 17, as I returned to my hospital room after gazing at my tiny son for about an hour, a nurse arrived to take my vitals.

"Great news," she chirped. The only "great" thing I could think of would be waking up to discover that the past thirty-six hours had been a bad dream.

Nope. Her news was a bit different. My fever had broken and after a consultation with Dr. Cherry, I could go home.

"Isn't that exciting?" she gushed.

Let's see. Hmmm. Exciting? My son was twenty-eight hours old. He weighed practically nothing. His lungs couldn't handle breathing on their own. Oh, did I mention that he had a heart murmur? No, I would not call my reaction "excited."

The nurse brought me a toothbrush and toothpaste so I could "freshen up."

Leon had gone home at some point in the middle of the night to get some sleep. And when we ran out of the house the night before, I didn't have a "go" bag ready. All I had with me were the clothes I wore when I got here. I dressed slowly.

I sat in the straight-backed guest chair that converted to a sleeper and waited.

Leon arrived shortly, wearing an expression on his face that I had never seen. He had the hungover look of someone who had been up all night, but this bore no resemblance to a drunken hangover. It was more like a "scared out of my mind" and "couldn't close my eyes for five minutes" look.

He gave me a wan smile. I wish I could have responded kindly. Instead, I stood up stiffly to accept the hug he offered.

"They said I could go home," I muttered into his shoulder.

"Already?"

"Yup. I'm apparently as healthy as a horse, except for whatever caused my fever. I have antibiotics and they see no reason for me to stay."

"Well, then," he said, "can we see the baby first?"

We had nothing to gather, except my little pharmacy bag of antibiotics, which he shoved in his jacket pocket.

"Ready?" he asked.

"Ready," I replied. And off we walked toward the elevator—past the nursery and its rows and rows of healthy babies, some with blue crib cards, some with pink crib cards, beaming family members standing at the gigantic window peering in, cooing, calling names, waving. I felt angry, sad, and guilty.

We waited for the elevator, and when the doors slid open, out came throngs of people with flowers, teddy bears, balloons, and smiles. Lots of smiles. Leon put a protective arm around me as we let the crowd of happy families and friends stream around us.

We stepped into the now-empty elevator. Leon had tears in his eyes. I stared stoically at our reflection in the elevator door.

In mine, I saw guilt-ridden failure. I had brought into this world a tiny boy who had compromised lungs and who knows what else and weighed less than a loaf of bread.

Reading my mind, Leon, whose arm still encircled my shoulders, squeezed hard.

"It's nobody's fault, you know."

Disagreeing, I stared silently at my reflection until the doors slid quietly open.

The corridor from the elevator to the locked doors that bisected it wasn't a short walk. I barely noticed the family lounge, but a bright photo array on the far wall caught my eye as we passed a water fountain, the men's and women's restrooms, and a few closed doors before we finally reached the floor-to-ceiling locked double doors. Were they trying to keep us out? Trying to keep the babies in? An image of isolettes wheeling themselves down the long hallway flew across my mind's eye as Leon buzzed the intercom.

What would soon become routine was still an ordeal. Waiting for the buzzer to unlock the gateway to our son. Making the first stop at the sterilization sink to wash our hands and arms up to our elbows. Donning the sterile gowns and the paper foot covers. Then we were permitted to walk past the outside nurses' station and outer nursery and into the inner section of the NICU. That's where the sickest, most fragile babies were, arranged in a hub-and-spoke layout around the room, a large nurses' station at the hub.

We walked to our son's isolette, the zoo exhibit that served as his womb away from home, and stood side by side looking down at him.

His body nearly vanished beneath the leads and monitors; the ventilator apparatus covered most of his miniature face. The vent breathed for him when he couldn't.

My heart hurt looking at him. Leon reached for my hand, and we held each other tightly, gazing at the miracle that lay before us, terrified of losing him, loving him completely.

"Look," exclaimed my husband. "He's shitting, I think!"

"Here in the NICU we use more scientific terms," came a female voice from behind us. "We prefer the term 'pooping.'"

The three of us smiled at that. It felt good to smile.

"You must be the Rodays. I'm Dr. Weintraub, the Neonatal Fellow taking care of Harrison."

Dr. Andrea, as she's known to us to this very day, stood about a head shorter than me. She looked to be about my age, had an open, pretty face with large, smart, soulful eyes, a quick smile, and a calm, easygoing demeanor. I liked her instantly.

"It's called meconium. And it's great. Babies his age usually take longer than term babies to pass their first stool. Since he's only about thirty hours old, this is a really good sign."

Dr. Andrea stood with us for quite a while as one of the nurses put on a pair of gloves from a box on the counter, out of a neat stack of different-colored boxes, each marked with the size S, M, L, or XL. The nurse pulled a small stack of baby wipes from a drawer in the isolette. She used one wipe to open the two portal doors and then set it aside. She took a fresh wipe off the pile, put each arm through one of the portholes, and began to gently clean up the dark green, almost black mess. Dr. Andrea reassured us as best she could, explaining that Harrison's weight loss was completely normal, that he burned a great many calories just being alive. She asked me if I planned to breastfeed. I hadn't given it a thought, but she explained how important it would be for him to have breast milk, even though it would be a while before he was ready for it.

She introduced me to a lactation specialist who escorted me to a small, cheerless room on the opposite side of the NICU floor. There I was presented with my very own milking machine, a hulking metal box with a heavy black cord neatly wound around it and attached to the handle with a twist tie. It reminded me of a slightly smaller version of my mother's Singer sewing machine, but the sheer weight of it surprised me and my arm wobbled slightly as I picked it up.

The lactation specialist showed me how to set it up, clean it, and store it. Then she asked, "Are you ready to try it out? Now don't expect anything. Your body isn't ready to produce milk yet. But you'll see. If you ask it to, it will."

After a soul-crushing ten minutes of nothing but suction pulling on my breasts, we stopped.

"You did great," she said cheerily.

"Yeah, great," I repeated. *Why don't we just add it to my nomination for the title of World's Worst Mother*, I thought.

She lugged the heavy machine back to the isolette where my husband continued to stand, head bowed, forehead leaning on the top of "the box."

"She did great!" exclaimed the lactation specialist. But I know my husband could see from the look on my face that it had gone anything but "great." I felt sore all over and suddenly drained and exhausted.

I wanted to stay and sit all day just looking at our son, memorizing every inch of him, just in case, you know, in case he died. But Dr. Andrea had a different idea. "You're no good to him if you aren't as alert as you can be. Go home, get some sleep. We'll be here when you get back," she said with a wry smile.

Leon agreed. He picked up my milking machine, its heft clearly a surprise to him, and held out his hand to take mine.

"You guys are going to be fine," Dr. Andrea said, lowering her voice. "I can always tell which couples are going to be wrecked by this experience and which ones are coming out the other side stronger than ever."

My professional interest was piqued by her comment. Too tired to ask what she meant, I made a mental note to ask her about it the next day.

My husband, my milking machine, and I headed out the enormous double swinging doors and down the long hallway to the elevators. Finding them blissfully empty, we got in and leaned heavily against each other. The car came to a stop and when the doors opened in the lobby, hordes of people were waiting for it to take them upstairs. I could tell by their smiling faces that these were the lucky many—the family and friends of healthy newborns going to see the newest addition to the family.

"Rose Schwartz"—my nickname for our car, a color that some Madison Avenue brand genius called "Rose Quartz"—stood parked directly across the street from the hospital door.

"What's the matter? You needed a dry run to find the right entrance?" I said to Leon, trying to be light but feeling bitter and angry about our lengthy loop around the bowels of the hospital during the wee hours of the night before.

His mouth set in a grim line, Leon grabbed my hand to guide me as we waited for traffic to pass so we could jaywalk across Fifth Avenue.

As we waited, I heard the hospital door open behind me and the sound of excited chattering. When I turned toward the source of the noise, the unexpected scene felt like a punch in the gut. A nurse pushed a wheelchair with a new mom, her arms full cradling her pink-blanketed newborn. Tied to one arm of the wheelchair, a giant bouquet of balloons heralded the news that "It's a girl!" Walking beside the chair, looking the picture of a proud new father, strode a very handsome man in madras shorts and a short-sleeved three-button polo shirt, a vase of flowers in each hand.

I felt a tug on my hand, and we crossed Fifth Avenue to our waiting car.

The milking machine got stowed in the back seat and I settled myself gingerly in the front passenger seat, my gaze falling on the new little family.

In that instant, it all came crashing down on me: the anguish of leaving my son in the care of others, the unrelenting fear that he might die, my overwhelming guilt that my womb inhospitably rejected him, the sheer terror of being out of control. I was shattered.

We drove home, the silence broken only by my sobs. Entering our house, I felt very unlike the person who had left forty hours earlier.

I felt so relieved that my mother was there to greet us. I hurt all over. I felt dreadful, physically and emotionally. All those years ago when I gave her so much grief, she would say, "Just wait. Wait until you have children of your own." And now I did. I knew I would never be the same—and neither would anything else in my life.

My mother gave me a sponge bath and helped me get into clean clothes. She tucked me under a blanket and gave me a cup of tea and a piece of white toast with a bit of grape jelly on it. The phone started ringing right about the same time that my mother had settled me on the couch.

Leon answered it. "Hello." A momentary pause, then "Yes, speaking." This preceded an extraordinarily long silence. And then, "We'll be right there."

The summons back to Mt. Sinai, the first of more than a few we would receive during our son's long NICU stay, didn't feel as terrifying as it should have.

7

The Darkest Hours

August 17, 1991

"The baby has a grade 3 brain bleed."

The words slid across the high polish of the twenty-foot-long conference table to where my husband and I huddled facing the ten or twelve doctors, nurses, and specialists arrayed at the other end.

"What does that mean?" Leon asked, breaking the silence that shrouded the conference room.

We were sitting so close together I felt his words vibrate in my body as if I had spoken them myself. Our feet, knees, and thighs were touching. Our shoulders were pressed together, our elbows hooked. The fingers of my right hand and his left intertwined in a mass of white knuckles. Only the arms of the oversized conference table chairs separated us as we clung to each other in the alien world we found ourselves in.

Leon directed his question to the Chief of the Neonatal Intensive Care Unit. The Chief had not introduced himself before his pronouncement, but I recognized him from atop the gallery of headshots in the visitors' lounge. Above the photos, in brightly colored letters, were the words "Meet the Team!" I had found the cheery exclamation point irritating when my husband had led me off the elevator for the first time the day before.

The Chief raised his chin slightly, cast his eyes at a kind-looking man who we later learned was one of two attending physicians in the Unit, and nodded at him. Having delivered the news, the Chief had completed his job.

For the next five minutes, Dr. Green gave us a crash course in intraventricular hemorrhages (IVH)—brain bleeds—explaining why they happen, what the different grades mean, what treatment options exist, and what the anticipated outcomes might include.

We learned that in nearly all cases, brain bleeds that happen to premature infants usually occur within the first few days following birth. It may happen to their fragile blood vessels because of repeated episodes of low blood oxygen levels or from exposure to greater fluctuations in blood pressure than happen to term babies.

Grade 1 bleeds, small bleeds limited to the capillaries near the ventricles in the brain (the cavities within the brain that produce and store cerebrospinal fluid), usually have no long-term impact.

Grade 2 bleeds are found in the ventricles, but the ventricles remain unchanged in size. These bleeds also usually do not result in any long-term impact.

Potentially catastrophic outcomes often result from grade 4 bleeds. Bleeding occurs in the ventricles, which become enlarged, as well as in nearby areas of the brain tissue. These hemorrhages can result in considerable permanent impairments.

And grade 3?

"Well," said the doctor slowly, "we really don't know. Only time will tell. It's possible he will have lifelong deficits; it's possible the blood will resorb and everything will be fine."

I felt my husband exhale—a long, slow sound. I realized that I, too, had been holding my breath.

"We just don't know," Dr. Green repeated for emphasis. "The more serious the deficit, the sooner it will show up," he added.

Exhausted from the raging infection and high fever, I felt clumsy leaving the conference room. My feet seemed too big. I tripped shuffling across the waxen sheen of the hospital floor.

I spilled half a bottle of the special soap we had washed with before we changed into sterile gowns to enter the NICU.

As I perched uncomfortably in a tall chair beside the isolette, gravity pulled painfully on my episiotomy, the cut Dr. Cherry had made in the tissue between my vaginal opening and my anus during childbirth. I combed back through the unread sections of the 1990s pregnancy bible, *What to Expect When You're Expecting*, the parts I had skipped over because "that" will never happen to me. Had I missed a clear sign? Had I failed to recognize a subtle one? What had I done to cause this beautiful boy to be born thirteen weeks too early?

Guilt nearly debilitated me when the lab results came back. I had listeria, a typically foodborne bacterial infection often found in unpasteurized cheeses, benign to nearly everyone, except pregnant women. I remembered a particularly delicious French triple crème cheese I'd eaten weeks before. Why wasn't *that* warning in the damn book?

My breath came heavily. Quick puffs punctuated by deep sighs. The room seemed airless.

And this insanely uncomfortable chair! Who was supposed to be able to sit in this chair?

In a slight variation on the Jewish tradition, we had named our son after dead relatives. His first name, Harrison, honored Leon's father, my father, and my maternal grandmother, all H's. His middle name, Nathaniel, honored my maternal grandfather. His polysyllabic first and middle names barely fit on his crib card. Staring at it, I thought to myself that if each of the twenty-two letters of his name weighed an ounce, we had burdened him with a name that weighed nearly as much as he did.

This cruel reminder that life changes in a split second, irrevocably altered with no way to rewind to "before," left me breathless. But it also made me furious. That I had been blindsided, that I didn't see this coming, that I hadn't even considered the possibility of it.

I twisted and turned in that ridiculous chair, berating myself. I knew better. I had learned from my dad's untimely and tragic death that life sometimes zigs when you're zagging.

I had deluded myself into believing I was coated with "Tragedy Teflon"—immune from anything *really* bad ever happening to me again.

Yet, less than forty-eight hours into motherhood, I felt terrified about the fickle brain bleed. That it could capriciously resorb or result in permanent damage made it seem all-powerful. That there wasn't a single thing I could do about it made me feel even more impotent and worthless than I felt before the conference room sit-down.

I looked over at Leon, tears dripping down his cheeks as he gazed down at our son, and I wondered if, like me, Leon felt clueless. So dense that we didn't even know what we didn't know.

Our son's health deteriorated or improved many times over the next few months, but the lingering fear that something dreadful lurked in his little brain waiting to reveal itself stubbornly clung to us just as it did that day.

It seemed like a strange time for her to appear, but as time waits for no man, the scheduled rounds of the lactation specialist seemed to wait for no woman. Minutes after we'd settled ourselves back at the isolette after the devastating news about the brain bleed, there she stood.

"Breast is best," chirped the lactation cheerleader as she guided me through round two of my unhappy introduction to expressing breast milk—an only slightly more painful version of round one, seeing as how it had not yet dawned on my body that I'd had a baby. This meant soreness, but no milk yet. The yanking suction from the pump felt like pummeling a fresh bruise.

Leon had already filled out the paperwork to rent *another* Medela Classic Hospital Grade Electric Breast Pump, marketed as being "the ideal pump for long-term and frequent pumping needs," so I'd have one for my office and one for at home.

Harrison lacked the sucking-swallowing-breathing coordination necessary for successful breastfeeding, but having been persuaded that feeding him breast milk via his nasogastric (NG) tube was the healthiest alternative for him when he grew ready for it, I felt determined to conquer the Medela Classic.

This brand of pump held the place of honor in the cheerless "pumping room," a curtained-off cubbyhole near the entrance to the unit that lacked a sign to indicate it was occupied. Privacy depended on the mechanical sound of the pump itself, and I had quickly figured out the uncomfortable way to position myself so that my back faced the curtain in case I got interrupted.

And since each plastic piece of hermetically sealed accessories weighed nearly nothing, and my coordination felt "challenged" at best, assembling all the necessary pieces and parts without knocking at least one "sterile" piece to the floor was nearly impossible. Not just that day, but for many days to come. The cubbyhole being barely wide enough to allow me to bend over to retrieve the fallen piece meant contorting over a sore tummy and a throbbing episiotomy.

Medela had cleverly created a dual breast-pumping system that allowed an all-thumbs klutz like me to cut pumping time in half by pumping both breasts simultaneously. Yes, multitasking had made it to the breast-pumping world. But the skilled coordination to manage both without spilling any of that precious, hard-to-come-by nectar eluded me.

Round two left me frustrated, crying and cursing. Despite the encouragement of the lactation specialist, this seemed like a cruel joke for Nature to play on me.

I listlessly walked back to Harrison, his tiny body quiet in his plexiglass box.

8

Reading in the Dark

August 18, 1991

Helpless.

Many words describe being the parent of a sick child in the NICU, but for me, someone so accustomed to being in control, the feeling of complete and utter helplessness captures the essence.

It felt so disorienting. Three days earlier, on Friday, August 15, I had successfully argued two motions in court, done three client meetings, written half of an appellate brief in a potentially landmark case, and attended an executive committee meeting of the New York Chapter of the American Academy of Matrimonial Lawyers by phone.

On Saturday, a full three months sooner than expected, I had become a mother. Well, technically a mother, but more like an untrained civilian crash-landing on an alien planet.

As a partner at a well-respected law firm in New York, not having control wasn't something I handled well. And not knowing anything about being the mother of an infant son with extremely low birth weight (except how poorly the odds of survival were stacked against him) left me reeling.

"Can't I *do* anything?" I asked Dr. Andrea.

"Talk to him. He knows your voice. Just open the porthole door and talk to him."

"But what do I say?" I asked, hearing the panic of uncertainty in my voice.

"It doesn't matter," she replied. "It's the idea of hearing a voice he knows. You'll see. You'll both find it soothing."

She walked off to attend to another of her teeny patients, leaving me to wonder what the hell I was going to say to the gravely ill little person lying naked in the isolette beside my chair.

Cautiously, I opened the porthole and put my mouth closer. "It's Mommy, sweet thing. You know I love you, right? The doctor wants me to talk to you, but I have no idea what to say." I felt like an idiot. I gently and carefully closed the porthole.

After three sentences, I was already stuck. Then I was suddenly inspired: *I'll read to him!* I picked up the handiest thing, opened the porthole again, and began to read from the front page of the Sunday *New York Times*. As I read the lead story about Iran taking center stage in the negotiations to free ten Western hostages, I thought, *This is great.* I was feeling better, useful, purposeful. A few minutes later, the doctor swung by. Quoting a Life cereal commercial, she quipped, "Mikey likes it," and gestured with a tilt of her head at the monitor that constantly tracked Harrison's vital signs.

I followed her gaze. Since Harrison was on a ventilator, a machine was breathing for him, so his heart rate and the oxygen level in his blood (saturation, or SATS) were mechanically controlled. The maze of numbers—blood pressure, heart rate, breathing rate, oxygen levels—and the assorted colors and lines for each were still a mystery to me after only a few days in this foreign world.

But two numbers—the heart rate and the saturation rate—were displayed in two boxes on the right side of the monitor, constantly reporting. I'd already learned the sound of the bradycardia alarm, the one that causes the nearest health professional to come running because the heart rate has dropped below one hundred.

The two boxes showed a steady one hundred and fifty beats per minute and a stable, unblinking ninety-nine as the oxygen saturation. Even as a neophyte to this technology, I knew this showed Harrison was calm, not at all agitated. I was elated. *I did this!*

"Nice work, Mommy," Dr. Andrea said with a smile. "Whatever you're doing, keep doing it!"

I picked up the folded newspaper and continued to read aloud, purposefully, as if dictating a memo. I found that it was soothing not only to the baby but also to me.

That night, the incubators were all covered with blankets like birdcages. Earlier that evening, I brought a proper book to read to Harrison.

I opened the worn copy of *Goodnight Moon* that I picked up from the family lounge and began to read aloud through the open porthole. As soon as I looked at the "great green room," my mind wandered to treasured memories of reading with my father.

Our nightly reading ritual started about the same time my brother was born and I earned my Big Sister honorific. Surely, our reading habit reflected a calculated parenting decision prompted by my brother's appearance—no doubt at the behest of the reigning parenting sage of the time, Dr. Benjamin Spock.

My father's lanky six-foot frame filled most of my twin-size bed, and my small four-year-old body found a perfect spot snuggling in the crook of his arm. The book of the night perched open on his stomach, which he used as a bookrest. His undivided attention filled me with joy and the words captivated me.

I remember him reading *Goodnight Moon* to me, him telling me that the astronauts were going to see the cow jumping over the moon. I know that "great green room" had a proud spot on my bookshelf for many years, alongside *Make Way for Ducklings* and *The Little Engine That Could.*

About a year later, our respective positions changed. My father sat upright with his back against the headboard, and I sat beside him, his left hand holding one side of the book and my right hand holding the other. The index finger of his right hand followed along with the words he spoke.

The Cat in the Hat and its many Seuss siblings heralded the next major change to our reading routine as *my* index finger pointed to the words that I read to Dad.

Years and books passed, and though the read-aloud-in-bed ritual eroded from nightly to occasionally, the reading bug had thoroughly infected me. Brushing my teeth, preparing my clothes for school the next day, and reading before bed were all on my nightly to-do list.

Somewhere along the way, Ari Ben Canaan came into my life within the two-inch-thick Leon Uris tome, *Exodus*. He captivated me. When my father left the room after our by-then infrequent read-alouds, I pulled the book from the bottom shelf of my night table, turned my lamp back on, and dove back into Ari's world.

Late one evening, my father poked his head in to remind me it was a school night. "One more chapter," I murmured as I kept reading. "Five more minutes," he countered firmly before turning to leave me aboard a ship with the book's heroine, Kitty Fremont. I was so absorbed that I didn't hear my father come back; only the abrupt darkness after he turned off my bedside lamp got me to stop.

"Tomorrow's another day," he said, walking out of my room toward his own. As quietly as I could, I got out of bed and tiptoed to the closet where my mother had stashed an emergency flashlight. Tiptoeing back to bed, grabbing the book from the night table, and turning my blankets and pillows into a makeshift tent—my head serving as the center pole—I read by flashlight until I couldn't keep my head up anymore.

Thrilled by the sweeping story, I fell asleep at "I have no idea" what time. The morning alarm clock seemed to ring more shrilly than usual, and as I waited my turn for the bathroom, I slumped against my bedroom door, all irritated and grumpy.

The bathroom door opened and my freshly showered, towel-clad father appeared, filling the air with the Canoe aftershave he always wore.

"How'd you sleep?" he asked conversationally.

"Okay, I guess," I answered without enthusiasm.

"Is the ship still blockaded in the harbor?" he inquired. A small smile showed first as crinkles around his hazel eyes before it appeared on his thin lips.

"But how—" I started to stammer, thinking back to the fraught chapters I had read the night before.

"Chip off the old block," he replied, his smile now wide. Without another word, he tousled my bedhead hair, kissed me lightly on the forehead, and strode into his bedroom, having given his blessing to my reading in the dark. Long before the universe became available with an Internet search, Dad got me hooked on the joy of exploring the worlds within the pages of books.

Now, sitting in the darkened NICU, the only light coming from the small bulb under the countertop behind the isolette, I read *Goodnight Moon* softly through the porthole to my tiny darling, feeling, at least for a few moments, like less of a failure and more like a mother. And when I finished the book, I couldn't help but wonder if my son would ever read to me as I had read to my father.

9

Elsie the Cow

August 19, 1991

Monday morning arrived. I had been a mother for two days. While nearly all that time had been spent at Mt. Sinai, during our drive back to Long Island on Sunday night, Leon had gently asked me if I wanted him to call my office to let them know I would be out for a while. After an exhausting discussion with him, I resolved not to waste my maternity leave while Harrison remained hospitalized.

My law practice hummed. In my fantasy "normal" pregnancy, I had prepared for a gradual transition of my caseload to several senior associates. My responsibilities as a partner would be handled by my colleagues. My volunteer responsibilities as a member of the Network for Women's Services, a program that provided pro bono legal representation to women who could not afford to pay for legal counsel, were to be spread among my fellow founding members. My duties on the executive committee of the New York Chapter of the American Academy of Matrimonial Lawyers would be handled by the other five lawyers in leadership—all men. In the fantasy pregnancy, the redistribution of my duties to the men on the executive committee made me feel like living proof of the stereotype that giving consequential jobs to women of childbearing age was a bad idea—they were just going to procreate and leave their male colleagues high and dry!

The plan looked good on paper on the corkboard in my office and might have worked, given the chance. But Harrison's arrival thirteen weeks ahead of schedule didn't allow for the soft transition we had envisioned.

Over tepid hospital coffee that Monday morning, Leon and I devised a schedule that sounded brutal in concept and turned out to be even more punishing in practice. I would be in my office on Madison and Twenty-Eighth Street most days between 10 a.m. and 4 p.m. That meant that to get my body on a "feeding schedule," at least one pumping session had to be done in my office, and somehow fit into the already insane schedule that my practice demanded.

The reality of pumping in the office turned out to be a comedy routine.

When I got off the elevator at my office with my Medela Classic breast pump in tow, our wisecracking receptionist, Sharon, asked me if that's where I stored my stash of kryptonite.

Lugging it down the long hallway past four open office doors, each occupied by one of my puzzled-looking law partners, I arrived at the desk of the indomitable Sandra Leslie, my very British, very stylish, very excellent legal assistant. Sandra epitomized professionalism when the occasion called for it. Most of the time, she had a devilishly delightful giggle and a dismissive, hand-waving "Go on!" when she thought I was being facetious.

She took one look at me and started clucking her tongue. "You look rough," she said softly, reaching for the pump. As I was warning, "Careful, it's heavy," she teetered slightly on her four-inch-high heels, balanced herself, and walked gracefully into my office.

"Let's get you settled," she said. "Can I bring you a cuppa?"

"No coffee for me." I sighed, dragging my tingling right arm out of the sleeve of my coat. "Water only from now on. I'm in the milk production business, apparently," I added, gesturing at the metal box she had set down at the side of my desk.

"Hot or cold? The water, I mean. Not the milk," she said with a giggle.

"Hot would be great," I said, easing slowly down onto my chair, my perineum throbbing with the effort of lugging the milking machine two city blocks from the parking garage.

By the time Sandra returned with my hot water, I had re-arranged my office so that I could plug the breast pump in beside me at my desk with my back to the radiator-to-ceiling windows that ran the full length of my office onto Madison Avenue. Except now I was a full-on frontal nudity show for anyone opening the office door.

"Awww," she teased. "I was going to charge a fiver for people to watch." She looked thoughtful for a moment. "How are we going to keep people from barging into your office like every-one does around here?"

She had a point. A closed office door nearly always meant a client sat on the other side, but that didn't seem to stop any of us from lightly rapping to announce that we were coming in anyway. None of us ever waited for a "come in" or a "not now." For a team of professionals in one of the most confidential of all areas of the law—divorce—we rarely gave one another any privacy.

That first morning, I waded through the pile of paper on my desk, reprioritizing what needed to be done right away and what would need deferring.

My aching breasts reached the point of complete distraction before I called out my door for Sandra.

She appeared instantly. "What do you need?"

"I need nobody to come in here until I tell you the coast is clear," I answered, hurriedly unpacking all the plas-tic-wrapped pieces and parts for the breast pump. Sandra watched wide-eyed.

"That looks awful," she summarized when I had finished setting up my personal torture device. "Alright, you go ahead and… whatever it is you do with all that. I'll stand by the door until you're finished."

"Get a chair," I suggested. "It will be a long half hour for you to stand in those heels."

She smiled and gently closed the door behind her. "Awful" didn't even begin to approach how much it hurt. But there wasn't anything I wouldn't do for Harrison, and if this had a chance of helping, I was "all in."

Three times I heard a small commotion outside my door. Each time I heard Sandra's firm, protective voice telling whoever was trying to gain access that he or she would have to wait.

When I finally finished, cleaned up all my gear, and snapped closed my nursing bra, it had been forty-five minutes from start to finish.

Looking at the pathetic output, still practically nothing for my labors, felt demoralizing.

Stashing the scantily filled bottles in the cooler pack under my desk, pressing my intercom, I told Sandra I was finished.

As though this were the most normal occurrence in the world, she opened the door, sat down, gave me my six phone messages and three in-person messages, asked me if I wanted her to bring me back any lunch, and was off.

The next four hours flew by in a rush of client phone calls, catching up on missed office news, and finishing a draft of an appellate brief I had started and stopped about ten times since I'd given birth. Finally, at 4 p.m. on the dot, Sandra appeared.

"You better get going, love, or you'll need to use that contraption again. Go see your bunny."

She was right. I had been concentrating so hard on my work that I hadn't noticed how sore I was getting. I'd soon learn my limits—every five hours was seriously pushing it—but I didn't know them yet.

I gathered my things and headed out the door.

"Do you need anything?" Sandra asked.

"Can you turn back time?" I asked, not kidding.

By the time I returned to work the next morning, there was a new addition to my office door. An eleven-by-fourteen-inch laminated color picture of Elsie the Cow hung from a string. Beneath the famous Borden's mascot, **DO NOT DISTURB** was neatly typed in all caps, in the unmistakable Times New Roman Bold font.

And so later that day, and every weekday for the next eighty-plus days, when I closed my door to pump, Sandra flipped the sign to show a beaming Elsie.

I felt enormously grateful for the moment of levity each day. Sandra's kindness made the brutal schedule a bit more bearable, even if just for a moment.

While the days were never typical, we did settle into a routine.

My pumping schedule provided the anchor for each day. Every four to four and a half hours, whether I was at home, at the hospital, or in the office, I stopped whatever I was doing and had a meaningful date with my Medela Classic.

The brutal daily schedule—an insanely jam-packed, at times chaotic, roster of activities—was intended to keep every spinning plate aloft. In retrospect, it was unreasonable to think I could successfully manage this juggling act, which looked something like this:

2 a.m. – Wake up to pump at home.

2:30 a.m. to 5 a.m. – Try to sleep.

5 a.m. – Wake up to shower, dress, and drive to the hospital.

6 a.m. – Spend "shift change" with Harrison.

6:30 a.m. – Pump at the hospital and then sit with Harrison until it was time to leave for work.

9:45 a.m. – Head to the office.

10 a.m. to 11 a.m. – Work.

11 a.m. – Pump.

11:30 a.m. to 4 p.m. – Work.

4 p.m. – Head to the hospital.

4:30 p.m. – Pump at the hospital.

6 p.m. – Spend "shift change" with Harrison.

8:30 p.m. – Pick up some food and eat in the car on the way home.

9:30 p.m. – Pump at home.

10 p.m. to 11 p.m. – Pay bills, catch up on paperwork (home and office).

11 p.m. – Call the hospital and talk to Harrison's nurse.

11:10 p.m. to 2 a.m. – Try to sleep.

And then I'd just grind it out again the next day, and the next day, and the next day for eighty more days. Throughout this time, my law partners were extremely supportive of my punishing routine and picked up the pieces of my case work that I invariably dropped along the way. They tried to cover my court appearances or have them postponed. I really hated to postpone them because that had a direct and detrimental impact on my clients. They all needed to continue to hurtle toward divorce, and every delay in their cases meant they were being ill-served. Whatever my guilt du jour, disappointing my clients was an added weight that rested heavily on my already exhausted shoulders.

10

Shades

One early morning when we arrived at the NICU, we came to Harrison's bedside to find him looking a bit like a hothouse plant under grow lights. Either that or Norma Desmond ready for her close-up.

There lay a nearly naked Harrison (by now he had the tiniest diaper known to humankind draped decorously over his genitals), wearing a pair of enormous sunglasses.

"Hyperbilirubinemia," proclaimed Dr. Andrea, quietly approaching us. "You might be more familiar with the term 'jaundice,'" she added. "Those are phototherapy lights."

Five minutes into another crash course in a medical condition we knew little to nothing about, Dr. Andrea explained that a high bilirubin value meant that Harrison's liver lacked sufficient maturity to rid his body of this compound, which is a normal byproduct found in bile. It is produced when the liver breaks down red blood cells and is typically removed by a well-functioning body through the stool.

But Harrison's bilirubin levels were dangerously high and could cause brain damage if left untreated.

Brain damage? Wasn't the brain bleed enough to worry about?

Dr. Andrea reassured us, telling us the lights were already having a positive impact on lowering his "bili." She added playfully, "And doesn't he look so cool?"

Within minutes, Leon had hand-lettered a sign that he hung on the isolette, adapting the title of a song that had been popular a few years before.

It said, "My future's so bright, I gotta wear shades."

Harrison's face was now obscured by both the ventilator and the enormous sunglasses; Dr. Andrea continued to try to allay our concerns by joking that he looked like a rock star.

I needed some air.

Wandering out of the hospital, I started to walk south on Fifth Avenue and soon found myself in the children's books section of The Corner Bookstore on Ninety-Third Street, my eyes filled with the kaleidoscope of colors beckoning me from the bookshelves. As I fingered the titles of familiar tales, and leafed through the pages of new ones, wondering how they would sound when read through the porthole door, I couldn't help but think about my father. Dad's fondness for reading, especially for reading aloud, created the spaces where I felt closest to him as a youngster. He read aloud with gusto and would have made a fortune as a narrator for Audible if he were still around.

When he read aloud, he voiced every character, read exposition with feeling, and at times felt compelled to act out sections of whatever he was reading. He could recite poetry from memory, and so convincingly withered in anguish as his knees buckled and he fell to the floor exclaiming, "Et tu, Brute," that my mother came running in from the kitchen to be sure he was alright. At her look of alarm, he leaped to his feet and launched into "Friends, Romans, countrymen, lend me your ears; I come to bury Caesar, not to praise him."

"The Charge of the Light Brigade," delivered theatrically one evening on the darkened screened-in porch, seemed so electrifyingly real that I felt the horse beneath me as I rode with Tennyson's "six hundred."

"Call me Ishmael," he thundered one night, as we began *Moby Dick*. I was enthralled by the timbre of his voice as we launched into Melville's classic.

My introduction to Robert Frost came, naturally, while Dad and I walked together in a yellow wood. He started at the end, although not knowing the poem, to me it might as well have been the beginning:

"Two roads diverged in a wood, and I—
I took the one less traveled by,
And that has made all the difference."

He asked me what I thought the poet intended. This question, posed to me when I was about eight, felt freighted with meaning. He seemed to be measuring me. My answer would determine—what exactly? I never asked him what he would have said or done differently had my answer been different.

I thought about it for a few minutes as we dragged four sneakered feet through the fallen leaves, not quite crunching yet as they would be after a few cold nights. Still soft and supple, they swished in the afternoon sunlight.

"It means that actions have consequences?" I timidly attempted.

"Are you asking me or telling me?" he said with a smile, using a favorite method of his to get me to be decisive.

"Telling you?" I replied, still unwilling to commit wholeheartedly to my answer.

"Would hearing the rest of it help you make up your mind?" he pressed. I nodded. We had come to Our Spot, a boulder big enough for both of us to sit on, resting at a small fork in a fast-moving shallow stream at the end of a path we walked each weekend morning when we were at my grandparents' vacation home in Milford, Pennsylvania.

The significance of where Our Spot lay juxtaposed with Frost's poem was lost on me at the time. Years later, while I was recounting the story to a boyfriend as we sat in that special place, he commented that my father "must have been a genius," waiting to teach me that poem in a place where two streams diverged in a yellow wood. Compliments about my father, especially welcome at the time, racked up significant brownie points for the boyfriend.

Dad began:

"Two roads diverged in a yellow wood,
And sorry I could not travel both,
And be one traveler, long I stood ..."

He recited the classic in its entirety, emphasizing the final stanza, which I had previously thought started the poem.

"Well, whaddya think?" he said when he'd finished.

I know I thought it was marvelous, that there couldn't be any other father on planet Earth who could recite that poem from memory, that I was the luckiest little girl in the entire world. What I said was, "I think I was right!"

He hugged me then. My head tucking in under his chin where we perched on the boulder in Our Spot, his pack of Kent 100s pressed against my ear where they nestled in his breast pocket, his jacket smelling of pine and cigarette smoke and Canoe, I felt safe and so loved.

He replied, "So next time, tell me, don't ask me." I didn't understand that some special lesson about having the courage of my convictions had passed from him to me. Long before I ever heard the phrase "teachable moment," Dad filled my life with them and, although I'm sure I didn't realize it at the time, this was just one of many that helped calibrate my moral compass.

I smiled at the memory and realized I'd been standing in the children's section for a very long time, holding *A Children's Book of Verse* in one hand and *The Velveteen Rabbit* in the other.

Knowing Dad would approve of both choices, I paid for my purchases and strode up Madison Avenue as purposefully as my episiotomy would allow. I was eager to get back to my perch to read to my "rock star."

11

Mama Bear

August 23, 1991

Never shy in my adult life, I knew that the strength to speak up and speak out for my voiceless baby came from a reliable source—my mother. I watched her advocate for my brother and me countless times, but never realized, until I needed it, how much I had learned from her.

One afternoon, watching Harrison twitching, agitated about something that he obviously could not express, I called the nurse over.

"Something's wrong. Look at him," I implored, suspecting that those erratic movements were his way of telling me something important.

The nurse glanced at him, then at the monitors, and patted me reassuringly on the shoulder.

"He's fine, Mommy. Don't worry so much," she said dismissively and walked away.

But it nagged at me. Something felt wrong.

The afternoon dragged on into the evening. Leon came from work looking tired and worn.

"Something is wrong with the baby," I said the instant he arrived at my side.

"What's the matter?"

"He's been twitchy all afternoon. Like something hurts. I told the nurse, but she said I was just worrying. I'm not just worrying, honey. There's something wrong with him."

"I believe you," Leon said soothingly, staring down at Harrison, who for the first time all day seemed quiet.

"Sure," I said to Harrison sarcastically, "make me look like a melodramatic Jewish mother."

Leon and I sat together beside the isolette for another few hours; Harrison seemed to be resting comfortably. Whatever irritation, pain, or annoyance troubled him earlier, it seemed to have disappeared. Still, something gnawed at me.

By now, Leon and I were staying in an apartment on Eighty-Sixth Street and Madison Avenue, a studio that Leon's brother Steve let us use. The mattress flopped flat on the floor, and the apartment didn't have much to recommend it other than its ideal "walking distance" to Mt. Sinai.

Leon encouraged me to get some sleep. I had to admit I felt exhausted, but I couldn't shake the feeling that something bad was going on with Harrison.

Lying in the dark, the noises of Manhattan invading the apartment through the open window, I found myself thinking about Eastern Parkway in Brooklyn circa 1967.

Modeled after the Champs-Élysées in Paris, Eastern Parkway boasts three lanes of traffic in each direction, bisected by a beautiful median lined with stately elm and sycamore trees, park benches, and pedestrian walkways.

My brother and I were in the back seat of the family car. My father was driving and my mother, seated beside him but as far across the front bench seat as possible, was smoking a cigarette. Courtesy of her open window, in the back seat I got a mix of wind and smoke in my face.

My brother and I were bickering about something—we frequently bickered. We had just left my mother's parents' house in the Midwood neighborhood of Brooklyn and were heading out to Belle Harbor, in Queens, to my father's parents' house. This trip was our family's Sunday ritual.

It was warm and my shorts-clad legs were sticking to the seat. There was tons of traffic and we seemed to be starting and stopping a lot. Between the heat, the cigarette smoke, and the speeding up and sudden slowdowns, I had a stomachache.

"Mom," I said, pulling gently at the back of her hair. "I don't feel very well. I think I need to throw up."

She turned around on the bench seat, sitting up on her knees so she could reach me. (I'm sure there were seat belts in that car in the '60s, but certainly none of us wore one.) She touched my head with the back of her cool hand and smiled.

"No fever," she pronounced. "We'll be there soon. Just close your eyes and rest."

"Harvey," she said, not unkindly to my ears. "Can you stop tailgating? Please?"

"I'm not tailgating," snapped my father. "You see how much traffic there is."

I heard the impatience in his voice.

My eyes were closed, but I felt the car accelerate and then suddenly slow down. My stomach lurched with the shifting momentum.

"See?" I heard my mother say. "If you weren't so close, you wouldn't need to slam on the brakes."

"Fine," my father roared. "You think you can do better? You drive."

I opened my eyes just in time to see my father open his door and get out of the car *in the left lane on Eastern Parkway.* He slammed the door. Horns started honking. My brother started crying. My mother started pleading. My father started walking.

My mother slid across the seat and gripped the steering wheel, inching forward to keep pace with my father.

"You're going to tell me how to drive?" he yelled at her accusingly.

"Harvey, please. You're scaring the children. Just get back in the car and drive," my mother implored.

"I don't need you to tell me how to drive," he shouted back at her.

She tried again. "Please, Harvey. I'm begging you. Please get back in the car."

"If you don't like the way I drive, you drive," he barked back, increasing his brisk walk to a light jog.

The light turned red. Mom stopped the car, but Dad continued his march up Eastern Parkway. My brother was hysterical. I think I heard my mother mutter, "Damn temper. Just like his father."

I instantly pictured my father's father, Sam. Sam had a very short fuse and instantly displayed his formidable temper. My father was slow to get angry, but once he crossed over to that side, his temper reached an impressive boiling point.

The Printz temper genetically reproduced itself in both my brother and me. Fortunately, in us it came in the Dad variety—lots of bark and no bite.

I wish I could say that his petulant walk down Eastern Parkway taught me something about controlling my own temper. *Au contraire.* I was the queen of door slamming, stair stomping, and other such childish demonstrations of anger. But Dad's zeal for dramatically making his point, and for articulating his position succinctly and unflinchingly, certainly worked its way into the lawyer I became.

The outburst on the Eastern Parkway shined the spotlight on my mother, the clear hero in this episode. In my parents' pretty typical '50s American marriage, that afternoon in Brooklyn gave me a chance to see my usually deferential mother standing up to my father, her mama-bear instinct on full display. I found it remarkable and inspiring to watch her.

My temper surely came to me directly from that Y chromosome. Sometimes, during an oral argument in court, I could feel myself fill with passion for the rightness of it and know that my father would be proud. The instinct to protect and advocate for my child at all costs, however, that's all my mother.

Who knew how much I would need it?

I felt myself smiling in the dark, giving in to the first real smile in days, as the sounds of New York City finally lulled me to sleep.

It was about 2 a.m. when Leon's phone began to ring. I got up to dress even as Leon answered it, knowing that something very wrong had happened to Harrison.

12

Trouble

Nobody sat us down to list all the possible complications that might or might not befall our beautiful baby during his NICU stay. Sometimes I wonder whether knowing what was possible might have steeled me for the many issues that did arise. Or whether not knowing spared me from the needless worry over the many things that did not happen.

Not knowing what could come exacerbated an endless series of crises that left me rattled and always on edge. On any given day, it seemed like some new terror might be revealed.

Rushing back to the hospital in the middle of the night, I reasoned with myself that the brain bleed gave us enough to worry about, that we had paid our NICU dues and were now immune from anything else "bad."

The nurse had told Leon that Harrison had a fever, abdominal distension, and some other "worrisome" symptoms. They wanted our permission to do a spinal tap to rule out meningitis. "Oh, and by the way, you might want to come right away ... "

A spinal tap. Meningitis.

What little I knew about meningitis I had learned watching *General Hospital* with my grandmother. Her favorite soap opera, replete with life-threatening conditions accompanied by dramatic music and overacting, offered up meningitis every several dozen episodes. Depending upon whether the actor was being written off the show, little good ever came to the character who got meningitis.

Yes, I was thinking this as we ran out of the elevator and down the highly polished hallway to the NICU doors.

Feeling pulled toward the spot where we had left Harrison just a few hours earlier, we both had to be scolded—gently reminded—about the need to wash, sterilize, and put on our gowns and booties.

If this were happening now, I would have already read everything I could on the Internet, would already know that in preemies, meningitis is rapidly fatal if not immediately treated, most commonly passed from an infected mother to her newborn, and that the most common bug happens to be listeria. Well, well, well, what do you know? Listeria! Back to that French triple crème cheese that caused me to deliver early in the first place.

But it was 1991. The immediate universe didn't yet live on a smartphone.

Rushing to Harrison's bedside, we didn't know anything except two words that scared us. Spinal tap.

We pulled up short, stopped by the phalanx of human beings surrounding him. Fleetingly, they reminded me of a huddled football team surrounding the quarterback.

One nurse stepped away from the group encircling our son.

She spoke swiftly, softly. I only heard a few of the words—fever, jittery, irritable, big belly, infection—enough to start me quaking where I stood.

"But I told his nurse this afternoon that something was wrong with him. She told me to stop worrying." I could feel my face flushing and I felt dizzy. I rushed on, "I knew it. I knew something was wrong. Why didn't anybody listen to me?"

Leon put an arm around me to steady me. He looked a bit sheepish. I don't think he had believed me either.

"We're doing a lumbar puncture; it's the only way to rule out meningitis."

"How long before we know?" Leon asked.

"We've already added another antibiotic to his drip," she responded, not answering.

I looked at the bags of liquids hanging on poles above the bowed heads of the bedside crowd. Now one of the bags had an ampicillin chaser.

"You guys might want to wait in the lounge. I'll come get you when we're all finished," the nurse said, gently taking my elbow in her hand and steering me away from Harrison.

"No," I said firmly, my feet planted where I stood. "I'm not leaving him again."

Leon had started to walk away, but he came back to where I stood solidly, immovable. "We'll just stand over by the changing room," he suggested, to the nurse's obvious relief.

We stood, leaning into each other, Leon's back supported by a wall, my back supported by Leon, my head burrowed under his arm. With my nose in Leon's armpit, I caught a whiff of something different about him. I think I smelled fear.

He stroked my hair absently, petting it really, more like he might be caressing one of our cats. While we waited there, my thoughts drifted back to that afternoon on Eastern Parkway. A mother for mere days, I knew where and how I had inherited my mama bear instinct.

The meningitis scare robbed us of a night's sleep, but it turned out to be just that—a scare. When the cultures came back, Harrison did not have meningitis. He had sepsis—I didn't know I should be just as scared of that—and I'd soon find out a whole list of new antibiotics intended to rid him of it.

Relief flooded me, and my shoulders dropped down about six inches. I hadn't realized that the tension and stress living in my body had found a home in my right trapezius, that I had hiked up my shoulders practically level with my ears, looking very much like the Teenage Mutant Ninja Turtles that would become popular a few years later.

That right trapezius has plagued me ever since. The hot poker stabbing me in the neck and shoulder is my body's not so subtle way of letting me know I've been subconsciously worrying.

13

Music to Soothe the Savage Beast

(AND A CRYING BABY)

August 31–September 2, 1991

Harrison looked fretful again. One tiny leg kept twitching and despite many efforts to gently hold his miniature foot, I couldn't calm him down. I knew that exertion meant calorie burn. Calorie burn meant no weight gain. No weight gain ... well ...

"He would love listening to music," one of the nurses suggested.

When I left the hospital that afternoon, I found the nearest Radio Shack and bought a cassette player and a box of batteries.

On the way home, I stopped at a record store and combed through the cassettes to find something "appropriate." I settled for *Peter and the Wolf*, a classical symphony for children by the Russian composer Sergei Prokofiev.

I put the batteries in the machine, then wiped down the cassette player with alcohol and put it in a zip-top bag. I wiped down the cassette itself with alcohol and put that in a separate zip-top bag. The extra batteries went into a third zip-top bag with a note: "These are not sterilized."

I felt so excited about going to the Unit the next day. I had music to leave behind so that Harrison would never feel like he was alone.

A nurse propped up the cassette player in the incubator, set it to the lowest volume, and hit play.

"I don't hear anything," I said.

She smiled. "Put your ear in the porthole," she suggested.

Sure enough, the sounds of the strings filled the ear next to the opening and I couldn't keep myself from smiling. My father, not exactly a classical music connoisseur, had given me a record album of *Peter and the Wolf* for my first Victrola.

Leon, who came by his love of classical music honestly—his father played it as a staple in their house while he grew up—insisted on adding Beethoven to our son's soundtrack.

The next day, in addition to Beethoven, we brought the *Brandenburg Concertos*, six lovely pieces by Bach.

Just as the nurse had anticipated, the music calmed our son.

A resting baby is a growing baby, I thought. Harrison seemed to be settling in; that night there was a discussion about adding some breast milk to his feeding tube.

The conversation abruptly ended with the arrival of Harrison's new "neighbor," heralded by a platoon of doctors, nurses, respiratory specialists, and the Chief, who strode behind the isolette with less than his customary bravado.

As hard as I tried to focus only on Harrison, the physical proximity of the activity behind me made it nearly impossible. I easily overheard that this new arrival had a gestational age of twenty-five weeks, a teenage mother who had no prenatal care, and a list of medical conditions, any one of which could kill him.

As I processed that the baby boy had slimmer chances of survival simply because of his gender, I felt a gentle hand on my shoulder—Dr. Andrea—asking me if I wouldn't mind waiting in the lounge for a bit.

I caught a glimpse of the tiny infant as I walked from the center of the action. Twenty-five weeks? I experienced my first pang of self-doubt about my long-held and strongly felt opinion about choice. The Supreme Court used twenty-four weeks as the bright line standard for viability. This demarcation felt inviolate to me because the Supremes had said so. In *Roe v. Wade*, the Court heard not only from lawyers on both sides, but also from *amici curiae*, otherwise known as "friends of the court," who filed briefs on behalf of twenty-three interested parties, organizations, and individuals, scientists, and physicians. That led the nine most learned minds in America to reach the conclusion that twenty-four weeks meant that a pregnancy could be terminated—an absolute right to be privately decided by a woman and her doctor. But did that one week really make the difference between when it was legal to choose to terminate a pregnancy and when it wasn't? Could viability be unambiguously measured with such precision?

Before that day, it had never entered my mind that there might be some fuzziness around when a fetus was viable. In the abstraction of a legal decision, the law clearly set a marker in the ground. Anything before the twenty-four-week mark wasn't viable, anything after the twenty-four-week mark was viable. As "simple" as that.

But the reality of that mark felt vastly different. Glimpsing what twenty-five weeks looked like, that tiny baby who seemed to have an entire unit of the hospital working to save him, I thought, *Well, maybe modern science has lapped the law. Maybe the bright line has dimmed.*

14

A Womb of Secrets

1970/1979

Never an issue of debate for me, a woman's right to choose simply stood as an absolute. I came of age in New York State, where abortion was legalized in 1970, the same year I got my first period. My passage into womanhood began auspiciously one afternoon when my eight-year-old brother pointed at my white Danskin shorts and loudly blurted, "Ughhhh. You sat in something gross."

This pronouncement propelled the other women in the household—an extended family of eleven of us packed cozily into a four-bedroom home built by my maternal grandparents in the early 1940s—into a flurry of activity.

Belts, clips, three-inch-thick sanitary napkins—none of the slim, peel-and-stick pads that grace pharmacy shelves today for "light" days, "heavy" days, or "maximum security" days. Nope. In 1970, the sanitary napkin came in a one-size-fits-all bulk that at first felt like I'd shoved a roll of paper towel between my legs. The enormous wad had long strips on the front and back that got threaded through two plastic clips hanging from an elastic waistband.

The contraption obviously had been designed by someone with a penis.

That a house with four women of menstruating age would have Modess pads stashed in every bathroom and linen closet came as no surprise. That I had never noticed them before that day speaks volumes about how unprepared I was to enter this next life stage.

My mother sat me down for "the talk," which I recall being more of her explanation of what to expect during my "time of the month." I soon learned this loosely translated into an agonizing few days of voluminous vaginal bleeding that arrived unannounced, accompanied by excruciating cramps and a miserable headache.

After about a year of truly awful, and unpredictable, menses, my mother took me to a gynecologist who diagnosed me with primary dysmenorrhea. His decision to put me on a birth control pill as the only way to regulate my body into a normal and less painful cycle earned him an unflattering nickname. When my mother shared this news with my father that evening in a hushed conversation, she referred to the doctor as "That Idiot." I overheard Dad say, "Well, at least we don't have to worry about her getting pregnant."

So began the daily ritual of dialing a white or apricot-colored pill out of the daisy wheel blister pack every day for the next twelve years. I gained a few pounds, my tiny breasts got a tiny bit less tiny, and my cycles became as regular as a Swiss timepiece.

I appreciated the fringe benefit of knowing I didn't need to worry about birth control. Especially so during the afternoon my high school boyfriend got frisky and suggested we "ya know, like, go all the way." I made a mental note of his failure to bring up birth control, adding it to an accumulating list of tits and tats that would eventually lead me to break up with him.

We screwed with reckless impunity for nearly five years. I felt secure in the knowledge that the Ortho-Novum genie watched over me.

In 1970, New York State permitted routine abortions during the first twenty-four weeks of pregnancy, and at any time if the woman's life was at risk. Three years later the Supreme Court issued its landmark ruling in *Roe v. Wade*. The Court held that a woman had the right to make her own reproductive

decisions, specifically, that the Constitution protected a pregnant woman's liberty to choose to have a safe, legal abortion
without excessive government restriction. The ruling adopted the twenty-four-week measuring stick and made legalized
abortion the law of the land. This ended a centuries-long
mishmash of laws that forced women into back alleys or the
offices of questionably competent providers or racing across a
patchwork of states to find a place where it was safe and legal
to choose to end an unwanted pregnancy.

Well, at least until 2022, when the Supremes, in their infi-
nite wisdom, undid fifty years of unquestioned access to safe
reproductive health self-determination in *Dobbs v. Jackson* in
favor of returning laws on such issues to the control of each
of the fifty states. Although millions celebrated the Court's
reversal, I mourned with the many millions of others who saw
this obscene one-eighty by the Court as a tone-deaf decision
completely out of step with the wishes of most Americans,
including those of us who never had to worry about our right
to choose for even a nanosecond of our sentient lives.

With the future undoing of *Roe* an unthinkable piece of
science fiction in 1976, I tightly held the hand of my hallmate,
a fellow college freshman, while she lay in stirrups at a Planned
Parenthood in Upstate New York preparing to undergo an
abortion. I applauded her decision and felt grateful that she
had access to a clean facility filled with compassionate and
helpful practitioners who let me don a gown, booties, and
gloves so that I could stay with my terrified but determined
friend during her procedure.

Highly focused on my role as the supportive distractor, I
kept up a constant stream of chatter throughout. The pre-pro-
cedure counseling and the prep took longer than the actual
procedure, which to me seemed brief and successful.

Terminating a pregnancy wasn't exactly something to shout
from the roof of the dorm at the time; perhaps it still isn't. Our
whispered discussions before and after the procedure reflected
my friend's wish for privacy and our shared belief that regard-

less of its legality, a stigma existed about being "that kind of girl."

The climate of judgment that hushed us then still leaves me indecisive about the wisdom of sharing this part of my past. But having kept it to myself for over forty-five years, I've concluded that I'm fine with being judged for my choices. My intention in sharing stems not from a desire to write a referendum on choice (although I do believe it to be a central freedom), but rather from a determination to bring into the light a previously hidden piece of my puzzle that hopefully helps make the remaining parts fit together—and to free myself from the weight of decades of lonely silence.

And in the "not-for-nothing" category, as I think of my own six nieces, all in their vulnerable twenties, and the millions of other teens and young women of childbearing age for whom access to safe reproductive care may literally mean the difference in how their lives turn out, I'm more motivated than ever to share my experience—warts and all.

So, when I missed my highly dependable period in the spring of 1979, a few years after my hallmate's visit to Planned Parenthood, I marched across the street from the off-campus apartment I shared with my boyfriend to the nearest pharmacy to buy a pregnancy test.

Thinking there must be some other explanation, that the contraceptives wouldn't let me down, I peed on the stick and stared in disbelief at the unmistakable pink line emerging in the results window.

Grabbing the small, thick folded packet glued to the back of my monthly wheel of pills, and leaving behind a small piece that stubbornly clung to the spot where it had been attached, I unfolded it and unfolded it, a paper version of a circus clown car. It grew ever larger until the tissue-paper-thin FDA-approved patient information sheet became a double-sided, two-page tome exceeding the dimensions of most major metropolitan newspapers and with a font so small that I practically needed a magnifying glass to read it. The entire document qualified as "fine print" except the extensive footnotes, which were written in infinitesimally fine print.

Had I bothered to read the patient information sheet at any point in the years prior to that day, I would have learned that my birth control pills had some fallibility. Between two and eight percent to be exact. Given the frequency of intercourse I had with my boyfriend, I figured the odds had finally caught up with me.

I didn't even share the "news" of my pregnancy with him, having no interest in his view on what I should or shouldn't do. Terminating that pregnancy was *this* woman's right to choose, I reasoned. The realization that since it took two of us to get pregnant, it should take two of us to decide what to do about the pregnancy didn't even occur to me until years later. At that red-hot minute, I had no doubt about what to do. I immediately called my former hallmate, who by then had transferred to a different university, and she made her way to be with me when I needed hand-holding for my appointment at Planned Parenthood.

The paperwork (in triplicate), the initials, the signatures, the takeaway reading material—all very thorough, I'm sure. I didn't read a word. I knew what I had to do. My vision for my future didn't include my quitting college to be someone's baby mommy. I didn't waffle. I didn't wonder if I had made the right decision.

That said, the theoretics of the choice didn't prepare me for the experience. Being the woman in the stirrups gave me quite a different perspective than the one I'd had being the supportive friend. As I was lying there, feet up in that insanely immodest and vulnerable position, the complete assault on my senses overwhelmed me.

More than the cold room chilling my skin (necessary for the equipment), the eyes of the kind nurse looking fixedly into my own (I recall not a single word she said), the clean smell of antiseptic, the reassuring friend's hand holding my own, and the gentle touch of the doctor and his play-by-play narration, the unmistakable sound of a vacuum stood out. That sound still takes me back to that day—to the intermittent but persistent pull in my uterus, the cramping, and that continuous sucking sound, the pitch changing as it grabbed at bits of my insides with workmanlike efficiency.

And then it was over.

"You did great," said the doctor, giving one of my knees a reassuring pat on his way out the door.

"You did great," echoed the lovely nurse as she helped me get my feet out of the stirrups and lifted the head of the table so I could rest for a few minutes.

"It's awful, isn't it?" said my friend, beginning to cry. "I'm so sorry you had to go through that." Surely, she didn't mean the five minutes of discomfort. No, she meant something altogether different, but whatever baggage she carried that had reduced her to tears about her own choice, I didn't ask.

It wasn't painless, but it *was* mercifully short. I squeezed my sobbing friend's hand and told her I felt fine, exhausted but incredibly relieved, and eager for a cup of tea, a hot shower, and a nap. I hoped that giving her a "to-do" list might take her mind off her own obvious demons. That, and I didn't want to tell her that I felt quite the opposite of what she apparently felt. I felt a liberating freedom that untethered me from an unwanted connection to a person I saw as merely passing through my life, not someone I wanted taking up permanent residence.

If I had read anything I'd been given during my pre-visit or the day of my procedure, I would not have found a single word warning me about the long-term impact of an abortion on future pregnancies. In 1979, there weren't any studies on the issue and certainly no known risks to consider other than the associated perils that accompanied any minor surgical procedure.

With the first of my uterus's many hidden secrets behind me, I recovered quickly and for another few years I continued to rely on the grace of my daily dose of Ortho-Novum.

I never once questioned either my right to choose or whether I had made the right decision—at least not until I came face-to-face with what happens in the NICU when a twenty-five-weeker meets modern medicine.

15

NEC

September 6, 1991

Central Park beckoned as a refuge of sanity during long afternoons. Walking out of the hospital, crossing the street, and being in the park felt like a B12 shot.

One early evening, after wandering aimlessly for quite a while and uncertain whether I now faced north, south, east, or west, I sat with exhausted exasperation on a bench, furious at myself for momentarily getting lost in the park.

Quickly getting stiff and sweaty on the bench, I couldn't resist the urge to briefly close my eyes. Was I insane? A woman alone in the park. Not much time had passed since the brutal attack on the Central Park jogger; hanging out by myself as dusk crept along the narrow pathways wasn't the smartest thing.

I exhaled a goodbye to my moments of peace, stood up to find the unmistakable profile of the Dakota just south of me on the west side of the park, and walked in the opposite direction back to the hospital and the crisis of the moment.

Within the hour, I ruefully realized that those peaceful moments on the bench might be the last I would have for a long time.

Necrotizing enterocolitis, known as NEC, is the most common and most serious intestinal disease a preemie can get. NEC occurs when intestinal tissue gets inflamed or injured; it can lead to the death of intestinal tissue and, in some cases, a perforation, or hole, in the intestinal wall.

The baby's bowel can't hold waste, and, like a toilet backing up, waste can get into the baby's stomach. As you might guess, this is bad. "Pooping" directly into a vein might be another way to think about it. They both boil down to the same result: a life-threatening infection.

I had barely finished the now familiar process of washing my hands, donning a sterile gown, and putting on a pair of sterile booties over my shoes when the Chief appeared in the doorway.

I had come to view any sighting of the Chief as a bad omen, and this time was no different. Harrison had too many of the signs of NEC to ignore: a tender belly, trouble feeding (which was nothing new), lethargy, and many A's and B's—apneas, during which he stopped breathing for short periods of time, and bradycardias, when his heart rate slowed.

"We suspect the baby might have NEC," he said, his tone lacking any empathy, just as when he had told Leon and me about the brain bleed.

"His name is Harrison," I replied, barely able to contain my fear about the possible diagnosis, but truly angry that this guy kept referring to Harrison as "the baby."

The Chief looked at me like I had two heads. For a fraction of a second, I thought he was going to apologize, or scold me for being sassy. Instead, he looked as serious as a heart attack and explained exactly how grave this potential diagnosis might be.

Harrison, who had valiantly fought his way through multiple infections already, now faced the fight of his very short life.

He was an ideal candidate for NEC. He was born very early, had been oxygen deprived for some unknown period of time, and—in an inexplicable phenomenon—had two NICU neighbors (albeit across the room) with NEC.

NEC "clusters" terrified parents and befuddled doctors and nurses, who did everything humanly possible to prevent the spread of infection.

The first intervention is perhaps the most alarming double-edged sword. Suspend feedings, period. Full stop. Nothing goes into that belly.

Harrison, barely back to his birth weight, could ill afford to miss a feeding, let alone days of feeds, while they monitored him for bloody stools, measured his little belly circumference, did X-ray after X-ray of his abdomen, and gave him the first of three blood transfusions.

Whenever the surgeon appeared in the Unit, the feeling of dread seemed to settle in like a dense fog. Despite his kind face, the sight of Dr. Dolgin terrified me. The Head of Surgery was someone I hoped to never have to meet.

In a gentle and reassuring voice, he explained to Leon and me that in case Harrison's temperature spiked or his belly grew any bigger, he had instructed the nurses to notify him immediately so that he could be ready for surgery. Leon stood behind me and held one arm protectively around my shoulders. His other hand, unseen, nervously jangled some coins and subway tokens, I guessed in his trouser pocket.

"I don't want you to exhaust yourselves by sitting here all night. Go home and get some rest. But just in case, can you sign the consent forms before you go so we don't have to wait if things take a turn?"

I understood that he was just trying to anticipate what might happen, but to me, signing those forms was giving Harrison a *kinehora*, cursing him with the Yiddish equivalent of the evil eye.

I know it was a silly superstition, but I couldn't bring myself to do it. Leon signed. I didn't.

The "watercooler" equivalent for NICU gossip among parents stood at the general location of the scrub room and the lactation cubby. Waiting to wash and gown or standing and waiting my turn for the Medela Classic Breast Pump offered some opportunity for interactions between parents.

One young mom, who didn't look much older than a teenager and had dark rings under deep-set, haunted eyes, began to cry the instant I said hello to her.

My reflexive reaction—to reach out one hand to touch her arm—resulted in her total physical collapse. She fell against me, sobbing uncontrollably, and I felt the sudden embarrassing sensation of my breast milk leaking from the pressure.

A nurse hurried over and gently put her arm around the girl. "I know it's been a long day. We'll hear something soon," she said soothingly.

I knew that no information would be coming to me from the nurse; anything would need to come directly from the mother, who clearly wasn't in any shape to talk. But that moment of contact, feeling her weight against me, made me feel connected to her. And I felt an even greater connection to her son, the twenty-five-weeker who had caused me to question everything I thought I knew about a woman's right to choose.

The nurse steered her back into the Unit, where a neatly made but empty isolette stood with the dreaded tall chair beside it. The chair was draped with a coat and scarf, which the young mom immediately put around her neck as she settled, still sobbing, onto the chair. I tried hard not to stare.

I hadn't noticed that the pump had ceased its unmistakable and precisely timed compression sounds until an extremely attractive woman pulled aside the thin privacy curtain. She wore a bit of makeup, even some lipstick. I recognized her, having seen her during the past few days across the Unit. She had made an impression on me; her clear efforts to be "put together" each day, so far from my own haphazard attempts at personal hygiene, let alone fashion, made her hard to miss. I recalled that her baby's bed stood adjacent to the still crying young mother.

"Excuse me," said the pretty mom as she stepped past me. "All yours," she added.

"Gee, thanks," I said with more than a touch of sarcasm. "I can't wait to get in there."

She paused, seemed to be considering something, and turned back toward me. "Dr. Dolgin came to take her baby earlier today," she began softly. I didn't have to ask whose baby. She lowered her voice even more and added, "He told her he might need to remove a large part of his intestine. My son has it too. NEC, I mean."

Just then, Dr. Dolgin walked briskly through the automatic doors. I could feel my stomach tighten. I felt sick for the young mom, who nearly fell from the chair in her haste to get up to greet him.

My attractive breast-pumping predecessor had managed to work her way back to her own spot, easily within earshot of Dr. Dolgin. I watched her face intently, looking for some sign that would tell me what happened to the young mother's baby.

When the pretty one looked away, opened the isolette door, and put a protective hand on her baby's foot, I knew the news wasn't great.

It took a few hours for it to make its way around the Unit. The young mom's baby had a badly damaged gut. Dr. Dolgin had to remove a large section of the bowel and create a stoma. If that sounds nasty, that's because it is. It means that the surgeon couldn't join the two healthy ends of the bowel together after he had removed the dead section of bowel.

Dr. Dolgin had taken the bowel out of the baby's stomach through a hole and placed it onto the skin with a small bag attached to it. If all went well, once the baby healed, Dr. Dolgin could again try to join the two healthy ends.

The rest of the day dragged on as I tried hard not to watch the near-constant activity around the two cribs across the Unit.

Later that night, Dr. Dolgin returned, this time to talk to the attractive mom. By now, a good-looking man had joined her, I assumed her husband, and the two stood on opposite sides of the isolette listening to Dr. Dolgin.

A pen, a clipboard, each one signing several pages—permission for surgery, I assumed—and moments later a small team came to take their infant.

I thought I would faint. NEC crept around the Unit, leaping from tiny bed to tiny bed.

I couldn't bring myself to leave Harrison that night. I reasoned that I'd stay only another few hours and then just hop in a cab to the apartment on Eighty-Sixth Street. At about 2 a.m., a time when tragedy seems to choose most frequently to strike, I startled awake in my chair, one arm fast asleep where it poked through the porthole keeping one finger on the back of Harrison's tiny hand.

Signaled by a frantic and relentless alarm on the heart monitor, across the Unit a baby had "coded," and an all-hands-on-deck effort to resuscitate the tiny human began. The area instantly flooded with light. Although it did not seem physically possible that so many people could fit in the small space around the now fully elevated bed, aptly called a Giraffe for the extending mechanism below that raised it, within a minute a team had assembled. I watched with the same sense of morbid fascination I might have watched a car accident. The professionals worked quietly, and their movements were swift. From where I sat watching in the semidarkness, it soon became clear that the effort was fruitless, and the team members backed away respectfully, reverently, at being bested by Death.

Having this front-row seat to a clash with the Grim Reaper immediately conjured thoughts of the night my father died, and shaken by what I had just witnessed, my mind began an endless loop of the scene.

Bleary from lack of sleep, I watched as a man arrived and wrapped the dead infant in a blanket, lifted it from the bed, and carried it gently in his arms. Without ceremony, he left the NICU cradling the infant as though it still breathed life. A group of nurses descended on the now empty bed and began to meticulously sterilize it, change out the mattress, and apply a fresh sheet. In moments, the bed stood ready to accept its next occupant. I couldn't help but press gently on Harrison's hand and hope that Death felt satisfied with the night's bounty.

In a heartbreaking second, my mind snagged on something it had missed before. *That bed, that baby... The young teen's baby has died. I don't know her, but I'm filled with grief for her. I think of that instant of connection we had at the pumping station, and I feel like I know her. I want to hold her, hug her, comfort her. I feel crazy with worry for her. Will someone be with her when the hospital calls,* I suddenly wonder.

Other babies have died in the several weeks since Harrison arrived. But the anonymity of the NICU made them seem like tragic misfortunes that befell a nameless family. I observed them with sadness but detachment.

Not this time. This feels so personal.

Karen, a skilled and talented nurse with a faint Jamaican accent, Harrison's duty nurse that night, gently put an arm around me and suggested it might be a good time to go get some sleep.

My mood, down and scared, didn't improve with the few hours of restless sleep I attempted that night, and I walked back in the morning just as the light began to fill the sky over Central Park.

The blood draws, tiny needle punctures referred to as "heel sticks," which already seemed annoyingly too frequent, became incessant. It felt like someone came to take Harrison's blood every hour, leaving his tiny heels bruised and purple. My heart ached from so many things, but for some reason, the sight of his purple heels tore at me.

After days of watchful waiting, antibiotics, no food, and many X-rays later, the Chief stopped by and announced that "the baby" didn't have NEC at all, just an intolerance to the human milk fortifier they had added to supplement my breast milk in his feedings.

As if reading my mind, Dr. Andrea, who had waited respectfully for the Chief to walk away after delivering his welcome news, said simply, "Quite the roller-coaster ride, isn't it?"

"What is it with him?" I couldn't help but ask. "Why doesn't he call Harrison by his name? I mean, it's right there on his crib card. How hard could it be to glance down and use his name?" I wondered aloud to Dr. Andrea, feeling the heat in my face as I said it.

She didn't look at me directly, a very unusual response considering the typically forthright and open style of communication I loved about her.

Decades later, when I became the March of Dimes NICU Family Support Specialist at a local hospital, I noticed that one of the doctors in that Unit did the same thing—she never called the infants by their given names. She referred to them as "the baby," not even "your baby" or "your son."

I was in a different stage in my life, older than she, and did not feel intimidated to ask her for an explanation.

Her answer surprised me. "If I call them by their names, I become too attached to them."

I thought back to the Chief. I had never considered the possibility that his choice of words masked his coping mechanism, that by keeping them generic "babies," he was trying to inoculate himself against the sadness and loss that were ever-present in the Unit. Now I understand that rather than being an unfeeling automaton, he was practicing self-care. He was a brilliant specialist who took phenomenal care of my kid and all those other vulnerable kids in the Unit. I know now that we were truly lucky to have landed in his NICU.

16

Milk, Milk Everywhere

September 15, 1991

With apologies to Coleridge, there truly was milk every-where, and for a long time, "nor any drop to drink." We tossed my hard-earned meager milk production down the drain for the first ten days, until I had completed my full course of antibiotics. And even then, Harrison, still too premature to get much more than his supercharged drip, demanded nothing, but I still had to supply milk. Among her many cheerily de-livered pieces of advice, the lactation specialist terrified me with warnings about my milk drying up if I didn't stay on a mimicked feeding schedule.

So, each day, I pumped—with three different machines, the one at home, the one at work, and the one at the hospital. It was incredibly challenging to remember where the accessories were at any given moment, so I finally broke down and bought cooler totes for each location. We bought a mini fridge for my office to keep the milk fresh. At the end of each afternoon at the office, I would pack up my tote with the expressed milk from that day, get my car from the lot on the corner of Twen-ty-Eighth and Park, drive to pick up Leon on the corner of Fifty-Third and Madison, and continue north for another fifty blocks to the hospital.

We'd sit with Harrison for a while until I'd have to go pump. Depending on that day's crisis, we would sit with him for a bit longer, then—always reluctantly—leave. I hated leaving him. In the early days, it felt like he might not be there when I got back. And even as his prognosis rocketed back and forth from unqualified disaster to stable, I always hated leaving him.

Many nights, we would grab dinner "to go" from a local specialty store and eat on the armrest in the front seat of the car as we crossed the Triborough Bridge to head home.

Did I mention that we were renovating the house at the time? That there wasn't a dust-free surface anywhere? That there were some nights when we got pizza and ate on top of the gigantic KNACK box that took up a sizable space in what would eventually be the sunroom?

A combination of Harrison's precarious and ever-changing medical status and going home to the wreck of the Hesperus made the sanctuary of Leon's brother's unused apartment on Eighty-Sixth Street even more of a godsend. It freed up at least three hours each day of hassling with the commute back and forth from Long Island, parking the car, unparking the car, garaging the car, re-garaging the car, parking the car, unparking the car, and so on. This got old extremely fast in our already exhausted lives.

Of course, my life would not be complete without the manual breast pump that we kept in the car. Since we spent so much time in the car going to and from wherever we happened to be going to and from that day, I always needed to know I could pump without electricity.

If the dual breast pumping took coordination, manually pumping on the Van Wyck Expressway practically took the skill of a diamond cutter.

When my breasts got the hang of it, breast milk could be found stashed in every corner of the freezer. I'd like to think this chaos was organized. At least I had the date and time in black marker on the outside of each freezer bag.

We needed a system.

The system included getting a freezer just for storing breast milk at home.

It also quickly became clear that the hospital didn't really have much of a system either. "Pump and dump" was the favored method of dealing with extra breast milk in the NICU. If your baby couldn't finish what you had pumped that day, down the sink it went. It broke my heart every time I watched a nurse take the milk I had worked so hard to produce and throw it down the drain like a cold cup of yesterday's coffee.

I decided that I needed to do something to make my life easier. Incidental to making my own life easier, my advocacy made it easier on other families to function in this alien and unfriendly place. It also made me feel somewhat less like a bit player in Harrison's life.

My first act as a family advocate was to buy a freezer for the NICU. Of course, this needed the blessing of the Chief, who deigned to give me a brief audience one afternoon as I sat miserably beside the isolette.

In general, his disposition seemed entirely unsuited to dealing with overwrought parents of incredibly sick kids. But I had dealt with far more imperious members of the New York bench and bar—I could handle this guy.

I pled my case. Most of the mothers here had children too ill to drink the milk they expressed. The nurses unrelentingly insisted that "breast is best." Yet those same nurses didn't give it a second thought when they tossed a batch of unused milk down the sink because they had no place else to put it. What if we had a refrigerator/freezer where all the lactating mothers could store and label their milk? And where all the nurses could put back the unused portion to be used at the next feeding? And for my grand finale: What if someone was willing to donate it to the NICU so the hospital didn't have to pay for it?

The Chief's expression went from dismissive to doubtful to approving as I quickly gave my *spiel*.

"Sure," he said. "As long as the nurses say it's okay and they can find a place to put it."

I glanced over at Dr. Andrea, who gave me a subtle thumbs-up sign. I then peeked over at the head nurse, who briefly eyed me with an expression somewhere between admiration and irritation—finding a place for this appliance and implementing a system for its use would fall to her. But when the Chief turned around to look at her, she beamed. "Of course, Doctor. What a wonderful idea! I'll be sure to take care of it with Maintenance right away."

I basked in my victory. Yes, I had made *my* life much easier. But I had made the lives of my sisters in breast pumping much easier, too. And those of the many who would come after us. I felt great for the first time since—wow, I really had to think—since the morning we cheerfully packed the truck with our lawn chairs and picnic blankets for the Paul Simon concert about a lifetime ago.

Now that storing milk at the hospital had become a reality, there was no more *schlepping* cooler bags and ice packs back and forth. I pumped milk faster than it went down Harrison's NG tube, so my twice-daily pumping sessions at the hospital kept a constant supply on hand.

I felt terrific satisfaction looking at the neatly stacked freezer bags of milk. The lactation specialist's early assurance that "breast is best" had convinced me that this visual manifestation of my motherhood would eventually be all the nourishment my baby needed.

17

Taking a Breath

September 27, 1991

I had never given much thought to breathing before I gave birth to Harrison. Breathing didn't seem to need any "help" to happen; it just seemed to me to be a naturally occurring phenomenon.

But Harrison taught me many things from the earliest instant of his life. Breathing just doesn't come naturally.

The morning Harrison was born, I don't recall anyone asking me if I wanted him to be resuscitated should anything go wrong.

Unlike the big black DNR sign on my grandmother's hospital door indicating her wish not to be kept alive artificially, no such DO NOT RESUSCITATE directive had been asked of me.

Looking back on it, I'm not sure what I would have said had I been asked "in the heat of the moment."

My grandmother was in her eighties, her body was ravaged by cancer, and she knew what she wanted and didn't want. Being on a respirator went easily in the unwanted category.

But the morning Harrison came quietly into the world, not breathing and not improving even after "bagging," he was intubated in the delivery room and *voilà*—a machine breathed for him.

He would likely have died if they didn't intubate him. But I lacked any understanding of the consequences to Harrison if they did intubate him.

Harrison remained on a ventilator for fifty days.

As a direct result of this artificial breath of life, he developed bronchopulmonary dysplasia (BPD). This is a respiratory disease that sometimes happens when an infant's lungs are undeveloped, making a ventilator or oxygen therapy necessary for support. High amounts of inhaled oxygen and pressure can tax the alveoli in the infant's lungs, resulting in damage to the inside lining of the airways, the alveoli, and the blood vessels around them. These side effects of being on a ventilator are especially pronounced in preemies. Most of the infants who develop BPD are born more than ten weeks early, weigh less than two pounds, and have breathing problems at birth.

Unlucky Harrison. He checked all the boxes. He would surely have died without the ventilator, but he got BPD because of the ventilator.

They finally extubated him on September 27, although he still needed respiratory support.

Later that afternoon, we got an exciting piece of good news; Harrison had a normal eye exam. I didn't dare ask what a normal eye exam meant in terms of his brain bleed. It felt like a tonic to hear something upbeat.

Well-meaning nurses, doctors, and friends advised against reading materials about health problems in infants, but I had previously devoured an article about retinopathy of prematurity. I felt elated to cross something off my list of things to worry about.

18

Does Anybody Really Know What Time It Is?

October 7, 1991

In the NICU, time takes on a different meaning than it has "outside." Often the only way I had any idea about the time of day came from watching the nursing shifts change. That went like clockwork.

The staff would double in size for about thirty minutes or so as each nurse "reported out" on his or her patients to the incoming nurse. The dyads moved isolette to isolette, crib to crib, heads inclined toward one another, their voices hushed to maintain patient privacy as they discussed confidential information.

Shift change had an elegance to it. It was like a dance; the couples moved in tandem across the polished floor, focused only on their partners. That is until an alarm went off, or the phone rang, or the entry door buzzed, or a dozen other interruptions caused the pairs to pause, to separate, but to always return to finish their dance.

The windowless inner room, where the most acutely ill babies arrayed around a central nurses' station, felt like an especially difficult space to appreciate time (or weather). I easily lost track of days of the week, times of the day; the only reminders were the nurses' shifts, the doctors' rounds in the morning, and the noticeable filling of my breasts, which didn't tell me the time, only that about four or five hours had passed. Occasionally, I felt the drag of time passing so slowly that it seemed like a day had gone by since I had last visited the pumping cubby.

The only other reliable indication that evening melted into night came when the lights dimmed and the blanket-covered isolettes mimicked the circadian rhythm of sleep time for the babies. That was the time for bedtime stories and lullabies, but for some reason Harrison tossed that night, and I gave up on bedtime stories after just a few pages.

"If you don't feel like reading, you can sing to him," suggested our nurse.

"You've never heard me sing," I replied dryly.

"He doesn't care how bad you are!" she said, gesturing at my restless son. "He'll have plenty of time to be embarrassed by you when he's older," she joked, one of the few times I recall her saying anything hopeful that even hinted at him getting out of here.

Singing to Harrison felt more awkward than that first day of reading the *New York Times* had felt, but I started singing the first song that popped into my head, the love song of all love songs, "As Time Goes By," a Dooley Wilson classic from the movie *Casablanca*, which Leon and I had watched together dozens of times.

Despite my former membership in the middle school chorus, my adult voice lacked the slightest musicality. Even as I crooned the tuneless words into the porthole, I thought to myself, *My God, I'm worse than Dad!*

My father sang. Embarrassingly, in public, mixing up the words, delivering hopelessly tuneless, off-tempo singing—with great gusto.

Even as I sang the familiar words to "As Time Goes By," my mind wandered to some of Dad's Greatest Hits.

"Love Is Blue"—the real version, most famously recorded in 1968 by Paul Mauriat—begins:
"Blue, blue, my world is blue
Blue is my world now I'm without you."

Dad's version began:
"Blue, blue, your eyes are blue
Blue are your eyes, and your brother's are too."
The additional verses center on the colors gray, red, green, and black, and Dad sang his own version for each color. I don't remember any of the other verses except for the "black" one. It was dark, macabre, and oddly prescient. I'm not sure if that's why it stuck with me all these years, but his version went like this:
"Black, black, my lungs are black
Black are my lungs, I'll have a heart attack."
I mean, really, Dad …

At the other end of the emotional spectrum, Dad, a romantic at heart, took me to see *Love Story* the day after its release because he knew I had a crush on Ryan O'Neal. The instrumental theme song, "Love Story" (otherwise called "Where Do I Begin?"), performed by Henry Mancini for the film, topped the Easy Listening charts in 1971 when Andy Williams did a soul-wrenching vocal version of it.

In Dad's version,
"Where do I begin
To tell the story of how great a love can be … "
morphed into:
"Where do I begin
To tell the story of how great a dad can be
The truest story that is older than the sea
The simple truth about how great a dad can be
Where do I start?"
He had endless variations on "My Favorite Things," the Rodgers and Hammerstein classic from *The Sound of Music*, depending on what we were doing at the time:
"Raindrops on roses and fresh huckleberries"
or
"A beautiful daughter with a father who sings
These are a few of my favorite things."

When my brother, Robert, got proficient enough to play it on the piano, he and Dad kept my mother and me entertained for hours with their energetic renditions.

And because my mother's nickname—short for Sandra—happened to sound like the title of a wildly popular song, Dad loved to serenade her with "Sunny." In the second verse, the singer thanks Sunny for the *"sunshine bouquet."* Dad either misheard it or just preferred his version: *"Sonny, thank you for the sunshine parade."*

Butch Cassidy and the Sundance Kid first appeared on the silver screen in 1969. The hit song from the movie, "Raindrops Keep Fallin' on My Head," sung by B. J. Thomas, won an Oscar for Best Original Song. Dad earnestly tried to sing it correctly, which made his mistakes even funnier. The best he could do sounded something like:

"Raindrops keep falling on my head
They keep falling
Those raindrops are falling on my head
And my feet are too big for the bed
Those raindrops keep falling on my head."

All those words are in the song, just not in the order Dad put them!

Helen Reddy famously covered a song in 1973 that happened to come along at a time when my moody streak threatened to carry on from months into years. As a fifteen-year-old awkward teen, I responded to practically anything anyone said with a clipped answer that segued into "Just leave me alone," typically followed by either me stomping up the stairs or me storming out of the room. On its way to becoming a million seller, "Leave Me Alone (Ruby Red Dress)" played endlessly, and Dad swore it had been written with me in mind.

In Dad's view, the monotonous chorus didn't need a word of tinkering. He considered it perfect just as written and made sure to sing a few bars to me every time I flashed my bad attitude. My whining, irritable, snappy "just leave me alone" retort had barely escaped my lips when Dad broke out in full-throated song:

"Leave me alone, won't you leave me alone
Please leave me alone, now leave me alone
Oh, leave me alone, please leave me alone
Yes, leave me, leave me alone."

Yes, those are the actual words, and right as he nearly always was, I got so sick of hearing him sing that song that I stopped telling everyone in the house to leave me alone just to get him to stop singing it!

As I finished "As Time Goes By" for about the tenth time, I gazed at my precious Harrison. Would I ever get to see him be mortified by my terrible singing?

Just then a familiar voice whispered close to my ear, "You're playing our song." I smiled at Leon's words. "Happy anniversary," he added.

I was touched that he had remembered, and told him so. Maybe this whole being a father thing had made him a little soft.

"Don't worry," he assured me, as if reading my thoughts. "I only know because your mother called!"

We sat together for the final hours of our seventh wedding anniversary, watching Harrison, who was finally sleeping peacefully, as I chided myself for not even knowing what day it was.

19

Brains Bleed

October 11, 1991

With sufficient distractions, worrying about the nameless, faceless, indistinct enemy called the Brain Bleed had receded in my mind. Just as it had been doing in Harrison's.

This was confirmed by science in the form of a smiling Dr. Andrea. Holding a single sheet of paper in her hand, she reported the results of the latest sonogram: the intraventricular hemorrhage that had measured 9 mm (the grade 3 bleed) now had reduced to 6 mm!

She went on to explain that Harrison's brain had slowly but measurably resorbed the bleed. The massive bleed that had worried everyone so much had become, well, less worrisome.

I immediately followed up with "Less worrisome as in 'he's going to be fine'? Or is there still some mysterious potential disaster, only smaller?"

Dr. Andrea looked at me inscrutably. Where a moment before she had been all smiles, when asked a direct question about the impact of the bleed, she slipped back into professional hedging.

I got the same noncommittal "We don't know," "It's still too early to tell," "This is an encouraging sign, but the damage may have already been done" series of answers that we had been given that very first day we were told about the Brain Bleed.

I felt the hot tears springing to my eyes unbidden, as they had so many times during the promised roller-coaster ride. The ambiguity of this information left me terrified and surprisingly furious.

I railed at Dr. Andrea for about five minutes, running out of steam before I ran out of emotion. I didn't even realize that she had deftly maneuvered us out of the middle of the Unit. And then she said something that stopped me in my tracks.

"I can't imagine what you're going through," she said kindly.

The bitter retort, "No, you can't," thankfully got caught by my inner filter.

I managed a feeble, teary, and exhausted "Thanks. I know you're just telling me what you know and not guessing."

"Right," she agreed. "With some things, we just have to wait and see what happens."

I hated the Brain Bleed. In that moment, later that afternoon as I recounted the story to Leon, and countless other times, I wondered how long before we knew just how ugly that dragon would be. My life experience had taught me how unexpectedly and unapologetically our bodies can betray us.

20

T-Minus Not Counting

Exhibit B—Betrayals

1984/1989–1990

Leon and I had been married only a few months when I went for my annual gynecology exam. In the forced banter that women have come to know and hate as our breasts are poked and prodded, Dr. Cherry paused—just a split second—over one spot.

"How long have you had this?" he asked, bringing my left hand up to a spot just over the areola of my right breast.

"No idea," I said honestly. I mean, really. I was twenty-six—who checks their breasts for lumps?

In 1984, with the one-stop shop for mammograms, sonograms, and immediate radiology results still in the distant future, the draining month long process of doing it the old-fashioned way began.

First, there was the referral to a radiologist. Then the wait for the appointment. Then the exam. Then the sonogram. Then the mammogram. Then the biopsy, in a hospital. Then the grueling and nerve-racking wait for results.

I felt terrified every day, and Leon counseled me against being "prematurely upset," a refrain he has hauled out on multiple occasions ever since. Since I had made the mistake of telling my mother somewhere along the way, she worried enough for all of us. She had read in a magazine that being on the Pill for long periods of time increased the chances of breast cancer. This gave her the opportunity to vent about how much she disliked That Idiot, the doctor who had put me on the pill when I was fourteen.

My first brush with a scary lump ended with a great diagnosis. Although I needed a lumpectomy, the lump turned out to be a harmless fibroadenoma. An outpatient hospital visit, several stitches, an ice pack, and a few new worry lines were all I had to show for the experience.

"See," Leon reiterated, "I told you not to get prematurely upset." My clenched fists were dangerously close to bashing him in the head.

Breast cancer ran in my family, I'd been on the birth control pill for over a decade, and I was only twenty-six—all of which made my gynecologist more cautious than he might have otherwise been. He took me off the Pill immediately, fitted me for a diaphragm, and counseled me on its proper fit.

Then came the annual follow-up mammograms, with their many "delights"—getting squeezed between those vise-grip steel plates, the empty apology from the technician for how cold they were, the awkward body positioning—feet pointing one way, head pointing the other way, one arm straining at the socket to hold a bar that felt about an inch too far out of reach—followed by the warning to "hold your breath," and then, my favorite part, the excruciating wait for results.

Thankfully, after several years of lump- and bump-free scans, the radiologist let me "graduate" to three years before my next dance with the mammography machine.

Visiting Dr. Cherry for my routine annual exam in the early months of 1989, I shared my excitement at finally being able to put the breast cancer scare in the rearview mirror.

When one of his nurses called me a few days later to tell me that my Pap smear had come back abnormal, my immediate reaction was disbelief. Surely there had been a mistake.

What now?

"He needs to see you right away," she told me. As hard as I tried to use my lawyerly powers of questioning, she wouldn't say another word.

Dutifully making an appointment, this time I didn't tell Leon about it. Another infuriating chiding from him that I shouldn't be "prematurely upset" would have just made matters worse.

My appointment was like a scene from a movie.

I sit across from my Park Avenue doctor, Sheldon Cherry. He looks serious.

"Lisa," he starts, "are you, um, sexually active outside your marriage?"

"What?" I respond in a huff. "No way. Why?"

"Well, your Pap test shows active abnormal cells that are consistent with a sexually transmitted disease—human papillomavirus, or HPV."

"I don't understand," I stammer. "I can't have an STD. I've had only one partner since, like, 1983."

He looks at me thoughtfully, measuring something in his mind. "There's only one way to get this, Lisa. And you'll need to tell all your partners so they can be tested. Untreated, it can be serious."

I have no idea what he could be talking about.

"How serious is it?" I ask.

"Left untreated, it leads to cervical cancer."

"What's the treatment?"

"Well, we have a doctor on staff who's trained in laser surgery. She'll cauterize the abnormal cell tissue and you'll be as good as new."

"When do I need to do this?"

"As soon as possible."

Yes, that could have been an episode of *General Hospital*, Grandma Hannah's favorite soap, but no, the actual conversation with Dr. Cherry happened just like that.

I left the Upper East Side brownstone and walked thirty blocks back to my office. How in the world could I have HPV? My mind raced. It could only be from Leon.

Did that mean ... wait ... what ... that he'd been cheating on me?

By that evening, my imagination was running wild, summoning all the times I had been out of town on a legal matter, all the instances when a lawsuit had taken him away from me. It was possible, right? No sooner had Leon walked through the front door than I went nuclear.

The accusations started flying. Screaming, crying, cursing at him, ranting about some surgical procedure that sounded horrible, I let it all out. When he looked at me blankly, my head felt like exploding.

"What are you talking about?"

"I have an STD," I hiss. "I know *I'm* not sleeping with anybody else. That only leaves you, you fucking cheater."

"Whoa. The only person I'm sleeping with is you," he says.

"Right."

"I'm serious," he insists. "Wait a second. They told me this might happen."

"Who told you what might happen?"

And out comes the full story. He had herpes during college—a decade before we even met. The campus infirmary doctor explained that because it's a virus (HSV), it might stay dormant in his body permanently or might reappear with no explanation.

"How come you never told me?" I ask.

"I don't know," he concedes. "I haven't had a flare up in so long, I just thought it had gone away."

I immediately called Dr. Cherry. The doctor on call got back to me within minutes. I described the situation and finished by asking if this "cockamamie story" my husband just told me could be true.

"Absolutely," confirmed the doctor. "In fact, if you've had multiple partners during your life, it's possible that *you* had it all along. We don't know for sure, but we think it's possible that HPV, like HSV, can stay dormant and undetectable for years without you having been previously symptomatic."

I thanked the doctor, hung up the phone, and slowly turned to my husband.

"Well?" he demanded. "What did he say?"

"He said it's possible that I didn't even get it from you. It's possible that I got it years ago and it's been lying low all this time."

I didn't apologize right then and there for leaping to the conclusion that he'd cheated. He didn't show an ounce of empathy. For weeks, our spacious two-bedroom apartment felt like a shoebox.

The day of the laser surgery, I told Leon I would be fine, that he should just go to the office and I would call him when I got finished. We parted wordlessly on the subway platform.

Later that evening, as I sat on my "donut" over a sitz bath filled with ice to ease the excruciating pain, I felt like I'd been punished, but for what, I didn't know.

The recovery took longer than I had anticipated, and the aftercare—painful, time-consuming, and messy—infuriated me anew each time I had to apply the antibiotic cream. The laser had cauterized an extremely sensitive area, the labia minora.

Back to being a gynecological problem child, I began to see Dr. Cherry once every six months for a repeat Pap.

I'd only gotten one clean Pap when the next one came back abnormal.

"How's that possible? I mean, we did that whole laser thing … " I trailed off, remembering the searing pain. Even as I sat across from Dr. Cherry, I could feel the continuous sensation of needles and pins in the spots where I had any feeling at all.

He patiently explained *again* that this might not be the last time the STD reared its ugly head and that I would once again need a laser procedure.

This time, the abnormal cells had parked themselves just inside the vaginal opening. When the numbing medication wore off, it felt like a red-hot poker had been rammed inside me. It took many months before I felt remotely like myself.

Although we didn't know which one of us had the virus to begin with, we both paid a heavy price for it. It took years for me to regain any pleasurable feeling in a spot designed for "feeling all the feelings." The multiple laser procedures had compromised the blood supply and nerve endings, so, during intercourse, my vagina felt like a freshly stripped piece of furniture getting its final going over with sandpaper.

Finding it impossible to enjoy intimacy, I withdrew. That made life difficult for both of us. I expected Leon to understand how the opposite of enjoyable intercourse had become, but I never bothered to explain it to him. I just put up a wall between us and became even more of a workaholic.

Abnormal had become my normal.

Things between us were tense, to say the least. We put up an incredibly good front, though. I threw Leon a surprise thirty-fifth birthday party, and I think we seemed the picture of happiness to the thirty or so friends and family in attendance.

It took most of 1989 to recover physically. It took much longer for *us* to recover. I had doubts about whether I still loved him.

My entire legal practice involved couples whose marriages ended up in the toilet. Usually, by the time one of them got to my office, at least one spouse had decided to call it quits. But before that, the spouse being left behind usually had an instinctive stress response to being threatened—stay and fight, or turn around and flee.

When a marriage goes through a rough patch, and one spouse reacts with "fight" and the other spouse reacts with "flight," reconciliation becomes nearly impossible. The two are heading in opposite directions.

And that's what happened to us. We each reacted very differently to the STD stressor. I fled, hiding behind the physical pain as an excuse for pulling away from Leon physically and emotionally. And in some small, dark place, I simply didn't believe him. That tiny bit of doubt, that miniscule mistrust can set a marriage to "self-destruct." Once I let my doubt about

Leon's fidelity creep into my mind, it took root there in all its noxious and destructive glory.

Leon stood his ground and fought for us.

Despite the prolonged strain we were under, we coped as best we each could. We both logged exceedingly long hours, using work as a reason to avoid each other, and explaining it away as being a critical time when each of us was in partnership contention at our respective law firms. Conveniently for me, Leon was the lead associate on an international matter that took him out of New York regularly and for long stretches of time.

He called me twice a day. My end of the conversation rarely included more than a few words strung together. My answers were curt and mostly monosyllabic.

Yet one day this same person insisted that the hotel security team let themselves into Leon's room because I was worried that he hadn't called me. I imagined him unconscious from a fall in the shower, or dead from drowning in the bathtub. I must have sounded convincingly frantic to get the hotel to agree. I can't imagine the look on Leon's face when he was awakened from a deep sleep by a security guard and the hotel manager standing over his bed. Only someone who deeply cared about the other person would have burst into tears, as I did, when he called me in the middle of the night. The relief I felt when I heard his voice from across the pond told me a great deal about my feelings. I was genuinely surprised. *My goodness. I love this man.*

My marital minefield, always one step from exploding around me, felt treacherously fragile. Although I'm sure there were many others, I cycled through six discernable emotions that ebbed and flowed like ocean tides, returning with unexpected intensity, like the rogue wave that somehow makes it further up the shore than its sister waves.

The various emotions that I experienced when I wasn't purposely drowning in work triggered some predictable reactions.

1. Fearful: Being scared, panicked, and even terrified are natural feelings during a marital meltdown. I was afraid of the unknown: Is he leaving me? Am I leaving him? And if we split, who gets the good china?

2. Furious: Being angry with Leon, with the world, and with my body's refusal to cooperate felt strangely liberating in the moment but did nothing to advance repairing the relationship. Throwing a piece of the good china may be satisfying momentarily, but when I host the whole family for Passover, I'll miss that twelfth dinner plate.

3. Frustrated: I felt emotionally, sexually, and mentally unfulfilled—simply exasperated with Leon and his inability to understand my *whys*: *Why am I scared? Why am I angry? Why doesn't he get it?*

4. Frosty: Not to be confused with *frigid*—which literally means "unable to achieve orgasm" (which in my case turned out to be true for a very long time)—*frosty* means that every time Leon came near me, I felt as warm toward him as the lasagna that had been in the freezer since last year.

5. Fatigued: It is exhausting to be afraid, incensed, irritated, *and* glacial, not necessarily in that order. I was bound to be exhausted. Just another reason why intercourse during this time felt like such a chore.

6. Forgiving: The path to forgiveness is paved with patience. In our case, several years of patience. We both felt wronged. We both felt misunderstood. We both felt alienated. The trouble with staying angry at each other for so long? We both lost sight of how we got to Siberia in the first place.

I don't mean to minimize how truly awful things were between Leon and me during those years by sharing a tongue-in-cheek cataloging of a time that I'd really like to forget. Dredging up the pain that took me years to get past feels daunting and not readily accessible to me. I will share what I recall, as imperfectly as I remember it, but spoiler alert—the headline reads, "Doomed Marriage Survives." When we finally came out the other side, a new and much more challenging test loomed around the next corner.

That our marriage withstood the physical and psychological pain that mostly *I* inflicted didn't just happen. Leon refused to give up. And while he can write his own account of his reasons for being so tenacious, I have long suspected that he didn't want his marriage to fail in the same way his parents had failed.

I don't really know for sure, and if pressed, I wonder if Leon would (or even could) articulate his parents' turbulent relationship as the reason he stood his ground and fought for us.

But fight he did in the ways he knew how. He enlisted my mother in a secret mission to help him buy me a full-length mink coat. He chose the fur, selected an elegant lining, and in a lovely finishing touch, had my initials embroidered inside. This was not yet the era of being anti-fur and the gift took my breath away. He tried hard to get us back on the same page, and he often did it with grand gestures. The mink certainly remains among the top five.

But there were other gestures that he knew would be meaningful to me. During the complex and gigantic hostile takeover deal he was working on, he was in England for Passover. He asked the client if he could have a few days off—and if he could take the Concorde and charge it to the client—so that he could surprise me by getting home in time for the first seder meal.

My adored grandmother, Hannah, my mother's mother, had become quite ill. She had cancer that had metastasized from her parotid gland to her bones, causing her excruciating pain. She had nursing at home around the clock and I saw her nearly every day. When Leon was in town, he never passed up a chance to visit Grandma Hannah with me.

Her death in late September 1990 hit me especially hard. I remember getting the call at the office that she had died. In tears, I instinctively called Leon. He immediately began to cry, and we sat together on the phone, separated by two avenues and five city blocks, listening to each other breathing and sobbing. Leon finally pulled himself together and directed me to meet him on a street corner so that we could drive back to Long Island as quickly as possible.

Looking back on it, Grandma Hannah's death marked the turning point for Leon and me. Leon loved her ferociously and knew that she was the dearest person in the world to me. He behaved with such tenderness, not only to me, but to my mother, that despite how sad I felt to lose Grandma, I saw clearly that it devastated him, too. I loved Grandma to my very core. Leon loved her dearly. That truth made me realize just how much I loved Leon.

His solid presence beside me during the funeral and *shiva* (week of mourning in the Jewish tradition), the endless number of things he took care of so that my mother, my brother, and I didn't have to, the support he gave me, and the vulnerability he showed in his own grief for Grandma's death just broke the dam I had built to hold him back.

When we emerged, he had convinced me that together we could do anything. At some point in the many couplings of makeup sex that followed, we got pregnant. We were ecstatic. But we also felt melancholy that the person who would have been happiest about this news, Grandma Hannah, wasn't around to see it.

Once we landed in the NICU, it quickly became clear that as a team we could face all the curveballs the Unit threw at us, leaning hard on each other for the strength that exponentially multiplied by being together.

Faced with the gravity of Harrison's minute-to-minute struggle for survival, I rarely thought about the horrendous laser procedures, or wondered about their potential long-term impact. They were just part of the growing basket of insults I had hurled at my uterus.

21

Maybe Just Breast Isn't Always Best

October 28, 1991

A spinal tap for meningitis, suspected NEC, BPD, possible sepsis, hyperbilirubinemia, conjunctivitis, and—oh, yeah, the brain bleed—what other surprises did Harrison have in store for us?

When Dr. Andrea approached us with what we had come to fear as her "grave" face, I heard myself say in my head, *Now what?*

I felt dumbstruck when she spoke.

"Harrison has rickets," she said solemnly.

Instantly, in a highly affected British accent, Leon boomed, "Avast, ye matey!" Every head turned in our direction.

"Don't sailors get *scurvy*?" I asked.

"Aye, lassie," agreed Leon, still using his all-purpose accent.

Dr. Andrea allowed herself a small smile.

She began to explain that Harrison had a vitamin D deficiency, likely a result of having only breast milk.

Here we go again, I thought. *My breast milk isn't good enough*. I could already feel hot tears stinging my eyes.

"He'll be okay," she assured me. "We just need to add more calcium and phosphorus to his diet." Dr. Andrea reminded me that it was Harrison's intolerance to the human milk fortifier that had caused his serious gastrointestinal issues, given him reflux, and distended his belly when he had the NEC scare.

Then she told us more about rickets. It was a bone disease that retarded growth. Because of his body's inability to properly absorb calcium and phosphorus, Harrison's bones were soft and allowed for bending and distortion. In other words, left untreated, he could have delayed bone growth and bowlegs, and in rare cases, spontaneous fractures.

"How did this even happen? I mean, you take blood from him about a thousand times a day, you test his pee, you study his poop ... " My voice trailed off. I felt exhausted.

It was Harrison's seventy-third day in the NICU.

I nearly couldn't bring myself to pump that day. I felt riddled with guilt that my milk hadn't been good enough for Harrison to begin with, that it needed human milk fortifier at all, that he'd been unable to tolerate the human milk fortifier, and now, on top of everything, he had rickets. I ran through this insane litany over and over, making it through my Medela Classic session in record time and wanting desperately to hurl the milk at the wall.

I didn't.

I stormed out of the Unit, bashed at the down button for the elevator, raced through the lobby, and fled across the street to Central Park. I plopped down on a bench, and for what seemed like the hundredth time since Harrison's early arrival, wondered what role I had played in his premature birth.

22

T-Minus Not Counting
EXHIBIT C—STAYING ON TRACK

April 26, 1988

Early in our marriage, Leon and I had agreed that we would hold off on having kids until I had made partner at my firm. The New York law firm culture of the '80s had only two tracks—the partnership track and the mommy track—and I knew I didn't want to end up on the track unfairly heading toward the end of the career line.

Waiting until we both became partners at our respective law firms seemed the most sensible insurance policy to me.

This meant long hours for both of us, all-nighters, car services home in the middle of the night, late nights at the legal printer waiting for copies of appellate briefs to be reproduced and bound, long trips out of town on a case, and so on. We saw way more of our colleagues than we saw of each other.

One such case found me on a flight heading south. My litigation bag, with my senior partner's initials, NMS, engraved on its flap, fit snugly between my feet. The "hand-me-down," a gift he had given me when he needed me to carry his bags for a while following an open-heart surgery that went sideways, contained everything I anticipated needing for the days ahead. As the plane raced through the cloudless April skies, I thought about the deposition that had consumed me for six months. Starting the next morning, I intended to meticulously uncover the millions of dollars that a budget box retail store mogul had attempted to shield from his wife, my client, Mrs. Mogul #4.

During her first appointment a year earlier, the client had declared that she had "inquired discreetly" among her "well-connected relations" where she could find the "best damn divorce lawyer in America." She was smart, sophisticated, and strong, and her detailed account of Mogul's dalliances clearly showed that being the woman scorned only made her more determined to exact the only revenge she knew her husband would understand—a swift kick in the wallet.

The demands of life as a sixth-year female associate on the partnership track at a New York City law firm only intensified during the many months I worked deep into the night to understand the intricacies of Mogul's financial empire. As I was already stress-filled, sleep-starved, caffeine-fueled, and nutritionally corrupt, my obsession with nailing Mogul at his deposition vastly improved only one aspect of my life. In a world in which time was sliced neatly into ten-minute increments of billable hours, the usually laborious task of filling out daily time sheets was radically simplified: *Mogul v. Mogul*—sixteen hours one day, fourteen hours the next day. My caseload was reassigned to other associates and my full attention was spent on the Moguls.

I knew my litigation bag held all I needed to get Mrs. Mogul #4 every penny she deserved.

Sudden cramping deep in my pelvis took my breath away. I started to stand, but the intense pain sent me falling back into my seat. My seatmate rang the call button and a flight attendant hurried down the aisle.

I felt hot and chilled at the same time. "Let's get you to the restroom," she said gently. She put her hand under my arm. I grabbed for the litigation bag. "Leave it," she barked. Then softly to my seatmate, "Sir, will you keep an eye on this for us?" The pain was so intense now that I let myself be pulled up and propelled forward.

As we reached the restroom door, I felt a warm rush between my legs. I pitched into the tiny cubicle; the flight attendant's elbows crooked under my armpits. I heard her murmuring, "I'm right here."

Time passed. A compress felt soothing against my neck. My nostrils filled with the scent of urine, something metallic, and White Shoulders. The fragrance, so out of place in the tiny space, clung sweetly to the flight attendant. I opened my eyes, and she squatted right in front of me, her back pressed up against the closed lavatory door. "There you are," White Shoulders said, her calm voice unable to mask the worry on her face.

She asked a single question: "When was your last period?"

I struggled to remember. When *was* my last period?

With her help, we maneuvered out of the restroom to the now vacant front row of seats in first class. Lying awkwardly across two seats, I drifted in and out of consciousness, trying to recall.

The first night of Hanukkah. Latke oil layered everything. As I cleaned the stove top, I felt the low back pain and abdominal cramps that signaled the onset of my period.

What day was it today? I envisioned the deposition notice dated April 27, 1988. That would make today April 26. In my semiconsciousness, I struggled with the math. Four months since ringing in the New Year with champagne, caviar, and sleepy sex. Could that really have been the last time I had made time for lovemaking?

With sudden clarity, I sputtered at White Shoulders, who was standing a few feet away from me in the open galley, "It's a baby, isn't it?" She looked so sad when she nodded.

"Where ... ?" I asked, hearing my voice rising as my question trailed off.

White Shoulders tenderly replied, "I'm not sure that's such a good idea."

"I'll decide what's a good idea," I snapped, immediately sorry for the harsh tone.

She turned back toward the galley and then faced me, handing me a neatly folded white cloth napkin. I opened the top flap, revealing two side flaps folded right over left. I pulled gently on the right one, then on the left. The bottom had been folded about a third of the way up to create a pouch. I hesitated at the obvious bulge.

Pulling down that final piece of cloth, I knew that someone had taken great care to clean the fluid from the tiny shape in my hand. Stinging tears blurred the miniaturized pieces and parts that would never grow into my living baby.

Love, guilt, grief, shame, anxiety, melancholy, anger, resentment, denial, wonder, emptiness, loneliness—waves of disjointed feelings overwhelmed me as my stomach and my throat swapped places. My lungs, caught in the crossfire, did their best, but my ragged breathing attested to how poorly they were doing their job.

I'm not sure how long I lay there crying, sighing, and gasping. White Shoulders gently pried open the hand I had unconsciously clasped, keeping the napkin and its contents tight to my heaving chest. She shifted my body so she could fasten my seat belt and quickly sat in the jump seat opposite me as the jet touched down. The roar of the reversing thrusters competed with the rush of blood thrumming in my ears.

The EMTs who boarded the plane were kind, efficient, and swift. Within minutes, I was snuggly strapped onto a stretcher, wrapped warmly in several layers of blankets with an oxygen mask covering my nose and mouth.

The stretcher lifted and I craned to find White Shoulders. She stood just inside the galley as the EMTs maneuvered me down the airstairs. She called out, "Wait!" and the stretcher stopped, making me feel suspended in midair. She reappeared, lugging my litigation bag.

"Y'all take good care of her," she said, and in one fluid motion touched her hand to her lips, then reached down to gently touch my forehead with her cool fingers. Her kindness overwhelmed me, and my tears began afresh. The stretcher resumed its lurching journey down the stairs to the open doors of the waiting ambulance. Both the bag and I were secured in place.

Racing across the tarmac, sirens blaring above me, I stared at the bag. Filling with rage, I suddenly saw it as a symbol of how my career-driven, myopic life had exacted its toll.

The ambulance took me to the nearest ER, where the resident put me on IV fluids and antibiotics, and after my insistence that he do nothing else until he spoke to Dr. Cherry in New York, agreed to discharge me to the care of my understanding client. After a day of rest at her manse, I felt strong enough to fly back to New York for a dreaded appointment with my OB-GYN. Given how many weeks pregnant I was when I miscarried, both the ER doctor and Dr. Cherry recommended that I have a D&C.

D&C, short for "dilation and curettage," is a surgical procedure to remove tissue from inside the uterus that, if left inside, could potentially cause a serious infection.

Dr. Cherry would dilate the lower, narrow part of my uterus. Then he would use a surgical instrument called a curette to scrape my uterine lining and, oh, I nearly forgot, he would also use a suction device to remove the uterine tissue he had scraped away. It was precisely the same procedure used to terminate my first pregnancy.

Although anatomically impossible, the vacuum aspirator felt like it had suctioned away a piece of my heart.

As I lay in the brightly lit office, breathing through the cramping, I remember thinking that my uterus had seen more than its fair share of scraping, lasering, and vacuuming. It didn't occur to me then to consider the impact it might have on my future ability to carry a baby in there, but years later, sitting on that bench in Central Park, I couldn't help but wonder. The tiny seed of guilt that Harrison's NICU stay had all been my fault started making me queasy.

23

That Face!

November 2, 1991

Despite coming off the ventilator, Harrison needed either a nasal cannula or continuous positive airway pressure (CPAP) for another six weeks. There were many failed attempts to wean him onto room air. After each failure, I could hear my father's voice saying failure was okay if I gave it my best effort. I soon found myself saying the same thing to my son.

Breathing did not come naturally to Harrison. He needed a combination of changing drug cocktails, getting older, and gaining weight before he finally managed to maintain his oxygen saturations on room air on November 2. It took seventy-eight days of breathing support before he could do it on his own.

On balance, though, having a dead baby versus a very much alive Harrison with lung disease seemed like a trade I'd make any day of the week.

And did I mention how incredibly adorable he looked? It took me a few minutes to put my finger on what was different. That day marked the very first time I saw my son's sweet face unadorned by anything. I couldn't stop kissing every inch of that soft skin, still chapped from the adhesive tape that had held his no-longer-needed apparatus. It felt so normal that it momentarily scared me.

But my mood shifted instantly at the sight of my mother, who had burst into tears seeing Harrison's face for the first time too. "What a *zeisah punim*," she exclaimed through her tears, using the Yiddish term for "sweet face."

We stood together gazing at that face for a long time, crying and smiling and crying some more.

We would have cried a good while longer, but a nurse appeared to tell us that Leon had gotten to the Unit and one of us would need to leave. The strict rule of two visitors at a bedside seemed inviolable and my mother reluctantly turned to go, but not before stroking her index finger along Harrison's cheek, looking up to the ceiling, and saying, "Thank you, Harvey."

I can only imagine what terror went through Leon's mind as he passed his crying mother-in-law on her way out the Unit door. By now he had put on his gown and rushed across to where Harrison lay in his open crib.

"What's the matter?" he started. And as he got close enough to see our son, I could tell from the tears springing to his eyes that he immediately understood we had reached a major milestone.

Harrison remained on room air from that day forward.

Going home felt possible.

The next day, we got Harrison a tape of Strauss. "The Blue Danube" waltz, a favorite of ours, seemed to be a favorite of his too. There he lay, in his open crib, stocking cap tilted jauntily on his bald head. While he was listening to the waltz, his SATS hit 99/100 and he looked as peaceful as can be.

Getting on room air seemed to go hand in hand with his steady weight gain. Despite his food intolerance, his reflux, and all the many medications they added to his feedings to be sure he not only kept it all down but also absorbed all the nutrients, Harrison started to "fill out." That grizzled old man I met on August 16 had been replaced by a baby.

24

There's No Place Like Home

November 5, 1991

Almost twelve weeks had gone by since the harrowing August day that our impossibly fragile son arrived silently into our lives.

I felt exhausted from the hours I'd been keeping—still working so I could save my maternity leave until Harrison came home (whenever that might be), commuting to the hospital multiple times each day, pumping breast milk on a "regular" feeding schedule so my body produced enough when Harrison grew sufficiently to be ready to nurse, and overseeing the construction in the house that would have been finished had he not been born three months early.

I was very superstitious about doing anything to decorate the nursery until Harrison's prognosis became more certain. When my mother tried to convince me to get going, I demurred.

Harrison had been off any respiratory support for only a few days when Dr. Andrea offhandedly said, "We think we're going to shoot for discharge on Saturday."

Discharged? What? In four days? But I'm not ready! My heart raced with this news. Home! Harrison was coming home!

"Are you sure he's ready?" I asked. "He's been on room air for only a few days."

"He's ready," she assured me. "And don't worry so much. You're ready, too." Once again, Dr. Andrea, mind reader extraordinaire, nailed it.

I left the Unit to call Leon, then my mother, then my brother, then Sandra, my secretary, then Norman, my senior partner.

Thinking of all the things I had to do at home, I kissed Harrison and for the first time since this ordeal had started, I left the hospital before dark, hopped in my car, and drove home, leaving Leon to find his own way home from Manhattan.

I changed into sweatpants and carefully unpacked the supplies that had been boxed and stored in the nursery.

First, I unpacked the bedding, crib sheet, bumpers, several receiving blankets and onesies, and ran downstairs to start a wash—with Downy. Everything that touched Harrison's sensitive skin had to be washed in Downy.

Next, I unpacked the rolls of wallpaper border, carefully laid down a drop cloth, and opened the bucket of paste. Hanging from a ladder in the nursery, putting up the whimsical beach scene border that Mom and I had chosen for Harrison, I let my mind wander as I measured, cut, slathered on wallpaper paste, and hung a strip.

I thought of my father and the many incarnations he had created for my bedroom over the years.

I could see the 1962 version of my bedroom with the double-arched canopy covered in white eyelet atop a white wood four-poster bed with gold leaf painted in the carved crevices. The dainty red-and-pink floral fabric adorning the windows and the coordinating coverlet on the bed (with matching wallpaper) were a testament to two truths: my mother's talent as a seamstress and decorator and my father's perception of me as his princess, for whom he had quite literally rolled out a red carpet and hung the flowered wallpaper.

The floral wallpaper was too girlie and juvenile, I argued one evening at dinner years later. My parents received this pronouncement without any discernible reaction. Little did I know that they had already planned a transformation: when I turned thirteen, the red and pink flowers gave way to two dramatic navy blue walls that took Dad a full weekend to paint. These provided a sophisticated counterpoint for the shiny white-and-navy abstract floral wallpaper he hung to cover the remaining walls.

My mother, once again showing her genius with fabric glue and her sewing machine, created arched window cornices upholstered in the matching fabric that she hung on the double windows facing the street and the single window facing the driveway. The four-poster bed remained, sans the canopy, and tall bookcases flanked the single window, from which protruded a bulky, noisy air conditioner.

It seemed like a fitting metamorphosis that paired well with the one happening to my changing body. Shedding the little girl's bedroom and receiving my first box of tampons at around the same time made sense to me.

My room was my sanctuary. It was the one place in our otherwise small and crowded house that I didn't have to share. That made the next change to my inner sanctum unforgettable.

One evening, following an especially spirited discussion about me getting a phone in my room, I insisted that "everyone" had their own phone. My mother volleyed back with "If everyone jumped off the Brooklyn Bridge, would you want to do that, too?"

The heated debate ended with me in tears stomping up the stairs in a huff and slamming the door of my private retreat as loudly as I possibly could.

Minutes later there was a knock. Expecting my mother, I barked a rude "What do you want?" The door swung open to reveal my father, his face a thundercloud. Saying nothing, he closed the door behind him, exposing the three brass hinges from which it hung. From his back pocket he produced a screwdriver and a hammer as he wordlessly removed each of the three pins, shimmied the door off its hinges, and leaned it up against the wall.

I watched in stunned silence, knowing that protesting would result in an even less palatable outcome.

From my bed, I could see into the small upstairs hallway, five doorways around its perimeter, each portal closed except mine. Feeling exposed and vulnerable, I cried myself to sleep, waking the next morning to the gaping maw.

I knew that no amount of reasoning, begging, or crying would move my father, but I didn't surrender immediately; it was only after a week of unconcealed life in my fishbowl that Dad won the battle of wills. Within minutes of my heartfelt apology for my unacceptable conduct to my mother, he re-hung the door on its hinges, restoring my precious privacy.

Not wanting to tempt fate, I didn't bring up the phone again. I'm certain it was no coincidence that my silence on the topic led to my sixteenth-birthday gift—a sleek white receiver that fit curvaceously into its cradle when not in use.

Having my own phone meant no longer having to straighten the twenty-foot coil of the kitchen phone practically to the breaking point in a (vain) attempt to have a private conversation with my boyfriend in the downstairs bathroom.

My haven got its final and most expansive transformation as high school ended. Graph paper in hand, my mother sketched her vision—a multi-level space with a mattress as the only furniture set at a stylish angle on the second step of a three-tiered platform.

Emptying the room down to the carpet tack, peeling the white-and-navy paper off the walls, ripping down the carefully constructed upholstered cornices, my parents hired professionals to install a floor-to-ceiling mirror on one small piece of wall and to carpet the floor and the three-level platform with a chic gray shag. My dad did everything else himself—including painting over the navy blue walls, an effort that took four coats of paint—completing the geometric platforms with the skill of a professional carpenter.

The true stroke of genius was the ocean.

One eight-foot-tall wall of gentle, rolling waves soundlessly and endlessly lapped onto a sandy beach on a mural that my mother had discovered during her many hours in the wallpaper store.

It took Dad the better part of a week to put that mural up. But once he completed it, the room was perfect.

Smiling at the memory, I added the final touches to what would soon be Harrison's bedroom. Filled with joy as I looked around at my handiwork, I wondered if this was how Dad felt when he finally finished that last panel of ocean on my bedroom wall.

I wondered, too, about my unintentional choice of a beach scene for Harrison's room—maybe not quite so unintentional. I felt like a tiny circle had been completed.

25

Million–Dollar Baby

November 9, 1991

Shift change in the nursing staff and the coterie of specialists and interns doing their daily rounds were the only dependable ways to mark time in the NICU.

The day shift hands off to the night shift in a practiced and thorough debriefing nearly always done crib-side. The written shift report contains everything the incoming nurse needs to know, but "shift reporting" is also a verbal ritual that provides the outgoing nurse the chance to describe your child's day, body system by body system, while also giving the incoming nurse the chance to ask any questions along the way.

It's also a chance for family members to ask questions, or to share observations about how their child looks to their keen eyes.

The nursing staff at Mt. Sinai ran like a well-oiled machine. They clearly loved what they did, had fondness for one another, and arranged their schedules so that there was a continuity of care that felt enormously comforting to me—and I'm sure made their tasks easier for them.

They came to know Harrison well, and I came to know them well. Once we got into a routine, rarely did I arrive to find a stranger caring for my son.

Some were quiet, some were chatty. All were professional and compassionate, and most worried as much about me and my well-being as they did about Harrison's.

It was not unusual for a nurse to hand me a glass of water, chiding me to "stay hydrated." Or to scold me about not getting enough sleep or not taking a break to go eat something.

Or to meet me in the changing room to warn me about the newest location of Harrison's IV.

That they could stick a needle into a vein as slender as a strand of hair was astonishing. And over time, as they ran out of veins in his arms and his ankles and the backs of his hands, one night he "blew" his IV and the night nurse didn't have any good choices left.

She placed the IV in his forehead.

As grotesque and upsetting as it looked, it turned out to be remarkably stable, lasting there for days.

These women were extraordinary. Keeping Harrison alive took the skills of dozens of doctors, respiratory therapists, X-ray technicians, feeding specialists, physical therapists, and lab technicians, but the nurses formed the bedrock of his care.

The twice-daily "changing of the guard," something we always tried to be present for, gave us a chance to hear exactly how our son was doing from the person who knew his condition at that moment in time better than anyone else on the planet.

It didn't take long to learn the verbal shorthand that at first sounded like another language. The early days in the Unit made me feel like I was watching a foreign film without subtitles, but I caught on quickly (another fringe benefit of all those hours watching *General Hospital* with Grandma Hannah).

The predictability of the shift change anchored me, well, at least twice a day. It gave me a grip on the world still turning out there—another twelve hours come and gone.

The other reliable measure of time—the morning rounds—did not occur with the precision of the shift change and varied a little from day to day. I often imagined the attending doctor for the day taking a little extra time over coffee or a quick look at the morning paper while the rest of the assembled team cooled their heels in the hallway waiting for him or her.

Mt. Sinai is a teaching hospital and rounds include a seeming cast of thousands, all crowded around that tiny space that "belongs" to my little family.

The chosen resident would begin the recitation formulaically. "Baby Boy Roday is a ___-day-old infant born by vaginal delivery, weighing 1,040 grams at birth at twenty-seven weeks gestation, to a mother suffering from fever and chills. The rupture of membranes was just prior to delivery, but the amniotic fluid was cloudy, and the baby emerged with poor respiratory effort and tone, which did not improve even after bagging. Baby was intubated in the delivery room and improved within two minutes and was transported to the NICU."

Then, depending on the resident, some would report chronologically, some system by system, and some by most acute condition first.

No matter how the reporting was structured, it was a daily reminder that it was my fault Harrison was born so early. I had powered through what I assumed was a summer cold, rather than pausing to consider it might have something to do with my pregnancy. And, as if I could forget, the ever-present Brain Bleed hung like the sword of Damocles over Harrison's head.

At first, the rounds took a long time. The report of the many things that were going wrong—for a while it felt like every day there was a new something going wrong—droned on and on.

Listening to the litany of things that were wrong with Harrison terrified me. How could he live through all of them? Or live through all of them and come out the other side without some long-term consequences?

Frankly, that's what scared me the most. I wasn't sure I was equipped for motherhood at all, let alone motherhood of a child with medical challenges.

There were times when fear overwhelmed me. The "what if" of the Brain Bleed, the aftereffects of the BPD, the potential retinopathy of prematurity, the impact of oxygen deprivation—if I allowed myself to dwell too long on any of these real prospective debilitating outcomes, I became filled with self-doubt and self-loathing. I bargained—not with God—with Dad to please not let Harrison suffer from a permanent disability. I didn't think I could cut it.

Even now I feel guilty for all those silent, one-sided conversations with my father, wondering if he thought less of me because I couldn't cope with the thought of a mentally or physically challenged child.

In the NICU, there's little in the way of speculation. Few statements are made that don't have a lab result, a physical exam, or an X-ray to support them.

So, strangely, over time the daily ritual of rounds became comforting. Fifteen pairs of professional eyes stared at my son every single morning, reciting saturation levels and hematocrit counts and how many millimeters his ventricle measured on his most recent head sonogram.

I saw many babies come and go during our stay. It felt bittersweet each time I watched a family excitedly take their little one, dutifully strapped into a car seat, hugging each of their caregivers and walking out those double doors without a backward glance.

I had not dared consider that one day that family would be us. That Leon, Harrison, and I would leave the Unit together, never to return. It didn't seem possible that the day had come to walk through that heavy NICU door—*with* Harrison.

The leaves had blown off the trees, and the soft shushing sound of the piles underfoot in Central Park had turned crunchy. Overnight lows were in the thirties and low forties, and crowds thronged Manhattan for the New York City Marathon.

Our feisty fighter who refused to give up was now twelve weeks old and weighed a bit over five pounds. He finally figured out how to suck-swallow-breathe and although never able to breastfeed, he was a breast milk champion with a hearty appetite.

On November 9, we posed for photos with the doctors and nurses as frightened families looked hopefully at us, the same way we had looked hopefully at departing families for many months before, and we said our farewells. Everyone fawned over Harrison, who looked adorable in a quilted yellow fleece sleep sack.

We got final hugs, and I spied a tear or two from these compassionate caregivers whose knowledge and talent had given us our son. The gratitude I felt overwhelmed me, and with each "thank you" I uttered, it felt inadequate. How could I properly and fully express my feelings about the extraordinary gift they had given me?

As we headed for the door, a young resident ran after us and handed us three very thick envelopes. I could see "Discharge Summary" on the outside of the top one.

I shoved the stack into what would soon become my ubiquitous diaper bag—the bag that would have scored big on *Let's Make a Deal*. There was nothing Monty Hall could have asked me for that I didn't have in that bag.

A nurse walked us to the car—hospital protocol—and watched as Leon nearly expertly snapped the rear-facing car seat into position. I slid in beside Harrison and waved as she closed the door.

She and Leon stood on the sidewalk, the wind blowing the leaves on the ground, the trees bare beyond them in the park, saying goodbye. Harrison slept peacefully through this momentous parting while I fumbled through the diaper bag for the envelopes.

"Discharge Summary" was followed by "Discharge Summary—Pediatrician's Copy," but the third envelope, the thickest of the three, was unmarked.

Naturally, that was the one I opened. It was a statement of charges. Pages and pages of them. I flipped to the last page just as Leon got in the car.

"Well," I said, "I sure hope you like this kid."

"What do you mean?" he asked, turning to me in the back seat.

I flicked the last page over and leaned closer to him so he could see it.

He whistled.

We had a million-dollar baby. More specifically, a baby with a million-dollar hospital bill.

I never, for one second, forget how fortunate we were. So many other people's lives would have been forever changed by the bill I held in my hand that day. Our lives would not be.

Our health insurance paid the whole thing, every penny above the deductible.

"How does it feel to have my precious grandson home?" my mother asked me later that day.

"Like a million bucks," I replied, winking at Leon.

Truth be told, I felt a little nauseated, and chalked it up to "new mom jitters," fear of not having a team of experts watching my every move, and terror about the ticking time bombs yet to explode as the issues du jour. While everyone had been extremely upbeat when we left the Unit earlier that day, I noticed that nobody said, "Don't worry about a thing. He's going to be totally fine." Harrison's still uncertain physical, mental, and developmental outcomes filled me with dread.

It didn't seem like a matter of "if" but rather of "when." The unpredictability of what additional deficits he had and when they would show up left me feeling edgy and worried.

26

The First Cut Is the Deepest

November 24, 1991

Phil Sherman, *mohel* to the "stars," as he had once been described in an article in the magazine *Manhattan, Inc.*, had been recommended to me by several well-meaning Jewish friends who took for granted that Harrison would survive and that I would need a mohel's services.

A *mohel* is trained in the Jewish ritual of circumcision, the surgical removal of the foreskin of a male infant to mark Abraham's covenant with God, usually performed on the eighth day after the baby's birth.

At the risk of sounding flippant about the most famous biblical example of faith, the covenant, literally the "contract" between God and Abraham, reminds me of a midnight infomercial for knives. At first, it's a good deal, then it's a great deal, and just when you think it can't possibly get any better comes the famous pitch line, "But wait, there's more."

For his part, God agreed to make Abraham the father of a great nation by promising him that he would be fruitful and multiply and that among his offspring would be kings. God also promised that he would be Abraham and his descendants' God everlasting and their protector. And if that wasn't enough, God promised Abraham and his people the land of Israel.

And what did God want Abraham to do to seal this deal? Abraham, who was ninety-nine years old, would be circumcised (ouch), and so would his thirteen-year-old son Ishmael, all the male children in his house, and every other male in his household—and then every Jewish male thereafter forever.

And so, as a descendant of Abraham, my son would have a *bris* to mark his entry into this ancient covenant. And what about that eight-day rule? Well, the rabbis had thought of everything.

If a baby is ill, the rabbis decided, the bris is postponed until the baby is deemed healthy enough to undergo the procedure. No free passes for the kid who spent the first twelve weeks of his life in the hospital.

Also, nowhere are there any rules about the health of the mother—mental, emotional, or otherwise.

Putting Harrison through an unanesthetized surgical procedure in my living room (with a catered brunch and a houseful of family and friends) did not sound like my idea of a fun day. In fact, I had been dreading it ever since Dr. Andrea first told me Harrison would be coming home.

"Look at the bright side," said a colleague. "You can pick the day you want to do it. You know the mohel will be available!"

Cantor Phil Sherman was famous, not only among mohels, but also among New York Jewish parents who only wanted the best for their precious boys. He had been featured in *Manhattan, Inc.* about a year before, and there wasn't a Jewish boy I knew whom Cantor Sherman hadn't "snipped," as Leon irreverently referred to it.

The *mohel* quickly returned my phone call, answered every one of my endless questions patiently and kindly, and assured me that although Harrison was more than three months old, this would be an uncomplicated and beautiful event.

We agreed on a date—November 24—and I realized there was a tiny silver lining. Unlike most mothers who were eight days postpartum with a nursing, crying, sleepless infant, I benefited from the fact that my son had been cared for by the fine doctors and nurses at Mt. Sinai Hospital for twelve weeks.

Admittedly, they were an incredibly stressful twelve weeks, but I slept some of every night, took an uninterrupted shower every day, and had a peripatetic schedule that left me physically fit and nearly back to my pre-pregnancy clothing size.

Cantor Sherman had been to this rodeo. I soon had in my hands a set of detailed instructions, a list of supplies I needed for aftercare, suggestions for the appropriate order of the ceremony—it's a very traditional tradition—and a request that we send him Harrison's Hebrew name so he could be sure to have the certificate prepared correctly.

The Hebrew name conversation turned out to be complicated. In English, the H for his first name honored my grandmother, Hannah, my father, Harvey, and my father-in-law, Harry. The N for his middle name honored my grandfather, Nathan. Using the H was an uncomplicated way to kill, I mean, honor three birds with one stone. In Hebrew, not so much.

Harry and Harvey both had different Hebrew names, and we floated the idea that Harrison's name in Hebrew be Harry's Hebrew name, Shimon, and Harvey's Hebrew name, Hanin.

"What? You want to leave my father's name out of it altogether?" asked my mother in a huff.

"No," I replied impatiently. "His middle name is still Nathaniel—directly for Grandpa Nat."

This was not a workable solution for my mother.

So we agreed that Harrison Nathaniel, already burdened by the longest possible English name, should also go through life with the preposterously hyphenated Hebrew name *Shimon-Hanin Nachum ben Yehuda 'veh Leah*, which translates as "Harry Harvey Nathan, son of Leon and Lisa."

With the Hebrew name finally settled, about a week before the *bris*, I ordered platters from the bakery, appetizers from the deli, and bagels from the bagel store.

We figured out the complexities of who was doing what during the ceremony—it seemed to me that Harrison would be treated like the football in a complicated double reverse in which he would be handed off multiple times—but everything was under control.

Cantor Sherman called me a few days before and ran me through a checklist. He seemed satisfied that I had everything covered.

During our first conversation, when I had asked the *mohel* if it was going to hurt Harrison, he said, to his credit, "Yes, but only for a few seconds." That sounded like a few too many seconds to me.

The big day arrived. I dreaded it. Leon was dispatched to pick up the food from the bakery, the deli, and the bagel store. I wasn't at the bakery, but since I have heard Leon tell the story about a thousand times, I feel like I *was* at the bakery. It's a little like an old Catskills comedy routine.

Leon goes into the bakery. Says to the guy behind the counter, "You have a couple of trays for Roday?"

"All set," says the baker. "But, if you don't mind my asking, what's this for?"

Proudly, Leon tells him it's the day of his son's bris.

Horrified, the baker says, "But you don't have the right challah!"

Leon points to the pile the baker has placed on the counter. "There's a challah right there."

"No, no," insists the baker. "That's the $4 challah. For a bris you need the $8 challah!" He disappears in the back and returns with an enormous challah. He presents it to Leon, wishes him a hearty mazel tov... and adds another $4 to the bill.

Leon gets home, and several trips out to the car later, the dining room appropriately looks like one in which a Jewish event is about to occur.

Coffee is brewing, accompanied by a veritable groaning board of food featuring bagels and lox, scallion and regular cream cheese, whitefish salad, egg salad, tuna salad, sable, a whole smoked whitefish, sliced tomato, sliced onion—very thin—Muenster cheese, Swiss cheese, cheddar cheese, two trays of assorted rugelach, and in the center of the table in a place of honor, the $8 challah.

Cantor Sherman gives me the high sign. I'd like to throw up. Or hide. Or both.

I nod to my mother, and she begins the perfectly choreo-graphed double reverse that would make Phil Simms, then the quarterback of the New York Football Giants, *kvell*.

My mother brings Harrison into the room and hands him off to Andrea, Harrison's godmother. Andrea carries Harrison to my brother, Robert, his godfather, who is also the *sandek*, the lucky guy who gets to hold Harrison during the actual pro-cedure. Usually, this falls to the grandfather, but both grand-fathers are "back to nature," as a dear friend likes to describe someone's passing.

Andrea deposits Harrison atop a pillow placed on Rob's lap. From where I'm hiding, all I can see are the sympathetic faces of the women watching, the pained expressions on the faces of the men watching, and a mixture of horror and fascination on the faces of our non-Jewish friends.

Cantor Sherman recites a few prayers and while his back is to me, I can see him leaning over Harrison, who immediately starts to cry.

The *mohel* had warned me about this; the baby is just unhap-py that his diaper is off, he's cold, whatever ... .

He instructs Leon to repeat after him: *Barukh Atah Adonai Elohenu melekh ha-olam, asher kideshanu be-mitsvotav ve-tsivanu le-hakhniso bivrito shel Avraham ovinu.* "Blessed are You, Lord our God, king of the universe, who has sanctified us with His commandments and commanded us to enter our son into the covenant of Abraham our forefather."

Then the *mohel* takes a cup of wine and recites a prayer for Harrison in which he gives Harrison his Hebrew name—every single syllable of it.

He puts a drop or two of the wine in Harrison's mouth, then gives the cup to Leon to drink.

And that's it. Leon says a few words of welcome, tells the collected onlookers whom Harrison is named after, and then gets too choked up to say much more.

My brother, Robert, hands Harrison off to Leon's brother Robert, who hands the baby back to my mother. With me close on their heels, we go upstairs to give Harrison a bottle of milk while our guests enjoy a delicious brunch and admire the $8 challah.

I'm not there for the *motzi*, the blessing over the bread, but by the time I get downstairs to the happy buzz of well-fed family and friends, there's only about $4 worth of challah left on the table.

Danken Got! Thank God the baker insisted that Leon get the $8 challah!

As Cantor Sherman warmly bids us goodbye—he's off to the next of the three more circumcisions he must perform that day—he holds my hand in both of his and asks, with genuine concern, "Are you okay?"

Honestly, I'm not. I think for an instant about whether I'm supposed to give the polite "Fine, thank you for asking" answer or the real one.

I decide on the latter and get no further than the first word before the unbidden tears I have been holding back for so long finally appear.

"My father... just another thing he didn't live to see," I blubber.

And, as I knew he would, Cantor Sherman looks earnestly into my eyes and says, "Oh, he sees, Lisa. He sees his grandson. I'm sure of that."

27

Mothers Say the Darndest Things

December 1991

There are few people on the planet Earth who have not been told by a mother, grandmother, or favorite aunt, "I'm cold. Put on a sweater." This presumptuous order must be immediately and dutifully obeyed by the donning of an appropriately warm garment or risk the wrath of Mom.

Sure, the first few times my mother said it, I grumbled, objected, even refused in the middle of a crowded department store—that didn't end well—and eventually, just acquiesced to the demand.

When I aged a bit, I swore to myself I would never say any number of things my parents said to me, but among my top ten "vow to never say" items was the insanely annoying order from Mom to put on some specified article of clothing because *she* was cold. (This is where my father would interject, "*She* has a name," and I would be in trouble for referring to my mother disrespectfully. Then I would be overheated *and* punished—this was long before "time-outs"—by being sent to my room for being sassy.)

While I haven't the vaguest idea who coined this adage, I have no trouble imagining that Abel was the favorite son because he put on a sweater when Eve got cold, a potential cause for the intense jealousy felt by his brother, Cain.

As it would turn out, I've broken all of the other nine of my top "vow to never say" promises to my children, including "wait until you have your own kids," "take your elbows off the table," "don't talk with food in your mouth," "because I said so, that's why," "when you're in my house, you live with my rules," "maybe when you're older," "don't you dare say another word," and my personal favorite—"If everyone else jumped off the Brooklyn Bridge, would you do that, too?"

But I'm confident that I never uttered the dreaded "I'm cold, put on a ... " whatever. In fact, I distinctly remember the time I didn't say it to my beloved son.

As a baby, I had a traditional coach-built pram. My Rolls-Royce for infants had a shiny, ivory-colored hard body with lovely gold leaf scrollwork, gigantic white-rubber-and-silver spoked wheels, and a gold-colored, hand-stitched folding leather hood with a distinctive silver frame. The body measured a whopping forty inches long by about a foot and a half wide, with a deep but firm mattress that lay low in the body, protecting the infant from anything Mother Nature might be throwing their way.

I don't remember this from infanthood. I remember it because the imposing rolling crib held a proud (and huge) spot in our garage for decades; my mother assured me that it had always been her plan that I would wheel her grandchildren in it. Now that's what I call vision.

Weighing in at a hefty seventy-ish pounds, the pram is not portable, packable, foldable into the trunk, or otherwise useful for anything except for taking long walks outside or using as an alternate crib in the house.

If you're unfamiliar with the British-designed perambulator, picture the Wells Fargo logo and you've got it—a stagecoach for babies. The hand-painted body is fixed to a steel suspension that is bent around C-shaped suspension members attached to the hard body with leather straps. It is the C-spring suspension and leather straps that create the unique and comforting coach-built pram "bounce." A folding leather hood, a bright-white-and-chrome pushing handle, and a fabric apron matching the hood are attached to the pram. The advanced safety feature was the foot-operated locking brake. My carriage came accessorized with a basket beneath and a secret compartment, a small hatch door that faced the handle. Once opened with a small thumb turn, the gold-lined cubicle perfectly fit a purse.

Huge wheels attached to the rolling chassis made for a smooth ride for the infant inside, and improved the ease of pushing the pram for the wheeling parent. The carriage was apparently a "must-have" for parents fortunate to be able to afford it (or, in my case, fortunate to have parents who were able to afford it!)

And so, about two weeks before it seemed like Harrison might come home, in addition to my long-postponed list of baby-related projects, like wallpapering his bedroom, I found myself heaving the carriage out of its cobwebbed home in the shed to try my best to clean it well enough to safely carry him.

It turned out to be a more complex project than I had anticipated. In addition to the leather hood and straps having dried to a weathered, brittle version of themselves, the high-gloss paint on the body had cracked in many places, and the glorious wheels had rusted significantly.

It took me the better part of an hour to steel-wool all the spokes clean on a single wheel. If the pram ever had a prayer of being restored to its former beauty, it would need more work than I had time for.

I decided I needed professional help. I immediately drove over to Gladstone's, the local paint store. The paint section was filled with mostly elderly gentlemen who knew everything there was to know about paint.

I had disassembled the carriage body and *schlepped* it into the store. The first man to spy me immediately came to relieve me of the unwieldy box, which he brought over to the paint counter while yelling to the cashier to "Page Jim to the paint counter." We hadn't yet made it more than a few feet when

I heard the amplified female voice: "Paging Jim. Jim to the paint counter." By the time we got to the paint counter, the embroidered shirt told me Jim stood beside it.

"Well, well. What do we have here? Looks like a pram. I'm guessing 1950s?" he said cheerfully. "Pretty rough shape, I see. Garage, wet basement?"

"Both, I think, over the years. Can you help me? I want to repaint it."

One hour and $125 in supplies later, I got home and went to work. Paint remover first. Scraper second. Light steel wool third. By the end of the first evening, I was ready for the fine sandpaper step. But my arms and lower back ached, so I decided to leave that last preparation step to the next night. By the end of the second evening, I had stripped that sucker right down to the base. Now all I had left was the priming, painting, decorating, and sealing. Piece of cake, right?

Paint Store Jim had assured me the painting would be the easy part. He had given me several spray cans of ivory paint with a high-gloss finish, a small can of gold leaf, and a can of high-gloss Minwax clear-coat varnish to complete the project.

"But," he warned, "you have to let the primer dry really good or when you spray on the paint, it will bubble."

Despite the cool November air, on night number three of this "little" project, I worked outside so the fumes from all the varnishes and turpentines wouldn't smell up the house. I worked with the music on and the light that indirectly shone onto the porch where I had set up my little refinishing station.

I read the directions for the primer and applied it liberally, as the can said. I went inside, caught up on a bit of office work, called the hospital to check on Harrison, and came back out to see if the primer had dried.

It looked dry. It wasn't tacky to the touch. *Well,* I thought, shaking the cans of spray paint like several maracas, *one more night and I'll be finished.* The sound of that steel ball bouncing around in the can as I shook it reminded me of the clicking sound of mah-jongg tiles. I plowed ahead. I got several old sheets and spread them out on the lawn, then I moved the carriage box onto the sheets. Nearing the edge of any usable light, I figured, how hard could it be to spray-paint?

If you crave immediate gratification, spray-painting is about as immediate as it gets. As I happily listened to the Rolling Stones, I finished spray-painting that baby in about twenty minutes. I felt incredibly satisfied—cold, but incredibly satisfied. I dragged the sheets back across the lawn, surrounded the whole thing with lawn furniture, and threw another sheet on top like a tent to protect it.

I fell into bed and woke at 4:45 the next morning to pump. I had by now perfected the art of transferring my expressed breast milk into pint-sized Ziploc freezer bags without spilling a drop, jotting down the date on the bags and tossing them into the freezer we had purchased solely for this use.

I hopped into a quick shower and dressed while Leon took his turn in the bathroom. Soon we would set off for our morning time in the hospital with Harrison. *But first,* I thought, *I'll have a look at my handiwork.*

In the predawn light, I could tell something had gone very wrong. I pulled away the furniture blockade and peered at the pockmarked carriage base. What looked like an evenly coated paint job the night before had become a moonscape pitted with craters and ballooning ridges. I cursed and stamped around the house.

"What's wrong?" asked Leon, coming down the stairs. "Is it Harrison?"

"No. It's the damn baby carriage. I ruined it. I have to start all over again."

Back I went to see Jim for additional supplies. "I did everything you told me to do," I complained. "I can't figure out why it bubbled."

"Too cold," he said. "It's my fault. I forgot to tell you that you couldn't paint unless it was warmer than 45 degrees." I thought back to the previous night and remembered shivering while I painted. "Says it right there on the can," he pointed, not willing to take all the blame.

Well, it went much faster the second time around. Not wanting to fall into the trap of applying the paint too soon, or when it was too cold, I waited until full daylight to do the painting.

With tremendous satisfaction, the night before Harrison got home I put the finishing touches on what I had come to think of as a chariot for my tiny conquering hero. It looked fantastic.

My mother insisted that the carriage air out for several days before putting the new mattress and quilted padding inside. She made me stick my head into the base for emphasis. I had to admit, it smelled like paint fumes.

It would be quite a few weeks before I felt ready to take Harrison for a spin in the carriage. But finally, on a blustery December day, I zippered him into his quilted New York Football Giants sleep sack, covered him with a blanket, placed him as far toward the head of the carriage as possible, and off we went. By now, he weighed nearly eight pounds and measured almost twenty-one inches long. His feet barely reached halfway to the end of the mattress.

Having set out with no destination in mind, I decided to walk to my cousin Abbie's house less than a mile away. As we perambulated along, Harrison snoozed away. It started softly snowing—gorgeous, gigantic snowflakes that gleamed for an instant as they fell on the gold leather hood of the carriage.

In the quaint era before the ubiquitous instant everything, I announced my arrival with a knock at the door. My cousin, thrilled and surprised to see us, helped me negotiate the carriage through her front door and said, "Let me call my mother. She'll be so excited to see you."

Aunt Gert worked about another mile further in Lawrence and appeared within minutes of my arrival, followed close behind by my mother, whom my aunt had called on her way out the door.

By now, I had folded down the giant hood of the stroller, taken the blanket off the baby, and unzipped his sleep sack. His little body radiated heat—not a fever kind of heat, just the comfortable, toasty warmth of a good nap kind of heat.

We had a great visit. Harrison woke briefly, drank a few ounces of milk fed to him by his doting grandmother, and promptly fell back to sleep on her shoulder.

I could see out the kitchen window that the snow had started to stick, and I wanted to head back home, unsure how the big rubber tires would fare in the snow.

I took the sleeping Harrison from my mother and laid him back into his sleep sack, zippered him up, and covered him with the blanket. I pulled up the giant hood that completely covered the sleeping infant and turned to kiss everyone goodbye.

In unison, my aunt and my mother asked, "He's not wearing a hat?"

I rolled my eyes at my cousin, who rolled her eyes back at me. "No," I said, "he's not wearing a hat."

"After everything he's been through. It's snowing. How could you take him out in the snow without a hat?" demanded Aunt Gert.

"Well, he's not exactly 'out in the snow.' He's all the way under the hood," I pointed out fruitlessly.

And then, just like that, my mother said, "Well, I'm freezing. Put a hat on him."

Of course, I didn't have a hat for him. I had an extra bottle of breast milk, a full supply of diapers, burp cloths, baby wipes, a change of clothes in case of a blowout poop, but no hat.

As it had always been in the past with me, this was a non-negotiable for my mother. She felt cold; the baby needed a hat. We were at an apparent impasse.

I was rescued by my cousin, an avid skier, who pulled a neck gaiter from her front hall coat-tree. She folded it in thirds, leaned into the carriage, and smiled broadly at her handiwork. It was a perfect fit for Harrison's head.

"There, Aunt Sonny," she said, "now he has a hat!"

Before my mother could say a word, we maneuvered through the front door and out into the falling snow. I waved goodbye to the three women standing in the doorway and pushed the carriage through what seemed like an inch of snow, gaining by the second.

The traction from the gigantic rubber carriage tires turned out to be pretty darn good. As I turned the corner and braced myself for the windy, snowy walk back home, I said aloud to my sleeping son, "I'm cold. I'm taking your hat!"

BOOK THREE

MY LIFE'S MAP

28

Reverse Engineering the Path from Point A to Point B

I wholeheartedly believe the old chestnut that getting from Point A to Point B isn't always a straight line, and that the twists and turns and detours along the way usually provide the most interesting and transformative sights and experiences.

It's a long-winded way of saying that things don't always turn out the way we planned.

My own life is filled with indirect routes that led me to right here. I wonder how much of the stories I tell myself are remotely close to what really happened. Why am I who I am? Why do I believe the things I believe? How did my past shape the person I am today? Were the moments I remember as being pivotal really just ordinary?

That my life was informed profoundly by seismic events seems obvious. And while it would be easy to break my life experiences down into BDD and ADD, Before Dad Died and After Dad Died, such a simplistic analysis leaves out the more ordinary things, like a tooth getting chipped or a tough breakup or a disagreement with a grade school friend that left profound fingerprints. Those fingerprints didn't always seem clear at the time but feel so consequential looking back.

Efforts to harness those experiences and order them in a sensible narrative proved to be both elusive and distracting. Memories diverted my attention, some for hours at a time, as I looked at photographs or read old letters and newspaper clippings or set off down a rabbit hole of Google searches. Other experiences took days or weeks to parse, so painful to examine that cleaning the garage and alphabetizing the spice cabinet were far more attractive alternatives. Looking back at my many false starts and half-hearted attempts to capture these formative events, I eventually realized that my reluctance stares back at me from the mirror each day.

Making sense of who I am in this moment requires me to turn back to find the formative moments along my meandering path, where they appear with disconcerting randomness.

I am certain of this: my path from there to here never hewed to a straight line, especially in the fog of the months and years after my father died. The twists, turns, and detours occasionally obscured the right track.

29

A Very Good, Very Bad, Very Formative Year

July–October 1969

Just days after the launch of Apollo 11, but before Neil Armstrong's historic walk on the moon, tragedy struck a young, vivacious woman named Mary Jo Kopechne, and shone a shocking spotlight on Ted Kennedy, the senator from Massachusetts, brother of assassinated president John F. Kennedy and assassinated presidential hopeful and former attorney general Robert F. Kennedy.

Ms. Kopechne drowned in a car crash in Chappaquiddick, Massachusetts, a crash that happened while Ted was driving. Adding to the drama—Ted walked away from the incident and didn't immediately report it.

My father, a JFK and RFK fan, couldn't abide Ted's conduct as it had been reported in the press.

Discussing it at breakfast the morning after Kennedy's hearing about a week after the accident, Dad reminded me that "honesty is the best policy." He seemed truly disgusted by Ted's lies.

We kids had a macabre fascination with the story. In the swimming pool, we invented a drowning game, in which one of us got picked to be Mary Jo, treading water in the deep end. Then another kid would cannonball off the diving board as close to "Mary Jo" as possible to create a giant wave. The cannonballer would grab "Mary Jo" by the ankle and start pulling her down. This sick, twisted game amused us for weeks.

I learned two things from the sad events at Chappaquiddick and their aftermath: to always tell the truth and to own up to my mistakes right from the start.

Telling the truth, no matter the cost, was a prized trait in our family. So much so that as a young lawyer, I was told by the senior partner in the firm that I needed to learn to be more diplomatic. In my professional life, this early lesson that truth-telling wasn't synonymous with brutal honesty made me a far more persuasive advocate and a more effective questioner.

Chappaquiddick also taught me that although everyone makes mistakes, the consequences are usually less harsh when you admit to those mistakes from the beginning.

We had barely tired of the drowning game when a tragedy happened that was so horrible that even we kids couldn't muster the bad taste to make fun of it.

On August 9, 1969, a pregnant actress named Sharon Tate and four others were found brutally murdered at the estate she shared with her husband, famous director Roman Polanski, who was traveling at the time of the deaths.

The media's frenzied obsession with the story, at a time when the killers' identities were still unknown, riveted the nation. The August 29 issue of *Life* magazine ran an interview with Roman Polanski that featured truly gruesome crime scene photos and a picture of him standing beside the word "PIG" painted in blood on the wall.

Although I was only eleven, these murders sparked my first interest in the law. Fascinated by the crime scene photos and the bits of evidence reported in the newspapers, I first dreamed of being a prosecutor. Putting away people who would commit crimes as horrible as these—I thought that would be a truly satisfying career.

I shared this news with my father. The hint of a smile passed across his face.

"What?" I asked. "Do you think that's a silly thing to want to do?"

"Not at all, honey. I once wanted to be a criminal lawyer, too." And out spilled the story of how he got his draft notice the same day he got his acceptance to law school. Looking back, I know that his story morphed my nascent desire to go to law school into a desire to fulfill my father's dream of being a lawyer. Admittedly not the greatest reason for a career choice, but it motivated me for a very long time. So much so that I never *decided* to go to law school; I took for granted that my path had been preordained. When other opportunities presented themselves, I ignored them because they weren't part of the plan. These nondecisions, occasionally pivotal turning points that in retrospect deserved consideration, resulted in many "roads not taken." But all that happened long after the Tate murders and long after one of the defining events of the summer—Woodstock.

A few years too young to fully appreciate Woodstock, I understood enough from my father about the war in Vietnam to grasp the significance of about half a million people spending a weekend on a dairy farm listening to some of the greatest voices in the world of music, most of them playing songs protesting the war.

By that point, the Vietnam War had already claimed about 47,000 American lives. Dad put that in perspective for me. During the Korean War, in which he had served, more than 30,000 GIs were known to have died in action.

In August 1969, there didn't seem to be an end in sight in Vietnam. When all was said and done, almost 60,000 Americans died in Vietnam. While hundreds of thousands of people gathered in the rain and mud at Yasgur's farm about eighty miles from our house, my father and I pored over the *New York Times*, the *Daily News*, and the *New York Post*, all of which provided front-page coverage of the festival of "music and peace."

Dad—no fuddy-duddy at thirty-seven—made a few light-hearted jokes about the absence of his favorite crooners, Elvis and Sinatra, but he was genuinely excited about Woodstock.

It provided a backdrop for us to talk about the war and about free speech and about standing up for what you believe in. There were earlier instances of these lessons, but during that wet, wild Woodstock weekend, Dad, who had so recently shared with me his own misdirected plan for law school, stoked a fire in me to be a voice for the voiceless and an advocate for others. That weekend, he told me for the first time, "There's a difference between knowing what's right and doing what's right. That's where change happens." I felt myself being pulled toward being a doer.

As Arlo Guthrie said in "Alice's Restaurant Massacree," "If you want to end war and stuff, you got to sing loud." That August weekend marks my earliest recollection of the beginning of an opinion that would inform many decisions I made throughout my life and career. Doing the right thing, an oft-repeated mantra of my father's, settled in to become the true north of my moral compass.

The Kopechne death was tragic, the moon landing was breathtaking, the Tate murders were horrific, Woodstock was a revelation, and then? Well, then came the Miracle Mets. The New York Mets joined Major League Baseball in 1962. In the seven seasons prior to 1969, the Mets finished tenth in the National League five times. The other two years, they finished ninth. Their abysmal performance from 1962 to 1968 made their '69 season all the more improbable.

The weekend of Woodstock began a remarkable run for the New York Mets, who had fifteen wins in seventeen games. And although they trailed the Chicago Cubs by four and a half games when September began, they managed a strong finish to the regular season, winning twenty-four of their last thirty-two games.

One favorite family activity was baseball card trivia, but the only stats I knew belonged to the Mets. Each morning at breakfast, in a form of flash card torture that my brother had invented, we quizzed each other on randomly drawn baseball cards.

When his card collection outgrew the rubber-banded piles in which he kept them, my mother bought him mini "foot-lockers" for them. He'd line them up at the banquette in the breakfast room and pick one to put on the table for the morning activity.

Growing up Mets fans made us resilient, hopeful, eternally optimistic, and able to accept defeat with a "we'll get 'em next year" attitude. Oh, wait. That's not it at all. Growing up Mets fans left us heartbroken season after season.

Until 1969.

In postseason play, the Mets handily dispatched the Atlanta Braves 3–0 to win the National League Championship. Only the heavily favored Baltimore Orioles stood between them and the title of World Series Champions.

The Orioles came out hot on October 11 and beat Tom Seaver, otherwise known as "Tom Terrific," in Game 1. But that would be the only win they would muster. The next day, Game 2 saw the Mets win on the arm of Jerry Koosman and a dramatic bottom of the ninth base hit by "Little Al Weis," a hometown kid from Long Island, who had played for Farmingdale High School as a student. The underdog player on the underdog team delivered the win.

On October 14, behind Gary Gentry, the Mets took Game 3, with the uber-talented Nolan Ryan getting the save. With "The Franchise," as Seaver was also known, back on the mound, the Mets took Game 4 and headed into the final game with a 3–1 advantage for the series.

Game 5. Shea Stadium. I was sitting next to my father along the right field line as Jerry Koosman rose to take the hill again for the Mets. Little Al Weis, with only four home runs in his seven years in the majors, hit a heart-stopping shot deep to left field in the bottom of the seventh inning to tie the game at 3–3. In the bottom of the eighth, the Mets scored two runs left unanswered by the Orioles in the top of the ninth. The Miracle Mets became world champions, and the stadium erupted in pandemonium. My father threw bodies aside to stop them from trampling me as fans stormed the field.

If we shared elation in July when Armstrong walked on the moon, we shared euphoria in October when the Mets took the World Series.

More than fifty years later, it remains a significant bone of contention that my father took me to two of the three home games against the Orioles, including Game 5, the series winner.

Bringing this up in front of my brother—well, enter at your own risk.

The Mets winning the World Series cemented my lifelong commitment to them. Their victory in October 1969 capped a year of tumultuous events that captivated people around the world and mesmerized an eleven-year-old girl in Cedarhurst, New York.

30

Not Bad for a Girl

1975

The late spring sun cast deep shadows across the driveway. The *thwump, thwump, thwump* of the Spalding basketball, perfectly inflated by my father, heralded the evening's game of H-O-R-S-E. The first one of the three of us to miss five shots was out. That was usually me, by then. My younger brother had overtaken my five-foot-six, and my father's lanky six-foot frame always gave him the height advantage. Oh, yeah, and he had played college ball for three years.

On any given evening, our post-dinner "friendly" game of H-O-R-S-E consisted of me being completely intimidated by the sheer size of my brother and the overwhelming skills of my father. If they thought it was a drag to have me play, neither one of them showed it. The trash talk began before dessert ended and was funny, competitive, and joyful.

"You're going DOWN!" exclaimed my brother, just past his thirteenth birthday and, as my father would say, "full of piss and vinegar."

As we headed outside, my father already had his Kennedy half-dollar in his hand. He always flipped, and my brother and I alternated "calling" it. The role of designated flipper fit Dad best. His shooting was so deadly accurate from everywhere on our makeshift court that if we let him go first, I would have

H-O-R-S-E in my first five (maybe six if I got lucky) attempts to follow him.

The court was hardly regulation. A seam in the concrete marked the free-throw line, and the small hedge below the kitchen window was the three-point line. It was as wide as the driveway—about twelve feet. Out of bounds were the grass median between our driveway and the next-door neighbor's home on the left and the small, grassy fenced-in area to the right.

The basketball net was mounted to a wooden backboard. Red paint demarcated a square box above the rim, which over my lifetime helped me develop my "go-to" shot—a bank shot off the intersection at the top right of the red square.

Tonight, I called heads. My father perched the coin gently on the foundation of his calloused thumb and index finger. He flipped it skyward, the sun catching silver on the way up and back down as we let it fall. JFK's profile faced up to us as we crowded together to peer down at the coin. Heads.

My father bounce-passed the ball to me, and I dribbled it idly as I tried to decide my first shot. I thought of my father as Bill Bradley, a starting forward for the New York Knicks and a Rhodes Scholar. Bradley is the whole package—smart, skilled, respected, graciously competitive, a champion, a leader, and a former Air Force reservist.

My brother fancied himself Walt Frazier, but in my biased opinion, he lacked the style, finesse, and ball-handling skills of the sartorially resplendent Knick known as "Clyde."

I didn't channel a Knick; if I had, it would have been Phil Jackson, I think—an overall good athlete with long arms who makes up for lack of supreme basketball skill with intelligence and hard work. I was just trying to hold it together. My brother got in my head already.

I took a deep breath. It was a foregone conclusion that I would take the bank shot first. Build my confidence. I picked my spot on the driveway, stared at the spot on the backboard, and sent the ball flying. In it went.

Sarcastically, Rob quipped, "Shocking choice of shot," and put it in on top of mine. Dad lazily banked his in, too.

Back to me.

I chose another easy spot—the free-throw line—and called "swish." The basket only counted if it's nothing but net. In it went.

"Nice!" cheered my father. My brother, with a slightly respectful nod, stepped up, dribbled it twice, and released it. It hit the front rim on its way through the net. He had an "H."

Our fortunes reversed a few times for the rest of the game. Finally, both my brother and I had "H-O-R-S-," and somehow, Dad had the ball.

He winked at me. "You got this, right?" He stood beyond the hedge on what he teasingly once called the four-point line. I swallowed hard, warmed by his confidence but thinking that he had to make it first. He dribbled once, bent his knees to spring-load his power, and as he flexed back up, released the ball gracefully, where seconds later it dropped through the hoop.

"You wanna just quit now?" taunted my brother.

"Then *you'll* still need to make it," said my father with a smile.

By now the ball was in my hand. The sun had practically disappeared behind the house across the street. Somewhere nearby I heard the bells of the Good Humor ice-cream truck. I heard our dog, Coco, inside start barking at the sound. I pictured her enjoying her evening entertainment. She stood at the dining room windows barking ferociously (and she meant it) at the neighborhood children and their parents gathered around the truck.

I knew I had less than a minute before the colorful truck made its way halfway down the block to the end of our driveway, the Good Humor man's usual stop.

I heard a screen door slam. I didn't need to turn around to know that our neighbor was running down his driveway to order the same vanilla ice cream sandwich he ordered every time.

"Tonight," egged on my brother because I was taking too long.

I had never attempted a shot from that distance ever before. But I looked at my father—he watched me with a smile and a nod.

I bounced the ball twice to calm my nerves. I didn't shoot it as much as I heaved it in the general direction of the hoop.

Rob channeled Marty Glickman, the play-by-play radio announcer for the Knicks. "The ball's up. It's got the distance. It hits the backboard and bounces off the front rim and... it's in. It's in. She's made the shot!"

Dad was ecstatic. "Told you, you had it!"

Behind me, I heard the ice cream man. His bells were ringing, and kids' voices were calling out orders.

"Your shot, I believe," I said to Rob, resisting the urge to throw the basketball right into his gut.

There was no way he could make it. There was too much noise, he'd already broken his concentration with his Glickman routine, and besides, it just wouldn't be fair.

The basketball gods agreed. His lame brick bounced harmlessly against the garage door. Game over for him.

Although the rules required that my father and I square off until the last "man" was standing, Dad had different ideas. "I could really go for a Toasted Almond bar. You guys want anything?" he called back over his shoulder, already halfway down the driveway.

Minutes later, savoring my Fudgsicle and my shot, I looked at Dad. He grinned, pieces of nuts and bits of chocolate caught in the picket fence of his teeth.

"Nice shot."

"Yeah," I replied.

"Not bad for a girl." We both laughed. My whole life he had emphasized that being "a girl" should never matter.

I missed many more "clutch shots" than I made over the years and was nearly always the first one to get H-O-R-S-E. My father and brother would occasionally take mercy on me and turn the game into H-O-R-S-E-S, but there were plenty of nights that had the game been H-O-R-S-E-F-A-R-M, I'd still be the first one out.

But I took my place on the court every night.

31

Playing the Jewish Card

Spring 1976

I was a high school student in the mid-1970s, but the conversation about whether I was going to college never happened—not in front of me, anyway. I took for granted that college loomed in my future. My mother assumed I was college-bound. To my teachers and guidance counselors it was a foregone conclusion.

This put my father in a tough spot.

It wasn't a question of *whether* I would go to college (and then law school, we both hoped), but *where.*

My father had famously meddled in the lives of each of my older cousins—eight of them, to be exact—and decreed that none of them could go "out of town" for college.

His argument centered around the importance of the "family unit." This coded phrase thinly disguised his preconceived notion that my cousins would forget they were Jewish if they ventured out of town.

I'm not sure what is more peculiar—that he held sway with his siblings on this issue or that my cousins went along with it.

Either way, it's one of the few examples of my father being small-minded and selfish that I can remember. His general notion of keeping the entire family within a ten-mile radius of one another, although quaint, seemed the complete opposite of everything he had ever taught me about being independent and having friends of every race and religion.

Yet cousin after cousin strayed no further than one of the five boroughs of New York. And as each one brought home a suitor, my father noted with great satisfaction that all of them were Jewish.

His advice on dating could be summarized in a single sentence: "If you only date Jewish people, you'll marry someone Jewish." (This in stark contrast to my mother's advice that "it is just as easy to fall in love with a rich man as it is to fall in love with a poor one.")

Dad didn't exactly forbid my cousins from dating people who weren't Jewish. He just increased the odds that they would date only other Jews by keeping them in New York. Mathematically, my father had a point. If you were growing up in New York at that time, there was a 13 percent chance that the next person you would randomly meet would be Jewish.

But, as things turned out, the conversation about where *I* was going to college was a brief one. My father mentioned a specific school at dinner one night. My mother, vocal and loyal cheerleader extraordinaire, knew that my high school sweetheart was already somewhere else, "out of town."

With great conviction, she firmly stated that there were more Jewish kids at the school my boyfriend attended.

This was good enough for my father, for whom being Jewish was central to the complex fabric of our nuclear and extended family. He certainly observed the religion but could hardly be called "observant." Yet culturally he wore his Judaism with pride. Having European parents, being first-generation American, and growing up in a world that saw six million Jews exterminated, being Jewish—they all mattered to him. A lot. And it mattered to him that my generation carry on our cultural (if not observant) heritage.

So, when my mother very matter-of-factly told him which university more Jewish students attended, he smacked his open hand on the dinner table and proclaimed, "Done!"

With a knowing wink in my direction, my mother congrat-ulated my father for making such a wise decision. I marveled at her maneuver; by playing the Jewish card, she had ensured that I would be the first of my generation to leave New York City for school *and* that I would be going to college with my boyfriend.

A half-century ago, the brevity with which my college desti-nation was dispatched—a matter of minutes—with zero com-ment from me, didn't feel awkward, strange, or unfair. Just the opposite. Thanks to my mother, I felt like I had won the college jackpot.

"How come Lisa gets to go away to college?" my cousins all wanted to know. I never heard my father's answer.

Maybe the fact that I already had a Jewish boyfriend tipped the scales; I never asked.

As much as I hated to admit it at the time, Dad was onto something with the Jewish thing. Heading off to college, during the five-hour drive to Upstate New York and away from every-thing I had ever known, it occurred to me that growing up in a place that boasted the highest concentration of Jews outside of Israel hadn't prepared me for the possibility that I might be the only Jewish girl at college. My mother had exaggerated. While many of my high school classmates ended up in the State University of New York system, my campus wouldn't exactly be teeming with other Jewish kids. I decided that I needed to brush up on a social interaction known as Jewish Geography.

Not to be confused with knowing where Tel Aviv is located, Jewish Geography is a conversational exchange designed to build cultural bridges. Played upon discovering that a new acquaintance was also Jewish, this comforting icebreaker had been a helpful conversation starter for me for as long as I could remember.

Within seconds, two former strangers—now having found common ground with our shared Jewish heritage—began the eons-old ritual of narrowing down just how closely our geo-graphic circles overlapped.

I don't remember anyone ever teaching me the "rules." Where I grew up on Long Island, New York, seemingly everyone knew them. Sitting in the back seat, heading north on I-81, I went over them in my head just to be sure.

1. Establish mutual Judaism.

2. Begin with the open-ended question "Where are you from?"

3. Be sure that all subsequent questions incorporate the answer to the previous question and require the subsequent answer to yield a narrower geographic location than the prior answer.

4. Never directly name the town where you grew up in answer to the question "Where are you from?" That would eliminate the building suspense that, just maybe, you and your new friend's circles overlap.

5. Tuck away information provided by the respondent that's not directly related to geography, but never comment on it in the moment. These other bits of data—consequential or otherwise—will provide the basis for future conversations.

6. Always end the game by saying, "Small world!" no matter how geographically close you got to the other player's hometown.

We arrived at school and followed the cheering greeters to my first-year dorm. Several strapping young men in sweaty T-shirts helped my parents and me, all of us trudging up two flights with the latest and greatest college supplies available from Bed 'n Bath, later known as Bed, Bath & Beyond, now known as bankrupt. But I digress.

The moment I'd been excited about, and dreading—meeting my roommate—had arrived. In an unwelcome surprise, I had not one, but two roommates. Three of us crammed into a room designed for two, and in what I feared spelled doom for our relationship, the two had already claimed their beds, leaving me with the top bunk. The cramped room felt stifling.

Could this get any worse?

I was homesick already, even though my parents stood twelve inches in front of me, my mother chatting brightly with the other parents.

It didn't take long to establish that both of my roommates were Jewish. After playing the requisite game of Jewish Geography, it turned out that one grew up about fifteen minutes from where I grew up and the other had a brother who went to the same summer camp as my cousin. Small world!

My parents beamed. My roommates' parents beamed. The three of us felt too nervous to beam, but we managed wan smiles.

With eight of us standing around among the many bins and boxes we had each brought, the room felt claustrophobically small. But as our parents chatted about the logistics of shipping bagels and cream cheese to us, I started to feel more at ease.

Although we were hundreds of miles from home, the conversation in our dorm room felt totally familiar. When one of the other dads exclaimed that he "couldn't *schlep* up those stairs one more time," everyone appeared more relaxed on this shared linguistic turf.

Despite the comforting discovery that my roommates were both Jewish, nothing had prepared me for the moment when my father said how long the drive was to get back home and that he and my mother needed to get on the road. He might as well have said he was leaving me in the woods to live out the rest of my days with a pack of wolves.

Our goodbyes were truncated by the appearance of a buoyant R.A. (resident assistant) who, at the exact instant when my stomach started folding over itself, made her grand entrance into our room holding balloons with our names on them (and smiley faces, of course).

The cramped room felt hot. August in Upstate New York in a non-air-conditioned room with one functioning window, nine adults, and three balloons jockeying for position made me regret that my mother had successfully argued for me to leave home and go away to college.

It seemed like the worst idea in the history of terrible ideas.

While the R.A. introduced herself to the parents, reassuring each of them that their "precious daughters" would be well taken care of, my roommates and I found ourselves edged out of the room and into the corridor.

I was just thinking I could make a break for it, hiding in the trunk of the car until we were back on Cedarhurst Avenue, when my plan was interrupted by a jovial guy in a funny hat who introduced himself as the M.E.R.A., "Most Excellent Resident Assistant." Pointing to the first door on the other side of the staircase, he told us that was his room, that he had an open-door policy, and that we should come by anytime. Wink, wink.

Wait a second. Boys lived on this floor? With the girls? With only a six-foot-wide staircase separating us?

This was my "get out of jail free" card. Wait until my father hears about this. He would never let me stay here.

And just as I was about to use honesty as the best policy for getting me out of staying in that godforsaken place, the parade of parents started filing out of my dorm room with Ms. Rah-rah R.A. bringing up the rear.

"Time to say goodbye, ladies," she said, her grating cheer making me want to rip her eyeballs out.

The mothers gave us each a hug, and I noticed that Dad had turned away and started coughing. "Just something caught in my throat," he explained when he faced me with red-rimmed eyes.

"I'm just a phone call away," he said. I wasn't sure which one of us was being reassured, me or him.

He took my mother's elbow and steered her toward the staircase. They didn't look back. I ran into the room to look out the window and watched as they got in the car. I stood there until I couldn't see the car anymore no matter how much I pressed my face up to the screen.

Finally noticing the loud sniffle behind me, I turned around to find one of my roommates openly weeping and the other quietly sitting on the bed and daintily dabbing at her eyes with a tissue. I was neither a dainty nor a showy crier. In fact, I wasn't much of a crier at all. I felt hollow and miserable, like this was all a terrible mistake. I took a swipe at the nearest balloon with an angry fist. It hit the corner of the metal locker that served as the third closet for our two-person room, and popped with a startlingly loud and extremely satisfying sound.

The three of us found this hilarious, and our tears quickly turned to laughter that turned into crying because we were laughing so hard. I'd like to say that was it, the turning point that put homesickness in the rearview mirror—but it wasn't.

It was, however, the icebreaker that we needed to relax and get to know one another as we unpacked our meager belongings.

For the first month of school, our trio was inseparable. We were away from home for the first time, in a small town in Upstate New York where the nearest synagogue was fifty miles away. Whatever else we did not have in common—which turned out to be nearly everything—our shared Judaism glued us together. It made us feel confident about jumping into every new first-year adventure because we jumped in together.

Of course, at college I quickly learned that "Fill in the Blank" Geography made for a fun and easy way to start *any* conversation with *any* new person. And to my naïve amazement, everyone played it the same way!

My Jewish boyfriend found a couple of other Jewish guys to fix my roommates up with, and it all was unfolding just as my father had envisioned it.

I wrote long letters home and couldn't wait until Sunday, the day we got to call home.

When it was my turn to use the pay phone at the end of the hall, my father always started the conversation by asking how things were at the *shtetl*, using the Yiddish word for a small Jewish village.

As much as I missed being home, my newfound freedom from my parents and their rules felt liberating. Within the first week away at college, I got so drunk on Mateus Rosé that I puked for two hours. I never drank Mateus Rosé again.

My boyfriend and I had sex so often that by the end of the second week away at college, I visited the infirmary twice to get antibiotics for urinary tract infections.

By the third week at college, I pulled the first of what would become habitual all-nighters to finish writing a paper.

And then it was Rosh Hashanah, the Jewish New Year—the first time I wouldn't be with my family at synagogue in Rockaway, wearing a new dress, seeing all my relatives, eating my grandmother's beautifully prepared dinners, seated at a table set with the good china and the best linens.

If that wasn't depressing enough, we had classes. It felt like a personal affront. Where I grew up, we didn't go to school on the holidays. My mother would write a note in her lovely cursive asking that "Lisa please be excused from school in order to observe the holiday."

Not the case at college.

The three of us considered the fifty-mile bus ride to the town with the nearest temple, then a taxi from the bus to the temple, but when we looked up the bus schedule, we realized we would have gotten there either two hours before services started or two hours after services started.

We sat staring at one another until one roommate said, "Well, what about Sandy Koufax? He didn't pitch on Yom Kippur. I don't think we should go to class tomorrow."

We agreed that staying in our room and saying the few prayers we could each remember (not very many) would be the right thing to do. I got drafted to write the letter to the Dean asking that we please be excused from classes to observe the holiday.

I wrote my first "legal" brief that night, explaining the meaning of the holiday, that we would not be attending classes, that our absences should not be recorded as "absent" but as "excused," and for good measure, I also mentioned that this would be the case on Yom Kippur ten days later and we would be making the same request. I concluded with the story of Sandy Koufax, the incomparable Dodgers ace pitcher, who refused to pitch Game 1 of the 1965 World Series against the Minnesota Twins because it coincided with Yom Kippur.

After proofreading my letter, the three of us marched up the hill to the Dean's office to deliver it in person. Walking out of the imposing building that housed the administrative offices of the university, I felt light, a little giddy. I knew I had done the right thing and couldn't wait to call my father to tell him.

On the way back to our dorm, one of my roommates had the brilliant idea to go to the library and see if they had a prayer book in their collection. No, they didn't, explained the librarian, who then suggested we go visit the professor who taught a class on world religions.

He didn't have a prayer book either, but he let us borrow his Tanakh—the book containing the Torah.

Over the next two days, we took turns reading it aloud. One of us got some apples from the cafeteria. Another one of us walked the short distance to the supermarket and got a jar of honey. Apples and honey are the traditional foods to herald the New Year with sweetness.

The next morning, the first day of Rosh Hashanah, and a day when we each had an 8 a.m. class, we sat on our beds looking at one another. "Are we really doing this?" asked one roommate.

"We are really doing this." My conviction that this was the right thing to do felt unshakable.

A few hours later there was a knock at our door. It was a student messenger bringing a letter from the Dean.

Dear Miss Printz,

Thank you for the thorough and instructive letter regarding your absence from class in observance of the Jewish Holy Days.

I appreciate you calling this to my attention and my office will notify your professors to mark these as excused absences.

I have asked my assistant to add this to the agenda for our next meeting of the administrative team so that we can proactively address this for our Jewish students in future years.

With best wishes for a happy holiday,
Dean _____

I reveled in my first successful official argument.

Although this was my first appeal to be permitted to observe my religion, it was hardly the last. The High Holidays, as Rosh Hashanah and Yom Kippur are collectively called, were a line in the sand that I would not cross.

I didn't intend to work on these holidays—ever. And I didn't. It turned out to be less of a big deal in my professional life than it had been that first year of college. True to his word, the Dean had the calendar for each of the following years annotated for the High Holidays with an asterisk that stated, "Jewish students are excused from class attendance. Please avoid administering any tests on this date."

I sped through college in three years. I wanted to graduate with my high school sweetheart, who I had followed to college. We stayed together throughout undergraduate school, but the plan to get engaged that next summer never materialized. We broke up and I met someone else. My new beau headed out of state for a job while I headed home to start law school.

32

The Group

Some legal rulings from my first year in law school, such as "If you dig, you must shore up," "Oh, Tree, I feel sick," "the last clear chance rule," and "the rule against perpetuities," as well as dozens of other legal principles, compete for space in my brain—along with the lyrics to endless '60s and '70s songs—not because they are memorable on their own, but because I can attach a specific law school classmate to each one of them.

In late August 1979, when law school classes began, we were divided into three sections. Clusters of students quickly began to form. With no recollection of how I "made it" into the group of students who, to my eyes, were the cool kids, there I found myself, amid a bunch of men and women who performed daily feats of intellectual magic.

Every member of The Group could juggle effortlessly between being a serious, brilliant student and a ne'er-do-well. Their transgressions—frequently taking place in class while the unsuspecting professor wasn't looking—and their unfailing ability to deliver the correct answer when called on by that very same professor made for a remarkable and very entertaining first semester.

How lucky to have this bunch of characters in my life! They invented a bingo game, not with your typical numeric squares, but rather with cartoonish descriptions of fellow classmates—girl with mousy glasses, chewing gum girl, tattoo dude—that provided hours of distracted entertainment.

One day they covered a seat in talcum powder, and when the target classmate plopped down, the resulting puffy white cloud had most of the cavernous lecture hall in stitches.

Despite their antics, though, they always knew the right answer, so calling them to task for their disruptive behavior rarely happened.

Some members of the basic group (who changed only slightly over time) played an important, though transient role, during my law school years. But a few fulfilled Dean I. Leo Glasser's prophecy and became lifelong friends.

Loyalty requires me to start with the lovely Loren, who favored White Shoulders perfume and whose entire wardrobe ran in tones of black, black, and sometimes black. Standing at five feet two, what she lacked in height she more than made up for in attitude. One would never consider crossing her. That said, she possessed (and still does) the kindest heart, a lightning-fast mind, and what I always found her most endearing quality, a raucous and thoroughly infectious laugh. I initially thought of her as Rizzo, the Stockard Channing character from the film *Grease*, a rebellious hellion with a tender side.

It was never easy for me to make friends with other girls or women, and Loren and I got off to a rocky start. She seemed cocky, until it became abundantly clear that she knew all the answers to every question that every professor asked. Loren was a badass with confidence.

Pichel (pronounced the Yiddish way, with a guttural sound of the "ch" as in "Bach"), so serious one minute and so funny the next, earned his nickname early on. His last name, Shapiro, got bastardized to Shapickle, and a short leap later got abbreviated to Pichel, a name he still answers to five decades later. A walking sports encyclopedia, his brash exterior and extremely short fuse barely concealed the heart of gold that beat inside his chest. Perhaps because our lives shared so many commonalities—we both hailed from closely knit Conservative Jewish families originally from Rockaway Beach, New York—I felt remarkably close to him and still do.

The ringleader of The Group, the Rogue Prince, a reckless, freewheeling, fun-loving, self-admitted cad, loved to create all sorts of mischief in and out of the classroom. While it seemed improbable that he could be book-smart and a smart-ass simultaneously, he pulled both off without a hitch. Our constitutional law professor seemed so disarmed by his charm and his invariably accurate answers that she acted smitten. Our property law professor, on the other hand, found the Rogue Prince's antics repugnant, but since he never caught him in the act, he could do nothing but fume.

This "merry band of miscreants," as one professor put it, ate together, drank together, watched football together, played together, and in general did everything together, but the ostensible purpose of The Group was to study together. We did this with a healthy mix of cookies from the Rogue Prince's cousin's bakery in Sheepshead Bay, long bouts of serious studying, and a heavy dose of gossip and laughter.

When I consider that Brooklyn Law School had no residence halls at the time and all of us commuted from somewhere, it's a wonder that any of us got any sleep. Conveniently, the Rogue Prince lived just a few blocks away, so it was in his apartment that we most often found ourselves when we needed to escape from the walls of the law school.

It was hardly surprising that couples would form within a group of people in their twenties who spent as much time together as we did. Some of the pairings were platonic, some of them were romantic, and at least one of them—mine and the Rogue Prince's—was purely flirtatious. All the double entendres and sidelong glances I exchanged with him seemed harmless and fun—at least until that wild kiss on the subway platform that made my knees weak. But when Dad died later that night, everything changed for me.

As soon as they heard the news about my father, the members of The Group surrounded me with protective arms and caring hearts. I needed "my people"—and I had found them.

33

The Dead Parent Club

1979 was a watershed year for my education. But my education did not come only in the form of Contracts, Torts, Property, or Constitutional Law. No, 1979 was the year I became a death expert.

By then I had attended with youthful detachment the funerals of an uncle and a grandfather. I was young for both and recall only bits of detail, mostly revolving around the platters of tuna fish and egg salad sent by thoughtful loved ones and visitors for our "meals of consolation." Grandma Rose's death in February 1979 hit closer to home; until I had left for college, I had visited her weekly my entire life. I came home from school for the funeral. It was a miserably freezing day, and her burial was the first one that I recall with any clarity.

My father, the youngest of four siblings, was committed to attending daily *minyan* so that he could say *Kaddish*, the mourner's prayer. According to Jewish tradition, this prayer is said daily for eleven months following a loved one's passing and requires a gathering of ten adult males, a *minyan*, to do so.

It was not only Dad's commitment to this daily ritual that filled me with reverence for the importance of it. The *minyan* also provided a concrete reminder of his mother's loss and allowed him to honor her memory. I respected and admired that.

After graduation, I returned home to live; I was set to start law school in the fall and planned to commute from home to save money.

I began accompanying my father each evening to the small chapel where the rabbi and (typically) twelve to fifteen other mourners gathered. And so I began to acquire arcane tidbits of knowledge and a very good grasp of the service.

At the time, because I was a woman, I didn't "count" toward the *minyan*. One rainy night, although there were ten of us in the chapel, in the rabbi's eyes there were only nine. We waited until a Jewish man who lived nearby was summoned so we could proceed.

My father and I often debated the unfairness of this Jewish practice. As a budding lawyer, I was eager to match wits with him. His favorite argument was that he didn't make the rules, he just followed them—that it was up to me to change them. This comment usually stalled me long enough for him to change the subject.

I enjoyed our time together in the small chapel. The group of mourners changed a bit from night to night. Some, like my father, were there regularly, fulfilling their commitment to honor their loved one for the traditional eleven-month period of mourning. Others attended for one night to observe the anniversary of their loved one's death.

Usually there were a few minutes of chatting among the mourners before the service started. I didn't realize how unusual it was to find a twenty-one-year-old at the nightly *minyan* until several months of being the only one. And on the many nights that my brother joined us, the two of us were clearly the exception, not the rule.

But when you see the same folks every night for months, the nods of acknowledgment evolve to more. Over time, Dad and I got to know the names of our fellow mourners, something about their family or their profession and, of course, whom they had come to say *Kaddish* for.

By late November, I had been coming to the little chapel with my father nearly every night for six months. I had memorized the short service, which varied only slightly depending on whether it was the Sabbath or a holiday. Eventually, I knew the prayers as well as my father and my brother did. Rob could actually read the Hebrew, rather than reciting it by rote, like I did.

But I never questioned the point of saying daily *Kaddish*, never thought that it was a silly tradition or that my father was wasting his time fulfilling this ritual.

In the way one's mind occasionally wanders, I once sat beside my father on the uncomfortable wooden pews and knew deep in my heart that when the time eventually came that I lost one of my parents, surely I would honor them by saying *Kaddish* every day for eleven months.

Sitting with my father all those months was like the dress rehearsal for the real thing. So, when the real thing befell us, as shocked and unprepared as I was, there was tremendous comfort going down the few stairs to the little chapel to say *Kaddish* for my father. The regulars had all heard the tragic news, and they welcomed me into their midst as a fellow mourner with words of condolence and comfort.

During my father's violent final moments, I know he suffered, but the anguished family he left behind ached with grief.

My seventeen-year-old brother was spared the worst of that night, or bore the brunt of it, depending on your vantage point. Not being in the room, hearing but not seeing what was happening, imagining it without knowing it... I'm not sure I would willingly have traded places with him.

The ensuing days, the decisions large and small, the call from the Dean, the visits from my law school study group, the cassette tapes of every lecture I missed, the funeral, the eulogy, the burial, that bone-chilling finality of dirt clods thudding on the coffin—I endured them all because they had to be endured. And when I took my spot on the hard wooden pew in the chapel, I embraced it. I didn't find it scary or uncomfortable but calming and peaceful. Although my father never said so, I wondered if he felt, as I did, that coming to synagogue was like opening a channel to speak directly to him.

Groucho Marx famously said he would refuse to join any club that would have him as a member. As a freshly minted card-carrying member of the Dead Parent Club, I could see his point.

Dad's death accelerated certain traits I may or may not have eventually developed. I faced the days and weeks after he died with execution-oriented stoicism and an obsessive need to get everything exactly right, from the tie my father would wear for eternity to the pitcher of water outside the house so that people could ceremonially wash after the funeral.

My need for perfection remains relentless. This pursuit of flawless execution drove every task I took on, every job I ever had, and certainly propelled my career. The demands I made on myself and the demands I placed on those who worked with me were precisely overlapping circles. Likely never to be described as an easy boss, I feel sure I'd be described as a fair one. I asked no more from my team than I asked from myself.

When my father died, the grief that gripped me made me only want to push through it harder, faster. If there was a barrier in front of me, I needed to figure out a way to run through it. I had always been strong-willed and hardheaded, but Dad's death made me tougher, grittier, and more resilient.

As newly inducted members in the DPC, my brother and I both grew up fast. My mother was unprepared to be the head of our shrunken household. The impact of dropping from a loving family of four to three emotionally wrecked individuals just trying to make it through each day was profound; it brought on a physical heaviness that we all visibly carried. Coco, typically a fiercely independent being most of her life, rarely left my mother's side after my father died.

My brother and I reacted quite differently to our father's untimely death, often spinning away from each other rather than sticking together. But the things we shared kept us close through the many rough patches. We shared—and still share—a deep love for each other, and we both have Type A personalities and a maniacal commitment to personal health. We also grew to share an abiding belief that you can't take anything for granted—nothing—because one day you may wake up and the father you thought would surely just "be" there... well, suddenly he isn't.

It is at this intersection that what I learned from my father's death and what I eventually learned from Aunt Vi's life converge, a mix between not taking anything for granted and *ozmer lebt, derle'bt*—if you live, you live to see.

Celebrating a forty-eighth birthday and a thirtieth wedding anniversary were life events that I'm sure my father took for granted would happen to him, but ones he never lived to see.

Perhaps that's why Aunt Vi repeated her mantra so often. She beat me over the head with it until I finally "got" it.

I returned to law school in the spring. The Group helped me through those times with copious amounts of baked goods and terrible jokes, all of which did little to lift my spirits but made me feel less alone. And although I didn't "count" in the eyes of our rabbi, I said *Kaddish* for my father every day, sitting in the same chapel pew we had sat in during the months my father said *Kaddish* for my grandmother.

Acceptance into the literal Men's Club never happened, but I do think that eventually the "regulars" arrived at grudging respect. I couldn't remake the rules—not at that time, anyway—but my very presence was just the sort of challenge that I knew my father would appreciate.

In May 1980, my mother's father died. It was cruel for many reasons. He had lived a long life, but died a long death, draining my mother. What must it feel like to bury a mother-in-law, a husband, and a father within a year of one another?

Since this happened so soon after my father's death, I was well prepared to find all the necessary legal documents, contact all the right people, and arrange what needed arranging. While my family swirled around in our triple whammy of grief, my newfound fastidiousness helped me do what had to be done.

Months later I got a call in the middle of the night from a panicked former boyfriend seeking my immediate help. His father had just died of a massive heart attack, and he was at a loss for what to do. When I told this story at the lunch table the next afternoon, The Group was characteristically irreverent. While giving someone a nickname can sometimes be a form of bullying, the nickname given to me that day by The Group felt like a term of endearment. With a penchant for dark humor as a coping mechanism, among them I was forever dubbed the Death Expert.

Soon after, further establishing my bona fides to The Group, my mother asked me to write the epitaph for my father's footstone. Jewish tradition requires an "unveiling" eleven months following a death. The unveiling is literal—a cloth is laid across the deceased's footstone, and then with a flourish the rabbi pulls off the cloth in a great reveal.

These words are not exactly written in water-soluble marker. They are etched in stone for all eternity. No pressure, Mom.

I struggled for days. When I was supposed to be studying, I struggled. When I was supposed to be sleeping, I struggled. I felt a great burden to get this right. No, not just right. Exactly right.

One afternoon, seeing that I was distracted by the still unwritten epitaph (while I was supposed to be studying torts), Loren asked, "What was special about him?"

"Everybody loved him," I replied without thinking.

"Well, that's it. Just say that."

That night, as I tried to fall asleep, I thought about what I had answered Loren. By the morning, it was there, fully formed, in my head.

When I committed it to paper and shared it with my mother and brother, they nodded in agreement.

I fretted about the words for weeks until it was too late to do anything about them. With my family and close friends surrounding the still recently turned earth and the yews we had planted in their infancy, the words were unveiled:

So much to so many. Most of all, loved.

As we walked away from the graveside a few minutes later, Loren took me by the arm, squeezed it, and said with a perfect mock-Yiddish accent, "Such a footstone! You must be some kind of Death Expert!"

34

Dad Stand-Ins

1979–1992

When I was about eighteen or nineteen, my parents, my brother, and I were at a Chinese restaurant for dinner. My father, immensely enjoying his egg roll with extra hot mustard, called the waiter over to ask him what was inside. The waiter proudly told us it was a house specialty called "imitation crab." Although ubiquitous now, imitation crab wasn't introduced in America until the late '70s. Dad and the waiter had a spirited discussion about the "crab sticks," which the waiter insisted were "real."

A very good substitute can be terrific, but at the end of the day it's not the genuine article.

After my father's death, many well-meaning men stepped in to try to fill his sneakers. Among the "imitation dads" were uncles (real and "adopted"), former boyfriends, college classmates of my father's, and law school friends of mine—all of whom kept me on my path and made me feel loved.

Without them, it's unlikely my career would have gotten the jump start it needed in a competitive, mostly man's, world, especially after the train wreck that was my law school GPA.

But in those early days, when merely surviving was my primary objective, my mother's brother, Uncle Julie, and my father's brother, Uncle Mel, swooped in right away. Physical proximity meant that Julie shared that crushing moment in the emergency room when the doctor came out to tell us what we already knew—Dad died and despite their best efforts, they couldn't do a thing. I felt tremendous relief that his firm hug held my mother for what seemed like ten minutes, his personal grief set aside to support her. This loss cut deeply for him, too. He and my father had worked together in the family business, desks facing each other, for over two and a half decades. He spent more time with my father than I did. Julie projected strength when we most needed it, and his ongoing, steadfast commitment to my brother and me in the days, weeks, months, and years thereafter demonstrated his unwavering love for us.

Mel, on the other hand, was wrecked by Dad's death. An emotional guy to begin with, he buried his baby brother with tears streaming down his cheeks, wedged between his petite wife, Joyce, and even more petite older sister, Gert. Uncle Mel and I had always enjoyed a close relationship, likely because he and my father, as well as Joyce and my mother, enjoyed a special bond. They were nearest to each other in age among the siblings, and one of their daughters and I were born just months apart.

It felt natural and logical for him to become a fixture in my life.

Then there were Uncle Mike, Uncle Norman, Uncle Alan, Uncle Gene... my father's fraternity brothers from college, spouses of my mother's closest friends, tennis buddies, and other friends—lawyers, doctors, accountants, printers, stock-brokers. They came from all walks of life, and each had something wise to impart.

Uncle Mike introduced me to one of his matrimonial lawyer buddies, and within minutes I had an offer for a summer internship. This was just one of the many instances when one of these men opened a door for me. I had a difficult time graciously accepting these as anything but favors; I thought they detracted from my desire to make it on my own.

I even challenged Uncle Norman once, petulantly refusing to meet a potential employer because "I want to do this myself."

He gave me some advice that day that I used as a parent later in life: "Someone might get you to the threshold, but only *you* can walk through the door. It is all up to you once you get inside." When he said it, it made sense to me, but I continued to be reluctant to accept these kindnesses.

The surprises came often from my assemblage of Dad Stand-Ins. A call, a note, a lunch, a dinner—moments that filled me with strength and hope.

There is a filament that I can clearly trace from my father's death through my entire legal career that runs through these men: the summer internship I got during my first summer of law school with a prominent Long Island divorce lawyer, the part-time job I got with him during law school, the full-time job he offered me and I took after law school, the article about child custody I wrote for the Chief Judge of the New York Supreme Court for the annual meeting of the New York State Bar Association, the first job I got in Manhattan with a prominent matrimonial lawyer, the next (and final) legal job I got with my favorite matrimonial lawyer, the invitation to become a member of the American Academy of Matrimonial Lawyers, being the youngest person (and woman) ever admitted to that organization, becoming a partner at my law firm, and having my name on the law firm letterhead and in bronze on the wall.

The unbroken throughline stretches from Dad through his cadre of wonderful friends. Their compassionate proffers of help were the most eloquent tribute to how well-regarded my father was.

35

Some Notable Casualties

I: Academic Success

January 1980

When I think about law school, I think about feeling the weight of darkness on the edge of down, pressing, pressing with its considerable heft against my fragility.

The way my first semester began stood in stark contrast to the way it ended. I had started law school filled with hope and promise and the joy of having my father share it all with me. But in January, with my father gone, I faced my semester grades with a mix of dread and inevitability.

My classmates jostled one another in the hallway where final exam grades hung from tape on the graying white walls. Exclamations of joy, surprise, relief, disappointment, and disbelief echoed off the concrete as each person found their name and grade on the sheets for our six required courses.

I reluctantly joined the mass of students clamoring to see their grades. The disorderly array of papers contradicted my idealistic perception of law school. I expected neat rows hanging in alphabetical order by course title. Instead, whoever had posted the sheets simply hung them in whatever random order they happened to be on his or her desk. I found Torts, Property, Constitutional Law, Legal Research and Writing, and Civil Procedure with little trouble. Scribbling each grade next to the course name I had scrawled out earlier on the first sheet of a yellow legal pad, I thought to myself, *So far, so good, all things considered.*

"All things" being that I had returned to school two weeks after my father's death and two weeks before my first semester final exams. I had firmly rejected the Dean's offer to wait to take my exams until the first semester of my *second* year. His alternative would have had me studying for twelve finals the following December, a prospect that struck me as both overwhelming and doomed to fail.

Having chosen to study only as much as my grieving attention span allowed, let's just say I hadn't exactly given the final exams my best effort. But the daily (and nightly) hard work during the semester and the support of The Group had clearly been enough to muster decent grades on my finals so far.

But something was missing. Where was Professor Gilbride's grading sheet for Contracts?

The course hadn't come easily to me all semester, and as I searched every list on the wall, I could still feel the sting of my first personal experience with the Socratic method of teaching. Professor Gilbride called on me during the first week of school to grill me about a case that I didn't understand. And he didn't just call on me. He butchered my name just enough for me to be sure it was mine, while sounding completely foreign and intentionally disrespectful. "Liza Prynz," he called, referring to his seating chart and using a long "I" sound in both my first and my last name.

It didn't occur to me to pretend I didn't know he meant me. Nor did I see it for the passive-aggressive intimidation tactic he intended it to be—skewing my attention just enough that he had me off-balance before I uttered a sound. I slowly got to my feet, Professor Gilbride having made clear on the first day of class that if called on, standing was the expected response. So I stood there, my cheeks flaming and my throat feeling like I just drank a glass of ocean water. I stammered and floundered with every question—something that delighted my professor and genuinely mortified my classmates, many of whom had physically sunk down in their seats or had one arm protectively shielding their faces. Nobody wanted to be next. Professor Gilbride grilled me on the first basic element of a contract: What constitutes an offer? It felt as if I had been standing there for an hour, but it couldn't have been more than a minute or so before he made a sweeping gesture to take in the lecture hall and asked, "Does anyone here know what constitutes an offer?" I sank into my chair, grateful that I hadn't fainted, although in retrospect fainting might have been better.

(I never knew, but always suspected, that was the very instant that I captured the attention of the Rogue Prince, who had an unobstructed view of my bare legs from his vantage point several rows in front of and to the right of me in the tiered theater-style room.)

Distracted by the memory, I finally found the grade sheet, scanning it for my name. My heart dropped to my toes when I saw the number beside it: 69, barely passing.

The supply of tears that seemed endlessly available, taking me from composed to weeping in an instant, obliged. Blubbering in the hallway, surrounded by hundreds of other students, I realized that the extraordinary law school career Dad and I planned had flamed out with my near failure in Contracts I.

I felt an arm around me and looked up to find the Rogue Prince. "Hey, Kid," he said. I turned and buried my sopping wet face into his chest and cried.

I felt another hand on my back and smelled the White Shoulders perfume announcing Loren's presence a second before I heard her soft, concerned voice. I blindly reached out a hand and she squeezed it. I felt another body press against my arm and turned to see Pichel's worried face. Within minutes, the tight circle of The Group was physically and emotionally holding me up.

I don't remember any words of reassurance, empathy, or support (although I'm certain they were said), but I do remember this liberating question: "Okay, who's ready for cookies?"

We took the elevator down to the cafeteria and commandeered several tables, pushing them together with scrapes and screeches as metal legs dragged against the shiny linoleum. The Rogue Prince deposited his bounty in the center—an enormous white box expertly tied with red-and-white twine.

The smell of butter and chocolate wafted from the box as soon as he lifted the lid. Inside, the overstuffed container held an assortment of cookies and rugelach from a bakery in Sheepshead Bay, Brooklyn. In what had become a weekly tradition, the baker, David—who just happened to be the Rogue Prince's cousin—sent a five-pound box of irresistible baked goods for us to enjoy at school.

Learning a new legal concept, gabbing about the Mets, gossiping about a classmate, or mourning a dead parent seemed a little easier in the company of a shortbread and a chocolate rugelach. Or two. Or five.

We demolished the entire box in minutes. I didn't have much to talk about during the grade-sharing conversation, but it seemed that Loren and the Rogue Prince both did great, as they tossed around the vaunted phrase "making *Law Review*."

Law Review was the most elite among academic measures of success. Impeccable grades usually presaged an invitation to write and publish a scholarly article, something I had aspired to until about an hour earlier when my Contracts grade tanked any chance of overall academic achievement—ever.

The realization brought a fresh wave of tears along with a tightness in my chest and a roiling in my stomach. I jumped up from the table and fled to the bathroom, where my body vengefully deposited the baked goods into the bottom of the toilet.

The heavy metal door to the bathroom, which I had neglected to lock in my haste to pray to the goddess of porcelain, slowly swung open. "Kid?" came the questioning voice of the Rogue Prince.

Wet wads of paper towel clenched in each fisted hand, I looked back at him through a mass of curly hair askew in my face, humiliated.

"C'mon," he said. "Let's get outta here."

He took my hand and walked me up the one flight of stairs to the lobby, past the massive glass-walled library, and out the doors onto the plaza. Neither of us said anything as we jaywalked across the street and made a left on Montague Street, the closest thing to a "retail" district in the mostly residential Brooklyn Heights, leaving the law school's imposing façade behind us.

We stopped for ice cream, and, despite the freezing January day, the ice cream soothed my raw throat. We ate and walked, and it wasn't until we stopped at his building that I gave any thought to where our ambling would lead. Although I had been there many times with The Group to study, watch football, or hang out, this first time alone with him felt different. Heading up in the elevator, and for the first time since the night my father died, I thought of that passionate first kiss on the subway platform just weeks before.

Once inside, he led me to the bathroom, offered me a fresh towel and toothbrush, and encouraged me to take a nice, long, hot shower. I felt grungy and painfully aware that I and my clothes smelled like Eau de Vomit.

Brushing my teeth felt great, and the hot shower felt even better. I didn't hear the bathroom door open and close, but when I pulled open the shower curtain, a neatly folded T-shirt and sweatpants sat in place of my pile of discarded clothing. This unexpected thoughtfulness and the kindness that lived behind it surprised me. I sat on the cold porcelain tub and cried some more. And when I finally pulled myself together to put on the clean clothes and walk out into the living room, the Rogue Prince sat on the couch with two cups, a pot of tea, and a plate of Cousin David's cookies. He picked up the plate and said, "Hair of the dog?"

At that moment the question truly felt hilarious and, like the clean clothes, unexpectedly empathetic. I sat on the couch beside him, drinking tea and eating cookies, but instead of expressing gratitude, I turned mean. It had occurred to me that the clean clothes fit me far too well to belong to the Rogue Prince. I said, "I see I'm not the first girl to take a shower in your apartment."

His face, beatific, didn't match his words. "No, and I'm sure you won't be the last." Hardly a pickup line, but something about the unashamed honesty of it was liberating. I was one in a procession of women, so rather than look for deeper meaning, I might as well just enjoy the afternoon.

The hours of cuddling, sex, more cuddling, and more sex induced a delightful case of amnesia. Both the sex and the amnesia continued for many months, during which a dangerously depressed Lisa Printz disappeared to make room for a reckless free spirit walking the halls of Brooklyn Law School.

Should I have hated and resented the Rogue Prince for taking advantage of a grieving and lost soul? No need: my brother had sufficient venom for the Rogue Prince to go around. Robert gave me an earful every time I left the house in Cedarhurst. And when I came skulking back in as dawn broke, he made it clear that he didn't approve of my letting myself be "used."

I didn't see it that way. While the Rogue Prince had made it no secret that I was one of many women in his life, often one of many in a single day, I truly didn't care. He wined and dined me, making me feel wanted. We went to neighborhood haunts and shared delicious steamed mussels in one place and chicken paprikash in another. We took long walks on the Brooklyn Promenade and admired the Manhattan skyline. Once we had a picnic on the roof of his building—a feast of strawberries, a hunk of cheese, and a bottle of wine atop a worn, raggedy blanket—almost like true romantics. He let me see a side of him he kept hidden behind his brash law school persona. A person capable of tremendous kindness lived behind that façade of a rule-breaking, heart-taking, mischief-making modern-day Don Juan.

For me, being with the Rogue Prince provided an emotional blank slate, an escape hatch that I dropped through only to emerge as someone different, someone alien but exciting to me. That other person felt desirable and mysterious. In hindsight, the Rogue Prince held all the cards, but in the many hours we spent together during those months, I felt like I wielded the power.

I must have been insane.

When I think back to those days, much of the time is a blur of eating cheeseburgers and ice cream, getting drunk and smoking dope (something I did for the first time with the Rogue Prince), and being in bed practically all the time—except for when we ate, drank, or got stoned.

The drinking and the drugs kept my demons at bay. I felt confident I had everything under control.

One particularly raucous night started with a bottle of champagne, a box of strawberries, and possibly some other un-inhibitors, which led to me dancing naked atop the bureau in the Rogue Prince's bedroom. The gigantic mirror that hung above the chest of drawers gave me an intimate glimpse into the stranger whirling, gyrating, and swaying to a soundtrack offered up by Bruce Springsteen.

The Rogue Prince's expression one of pure desire, the woman in the mirror—hair wild, eyes bright—moved seductively as Springsteen crooned:

There's a sadness hidden in that pretty face
A sadness all her own from which no man can keep Candy safe.
We kiss, my heart rushes through my brain
And the blood rushes in my veins,
The fire rushes towards the sky
And we go driving,
driving deep into the night
I go driving deep into the light in Candy's eyes.

And I spun like a dervish, with the music, fast and up-tempo, carrying my body. The song sped up like a freight train with an explosion of musical sound, and my bare feet on the polished wood occasionally squeaked as I whirled and saw a slice of mirror—the other girl—and whirled again as Springsteen growled out the words—

She has men who give her anything she wants
But they don't see
That what she wants is me
Oh, and I want her so
I'll never let her go, no-no-no
She knows that I'd give
All that I've got to give
All that I want, all that I live.

And I looked at the Rogue Prince, hungry, wanting me, needing me, and in that instant I knew I had crossed a line, falling in love with him. Just as Springsteen's voice lowered, Bruce whispered his heart's desire:

To make Candy mine
Tonight.

Taking one last look at the girl in the mirror, and twirling away from her one final time, I leaped from the top of the dresser to the bed, my short-lived control completely ceded to the Rogue Prince. He made love to me slowly and carefully. When we were both sated, he brought over his extra-long navy velour robe and draped it over me tenderly. The shift in the air between us felt real to me that night. But what seemed like the beginning of something new between us turned out to be mostly just more of the same. In today's parlance, we were friends with benefits and as time went by, it became clear that he didn't intend it to be anything more.

It would take another six months for my one-sided love affair (his one-sided lust affair) to come to a crashing and crushing halt.

II: Rob

November 1979

When our father died, my brother suffered an incalculable loss. This catastrophe still looms monumentally large in his life. His every waking breath is a testament to living every moment as if it were the last. Rob embodies kinetic energy. And when my mother wonders aloud why he pushes himself so hard, why he drives himself so fiercely at work, at play, at fatherhood, the simplistic answer is that Rob, barely seventeen when our father died, understands at the cellular level that it all changes in a heartbeat—or a missing beat.

As a member of the Dead Parent Club, my brother has a unique perspective on life. He has an unparalleled capacity for fun, for wringing every bit of joy from each experience. Some might say his "live every day to the fullest" strategy is enviable. The trunk of his car is filled with so much sports equipment that he earned the nickname "Toys R Us," after the famed toy and sporting goods chain. But his peripatetic need to be in motion until he drops with exhaustion has always struck me as a coping strategy. What started as Rob keeping himself so busy that he didn't leave time to be sad became a way of life.

The collateral damage from my father's death, vast and far-flung, had the greatest impact on those closest to him, but on no one more than on Rob.

When I think back to that night, to my mother wailing with terror, I knew her screams would wake my brother. I heard Coco starting to bark frantically from wherever she'd been sleeping. But I knew I didn't have time to worry about Rob.

Yet, as I raced from the phone to my stricken father, Rob's face flashed in front of me, freckled from hours of shooting hoops with our father, or shagging fly balls that Dad launched his way, or fishing beside Dad from the wooden bridge in the country.

I remember thinking, *He can't see this. I know that if he sees this, he will never unsee it.* I yelled to Rob, "Get the dog!" I heard footsteps heading down the stairs as I leaped across my mother's side of the bed.

In the frantic minutes that followed, while I tried but failed to save our father, while the paramedics failed to save our father, when I suddenly heard footsteps running up the stairs, I prayed it wasn't Rob. Twice as relieved when it turned out to be Dr. M, the father of one of Rob's best friends, I felt a rush of pride that my brother had such a clear head in this emergency to make that phone call.

Rob apparently made two calls while I tried vainly to save our father—first to Dr. M and then to Uncle Julie, my mother's brother, who appeared at the front door, tan raincoat over a bare chest and pajama bottoms, at the very moment Rob, my mother, and I were rushing out the front door. Bruce, my twenty-four-year-old cousin, trailed behind, looking dazed.

By then we stood clumped together in the tiny foyer, unsure what to do next. Uncle Julie took charge and herded us all to his waiting car.

We piled in and I stared out the window most of the way to the hospital, my mother's sobs the only sound. Rob and Bruce squeezed together beside me in the back seat. Rob sat right next to me, not even inches between us. I glanced at him. He looked straight ahead, no emotion. I thought about taking his hand, but I didn't. Maybe had I reached for him in that moment, that tiny space between my hand and his would never have opened into the resulting gulf between us. Surely the saddest and most preventable casualty, the big losers in the Dead Parent Club turned out to be Rob and me.

Just hours later, returning home, all of us numb with shock, we sat together in the den, facing one another, lost in our own grief. A fire had been started in the fireplace and the lights had been dimmed, so the room glowed with a warm, yellow light—such a contrast to the room where I left my father.

I suddenly remembered what my parents' bedroom looked like, the wreckage we left as we rushed from the house. *Rob can't see that*, I thought as I raced up the stairs, two at a time.

But I worried needlessly.

In the first of many kindnesses that came my way in the aftermath, Uncle Julie's wife, Aunt Lee, had come to the house while we were at the hospital. She had changed the sheets and made the bed, picked up all the detritus from the EMTs, sprayed the room with air freshener, spot-cleaned the carpet, and vacuumed.

She turned as she heard me in the doorway, her gloved hands holding a large trash bag, her eyes puffy, her face red.

"Thank you," I managed to say and fled back downstairs to the silent circle.

My gaze caught Rob's face, still expressionlessly staring off into space. I wanted to apologize to him for not saving his best friend, his favorite playmate, his idol. It was my fault that he didn't have a father anymore. I slumped into a tub chair, just wanting to disappear. I felt the responsibility for it, the gravity of my failure, and the weight of having to take on the leadership mantle of our little family.

I could never make this up to my brother—ever. How could he ever forgive me?

Any normal fissures and chinks that dented and bruised me for twenty-one years vanished, obliterated by the void in my chest where my heart had been shattered both by the loss of my darling father and by a guilt that I still carry for being the worst big sister in the world. It was my job to take care of Rob. By not saving our father, I failed miserably. But the truly unforgivable failure came when I let the grief create a gulf between us that opened wider whenever I selfishly took care of me at the expense of paying closer attention to Rob.

I know I could have fixed things in the chaotic weeks and months after our father died. But I didn't try. We turned away from each other and did whatever we had to do to survive. I know what I did, where I ran, what I drank, how often I got high, whom I had sex with, when I took reckless chances. The one question I can't answer—why did I leave Rob to fend for himself, to figure it all out, to grow up overnight to be the knight in shining armor for my mother?

As the only one missing from the scene who could come close to understanding what Rob lost, not just that night, but for the rest of our lives, I cavorted in Brooklyn Heights with the Rogue Prince.

Small wonder that Rob despised him during those dark years.

III: A Long-Standing Friendship

1981

Growing up, my best friend, Lisa, and I loved to cause the confusion and mischief that sharing the same first name affords. Sometimes we deliberately got out of a chore or a homework assignment by telling the relevant adult that we thought he or she meant "the other Lisa." My friend held a beloved spot in my family and I'm quite sure I held one in hers.

She grew up in a strict Italian household, and I grew up in a strict Jewish household. In other words, we grew up nearly identically, with family, religion, and food the driving forces in both our lives.

Lisa lived around the corner from me, and we walked to school and home again together every day from kindergarten through sixth grade.

Lisa's mother, Pat, made excellent snacks, led our 4-H troop, and let us watch *Dark Shadows* on television while we were eating. Lisa and I both loved this campy, scary soap opera about a vampire named Barnabas Collins who returned to haunt his family home in Maine.

Lisa remained part of my inner circle for most of my young life. And while never as close as we had been during the elementary school days, we shared a bond that seemed unbreakable.

Until it broke. Beyond repair. Over what else? A boy.

Worlds collide, and when they do, sometimes magic happens, and sometimes disaster.

So, on a lovely, warm evening in 1981, when Lisa arrived back in Cedarhurst after a terrible breakup, I thought I would cheer her up by inviting her to a party at Brooklyn Law School. She looked terrific with her long, straight blond hair brushed to a shine, her makeup simple—eyes shaded to perfection, lashes long—and a colorful button-down shirt tucked into a pair of very skinny Jordache jeans.

History favors its teller. I swear that going up in the elevator to the party, I told her that I had a crush on the Rogue Prince but that everyone else was fair game. Had I not been still fragile after my father's early exit the year before, perhaps my devastation at the sight of Lisa leaving the party with the Rogue Prince might not have felt like the dastardly betrayal it did.

Not by him. He was an honest scoundrel who made no bones about his extremely loose idea of fidelity. As in, the word "fidelity" was not in his vocabulary.

No, I was betrayed by her. She broke the cardinal rule of sisterhood. She purposely took a guy she knew I had a crush on. This crossed a line that could never be walked back.

A seventeen-year friendship destroyed by one tightly jean-clad ass.

IV: Passing the Bar Exam

1982–1984

Sometimes I wonder if the members of the New York State Board of Law Examiners are recruited based on a genetic tendency toward sadism. I mean no disrespect. I'm sure they are all decent people with families who love them. But just look at the evidence.

Twice every year, they create this test that they administer in intimidating surroundings, with exam-day regulations and security policies that make the most honest person feel like they are suspected of being a serial killer. Then, in the most widely read legal newspaper in the state, they publish a list detailing the names of the thousands of people who took the exam, and whether they passed or failed. I wonder if they share a bottle of champagne in the years when 33 percent of the test takers have a "Fail" next to their names.

For two years straight, I really, truly hated those guys. And I can trace the start of my hate-hate relationship with the bar exam directly back to Contracts I.

In the weeks after my father died, I couldn't muster the energy to study despite the best efforts of The Group. And they really tried.

One long afternoon, they attempted to teach me the principles of *Lawrence v. Fox*—an old case from the 1850s about third-party beneficiary contracts—using raspberry, chocolate, and cinnamon rugelach as stand-ins for each of the people involved in the case.

I didn't get to answer the question correctly on the exam, but nearly five decades later I can tell you everything you need to know about the case.

That I remember the essential facts of the case and the doctrine that it established proves only that I have a good memory (and maybe that I love rugelach).

When the final exam asked for an exposition on the case, I froze. Nada, zero, zippo, zilch. Maybe because it was the first exam I took after returning to law school after my father died. Maybe I was just nervous. Maybe all I remembered was the rugelach.

Either way, having the grades posted on the wall in the hallway made my humiliation even more crushing.

Beside my name was a 69, the lowest grade in the class. Just enough to pass, but by so little that the math made trying to do well in law school—ever—a cruel joke. Four credits of a D minus coupled with my mediocre grades in Torts, Property, Civil Procedure, and Legal Writing gave me a demoralizing average. Even if I had received straight A's the rest of the way through (a highly unlikely result), a graceful recovery from those first semester grades was nearly impossible.

So I stopped trying for academic success. I took that 69 as an excuse not to work hard another day of law school and just do what needed to be done to get by academically.

In the meantime, I poured my heart and soul into two very time-consuming labors of love. I became the editor in chief of the law school newspaper, and because I still had plenty of free time, I started the first-ever Brooklyn Law School yearbook.

While the other members of The Group started contributing to the prestigious *Law Review* and joined the National Moot Court Honor Society, I ate mouth-watering pastries and worked deep into the night on the newspaper and the yearbook.

The rest of my free time (about ten hours a week) I spent interning for a matrimonial lawyer on Long Island. He was also an adjunct professor at Brooklyn Law School and had been introduced to me by one of my Dad Stand-Ins, Uncle Mike, a fraternity brother of my father's. My second-year internship turned into a summer job, followed by a third-year internship and most third-year students' dream come true—an offer of full-time employment when I graduated.

I was set. I did the minimum necessary to pass and I barely made it through. But all that mattered was the stride across the Carnegie Hall stage where we graduated. Looking up at my mother and brother, seeing them beaming, crying, so proud, made the preceding three years worth it. And I comforted myself with the knowledge that nobody but me (and a few of my best law school friends) knew where I had finished in the class, that the 69 in Contracts wasn't relevant anymore. My law school classmates and I were on equal footing again: we all had to take the bar exam.

But those bar examiners had other ideas.

Sitting for the bar exam in July 1982 had only one redeeming feature—the Bar Review course I took with some friends in New York City was across from Nathan's Famous Hot Dogs. The nightly ritual of getting a knish and a hot dog was truly comforting—like a warm culinary hug.

The course was excellent. The materials were clear and concise, the mnemonic devices clever and helpful, the camaraderie of the very large group apparent—we were all in this together, and there seemed to be a sincere desire to see one another pass the dreaded exam.

The heavily proctored exam, given in a cavernous space on the Hudson River piers in Manhattan, had beaten me before I even sat down. I had never been a big fan of standardized tests in the first place, but sitting for the bar exam heightened my nervousness manyfold.

Had I realized at the time how little it mattered to my employer whether I passed the first time, I might have been relaxed enough to have done fine. As was the custom, those of us who were fortunate to have a job when we graduated from law school had already committed to start work long before the bar exam results would be released. There was plenty of work to be done, just none that involved going to court on behalf of a client. That was reserved for lawyers who had been admitted to the bar. But first there was that pesky test.

Rather than feeling relaxed and prepared, I spent several excruciating hours trying to make it through without fainting.

While my friends waited impatiently for the results to be printed in the *New York Law Journal* (*NYLJ*), I was already looking up the upcoming dates for the next exam and developed an isolation strategy for studying.

On the day the results hit the *NYLJ*, I spent the morning in the library at the law firm I worked at researching and drafting a brief about international custody laws and the Hague Convention's applicability to child abduction by a parent. The hours disappeared, as they often do when I'm buried deep in a project, and at about 6:30 p.m. my boss strolled into the library.

"I'm glad you're still here," he said. "I know you must be disappointed, but it's not a big deal. I want to reassure you that your spot here is secure. You'll get 'em next time."

I must have had a blank expression on my face because he quickly realized I had no idea what he was talking about!

"You haven't checked the paper, have you?"

"No," I replied. "I assume I failed?"

"You did," he answered. "I'm sorry."

"Don't be sorry. I expected it. I have a plan for next time."

The next test was being given in February 1983, and I asked my boss for three weeks off immediately before the exam. Once I got the green light to hole up in a friend's apartment in Florida, I gathered my notebooks, mnemonic devices, and study sheets, and I split for Boca Raton.

My determination to spend the entire three weeks doing nothing but studying was challenged early on. About a day in, the Rogue Prince showed up, not exactly unannounced, but close. He had ended things with the other Lisa (and likely a few other women) and had called me a couple of weeks earlier to say hello. I mentioned my three weeks in a free apartment on a golf course and, trying to sound casual about it, suggested he come for a few days. He encamped with me at the apartment for the rest of my stay, distracting me to no end.

Studying at the same time he and I ate, drank, and had sex-filled study breaks proved impossible. I decided, once again, that I really didn't care. I felt like my job at the firm was safe, so I didn't feel any pressure to pass.

It came as no surprise that the February results were the same failing ones as the previous July's.

My boss's visit to my office didn't have quite the same warmth as his visit to the library had six months earlier. He said supportive words, just without the same enthusiasm behind them.

On the theory that the third time's the charm, I planned to take the test again in July 1983, but decided to make a few adjustments.

I registered for a different and far more expensive Bar Review course than the one I had previously taken.

I also tried to sequester myself at work, at the Bar Review class, or at home. Period. No extracurricular activities. And with just a few exceptions, I did just that.

Despite what I thought were my best efforts, when the results got published, I had failed again.

Failing once seemed okay. Failing twice seemed less okay, but not catastrophic. Failing three times pushed me to the point of hopelessness.

My boss, Steve, invited me to lunch. I knew this didn't bode well. The ultimatum came before the waiter put down my salad—pass the exam the next time or find a new job. The firm, only about eighteen lawyers total, had an active litigation practice. I couldn't go to court if I didn't pass the bar. Simple as all that.

No pressure.

I had skipped my first law school reunion, ashamed to face my peers after failing the exam twice. What rock could I hide under now that I'd failed a third time?

Lacking a template from Dad's many life lessons, I decided the only clear path meant pitching the legal career—just giving up—and finding something else.

My grandmother, Hannah, knocked some sense into me. Visiting her apartment one Saturday afternoon, I sat my sorry ass on the couch and spilled out my whole sad tale.

"So, if I take it again in February and I fail, I get fired. What if this is a sign that I'm not cut out to be a lawyer?" I finished, waiting for an affirmation that getting out of the law was the exact right conclusion.

She said the one thing that screwed my head on straight.

"Your father would have said to take the test again and pass it. If you still want to quit, it's your decision, not an excuse."

That's exactly what he would have said.

I took the exam again in February 1984, passed it—finally—and didn't realize until I had passed it just how much I wanted to be a lawyer. What had started out as something I wanted just to please my father had become my true passion.

With several years of practice already behind me, years in which I got to work on all sorts of fascinating issues, now that I was official, I set my sights high.

So, despite their best efforts, the ladies and gentlemen of the Board couldn't beat me into submission. And dear Loren once reassured me there's no asterisk next to my name on the rolls of admitted lawyers in New York State that says, "Lisa E. Printz*—*three-time loser, passed on the fourth attempt."

36

Quitting, Engaged, Fired, and Hired

1980–1984

With dizzying speed, I quit one job, moved in with my life partner, got fired from another job, then got hired by my professional partner.

My law school/post–law school job working with a well-known divorce lawyer on Long Island was an excellent training ground. As the most junior person on the totem pole, I often got tedious tasks, like putting bank statements in chronological order or running down to the county clerk's office to fetch a judge's decision. Even though I had repeatedly failed the bar exam, because the firm was small, I still had the chance to do amazing things and tackle the kinds of legal issues that my peers in Manhattan were years away from dealing with as they toiled in their top-tier law firms.

My boss, Steve, one of the senior partners in the law firm, introduced me to everyone remotely connected to matrimonial law in Nassau County: every other lawyer, every court clerk, every judge, every court reporter. Steve also imparted a piece of advice that I later shared with my children. He told me that it was important to be nice to everyone—and that really meant everyone, from the highest justice to the person who ran the photocopy machine. No difference: treat everyone politely and with respect. This life lesson continues to serve me well no matter what hat I'm wearing.

The doors that Steve led me to, the ones that opened into rooms of opportunity, were many. But no door was more important in my fledgling career than the one bearing the name of the Chief Judge of the Supreme Court for Nassau County.

I wasn't nervous meeting Judge Meyer for the first time. Perhaps because Steve didn't tell me that's what we were about to do until we were two feet from Judge Meyer's office.

Steve had clerked for the judge as his first job out of law school and the two had remained friends. Judge Meyer had just been tapped as the keynote speaker for the annual meeting of the New York Chapter of the American Bar Association, and he wanted Steve to draft his speech. The two chatted for about thirty minutes as I furiously took notes, trying to capture everything each man said during the conversation.

When we left the courthouse, Steve told me to have a draft of the speech on his desk by the following Friday. Taking all those notes suddenly felt less nerdy and way smarter.

Judge Meyer knew what he wanted to talk about. He felt the child custody laws needed to be addressed in a way that was more inclusive of both parents so that children do not fall victim to the dissolution of their parents' marriage.

During our meeting, Judge Meyer had remarked that making custody decisions was a "sticky wicket" and that "the best interests of the child" most certainly changed continuously. He felt the court had been given too much judicial discretion in determining best interests.

That tumbled around in my head for a few days, and the more research I did, the more I understood what he meant. Words like "thorny" and "prickly" kept coming to mind. I had written a good chunk of the speech when I considered what it must feel like to be the judge—hearing only the evidence as it is presented to you, relying on experts who have examined the child, and knowing that in your hands you hold this whole nettlesome mess that you need to sort out to decide this child's fate.

At the top of the first page, I wrote the word "Nettle" and, a day earlier than requested, I left the draft on Steve's desk.

Coming into the office on Monday, I found the speech on my desk. Expecting it to be awash in red ink, I noticed with relief only several awkward sentences that Steve had vastly improved, three punctuation mistakes and, in a scrawl that rivaled mine, "How Grasp the" written at the top, in front of my "Nettle."

Steve's assistant retyped the speech, with the title "How Grasp the Nettle" and the byline "Judge Bernard S. Meyer, Chief Judge, Supreme Court, Nassau County*."

When she gave me a copy for my review, I saw what the asterisk referred to. Right there, on the title page of the keynote address, were these words: "The author wishes to thank Stephen W. Schlissel for his invaluable assistance and Lisa E. Printz, without whom this would never have been written."

I was stupefied by this recognition and felt sure that Judge Meyer would take it off before he sent it on to the Bar Association for printing.

Steve invited me to come to Saratoga Springs, New York, where the meeting was being held, to hear the speech. "After all," he said, "you wrote it."

The weekend was a whirlwind of introductions to what seemed like every lawyer in the state and a few from out of state. When the time came for the keynote address, Steve and I had seats in the front of the audience.

Judge Meyer's delivery was nearly perfectly faithful to the words I had written, and he finished to thunderous applause. He waved it off and said, "Before I leave you all, I'd like to acknowledge my former law clerk, Steve Schlissel, and his associate, Lisa Printz. Didn't she do an amazing job?" His question was answered with more applause. It wasn't too shabby for a coming-out party, my debut as an authority on child custody.

Steve and I soon found ourselves embroiled in a terribly difficult case. As it was widely reported in the press at the time, Mandi Liebling was taken off the school bus by her father. He drove to Kennedy Airport, where he and Mandi boarded a plane bound for Costa Rica. We had been retained by Mandi's mother, Nadine, to get her daughter back.

Steve was the partner in charge, and I was the lead (and only associate) in *Liebling v. Liebling*. The case provided me with an incredible education. I became conversant in the Hague Convention and what could and couldn't be done in international kidnapping cases.

Soon it was the only case I worked on, and while it felt fascinating for a long time, and a young child's life was at stake, after several years of working on it, I started to feel a restless pull. I wanted to see if I could make my name in Manhattan. Leaving aside the failed bar exams, a career in Manhattan seemed naïvely within reach.

Still living in the house where my father died, with my brother away at college and my mother and I not exactly feeding each other positive energy, I felt it was high time for a radical change in my work life and my home life.

The details are a bit fuzzy. Did I quit my job and then ask my boyfriend if I could move in with him? Did my boyfriend notice how unhappy I seemed and ask me to move in with him until I could figure my life out?

Whatever the precise sequence of events, I thanked Steve profusely for everything he had taught me, and all the opportunities he had given me, and then I quit my job, packed up my Nissan Sentra, and drove away from my childhood home and toward whatever my future might bring.

During the first month with my new roommate, I ventured to the supermarket every day to buy ingredients for a curry dinner.

Green curries, red curries, yellow curries ... I have no clue what possessed me to dive headlong into this marvelous cuisine, but by the end of a month, both of us had eaten enough curry to last many decades.

No job hunting, no networking, no work-related efforts of any kind happened for months.

There were no complaints from my "roomie"—the shopping, cooking, cleaning, dry-cleaning, and laundry activities now being done exclusively by me seemed to suit him fine.

And there was also a noticeable shift in our relationship. Once reluctant to the point of reclusive about spending any time with my family, he often visited my mom with me and became #1 on the list my grandmother kept of my boyfriends.

One lovely weekend, packing up the trunk of the car in the middle of East Fifty-Third Street, my roomie, Leon, in his high-powered Manhattan law firm suit and tie—next to me in my unemployed jeans and T-shirt—gave nothing away about his weekend surprise.

We borrowed the charming Upstate New York cottage of a partner at his firm, who graciously let us stay there amidst the woods, the birds, and the early May flowers.

Some champagne, a single red rose with an engagement ring dangling from a leaf, and suddenly my heart, the place where actual feelings "felt," opened again for what seemed like the first time in nearly five years. The tears flowed freely from us both and my first excited call went to Grandma Hannah, who had been sitting beside the phone waiting for it.

It seemed that my grandmother, my mother, my brother, Leon's father, his stepmother—well pretty much the whole family—knew about his perfectly executed plan.

Engaged, still unemployed, but finally a card-carrying member of the New York State Bar, I determined during the car ride back to New York that I had sloughed off long enough. By Monday morning, armed with a list of the top divorce lawyers in New York City, I set about to find a job.

My first interview, with an extremely gifted, incredibly smart, and supremely talented lawyer, didn't last very long. He had my résumé and knew both Judge Meyer, for whom I had written the speech on child custody that planted me in matrimonial law, and Steve, the lawyer on Long Island I'd worked for during and after law school.

In 1984, the men's club of quality, high-end matrimonial lawyers could fit into a stretch limo. They knew one another well as adversaries and as friends. The same men who duked it out in the courthouse in the morning could be found strolling along the golf course together in the afternoon.

As the interview was abruptly ended by a sharp knock on the door from the lawyer's secretary, in what I assumed to be a prearranged signal that the interview bombed, I hastily stood to shake the hand of the well-dressed man in the red suspenders.

"I'm sorry about the interruption. I need to take a call from a client," he said. "My secretary can show you out."

"Thank you for your time," I said, turning to leave.

"Oh, one more thing," he said. "When can you start?"

Before I could think of what to say, he had instructed me to work it out with his secretary, and even as I walked beside her across the broad expanse of the Park Avenue office, he had picked up the phone and the last words I heard before she closed the door behind us were, "Fuck him!"

What had I gotten myself into?

I lasted less than six months. I hated the scorched-earth tactics, the belligerence, the narcissism, the holier-than-thou attitude. But what I hated most was his treatment of everyone like we were a piece of bubble gum on the bottom of his Cole Haan shoes. Between that and the brilliant way in which he skated the legal line so artfully—*always* remaining on the side of the lawful—I started to feel like an accessory to the deliberate dismemberment of our clients' spouses.

The day I decided to quit, I asked his secretary if I could get in for a brief audience. No sooner had I walked into his office and said, "Good morning," than he said, "You're fired." Stunned and deeply hurt, I realized that not one minute before I had come into this office to quit.

Gruffly—one tone in his short repertoire of verbal inflections—he added, "Don't worry, I'll give you a great reference. You're a terrific lawyer. You're just too *nice*." He practically spat out that last word, distasteful in his mouth, a quality he neither admired nor could abide in his associates.

I called Grandma. She tutted a few times in sympathy and then buoyed my spirits by assuring me that most people would view being "nice" as a laudable quality.

I packed my meager belongings and took the subway back to the apartment, thinking that despite my wounded pride, the result mattered most. And besides, I had a wedding to finish planning!

Leon and I had elected to go with an abbreviated engagement and planned a Columbus Day weekend wedding—on October 7, 1984—the day after Yom Kippur. Neither of us had two nickels to rub together and between us we had a pile of student loans, but we decided we wanted a big wedding with all the trimmings at the synagogue I grew up in. We planned to use our wedding gifts to pay for it, fully expecting to end the evening with the same two nickels we had started with—but after one great party.

In early September, I decided that I better get my act together and look for a job. I really didn't want to come back from my honeymoon still unemployed.

I returned to my carefully curated list of top matrimonial lawyers in Manhattan.

This time, instead of going through the list alphabetically, I went straight to the name of the man I most coveted working for.

Norman Sheresky had a well-earned reputation as being the best of the best. A Harvard graduate, his storied career began in securities law and over time he developed a niche specialty as a divorce lawyer with a Rolodex that read like "America's Everybody Who's Anybody."

I later teased him that he took only cases where one of the spouses had a spot on the Forbes 500 list—a tongue-in-cheek joke that had more than a ring of truth to it.

Author, lecturer, founder and president-elect of the American College of Family Trial Lawyers, and former president of the New York Chapter of the American Academy of Matrimonial Lawyers, Norman epitomized my rose-colored view of how divorce law should be practiced. I had seen him in court plenty of times, watched him on television giving interviews, and read articles about him in local and national newspapers, gossip columns, and glossy magazines. He was a legend in the field and first on my list of wished-for employers, so I decided I had nothing to lose but my pride by reaching out to him.

I called one of Dad's fraternity brothers from college, a divorce lawyer on Long Island, and asked if he would mind making an introduction for me.

Within an hour, he called back to tell me that Norman expected my call.

"Nervous" doesn't quite capture my feelings riding up in the elevator to the offices on the corner of Fifty-Ninth and Park Avenue.

For the first time ever, I really wanted this job. It felt crucially important to get it. I felt butterflies in my stomach, a touch of nausea, and a deep need to ask my father for his advice on what to say during the interview.

Meeting Norman that first day didn't disappoint. His clothing was stylish, elegant, and expensive; his wit dry; his silver hair perfectly coiffed; his eyes sparkling with amusement, interest, and intellectual curiosity.

I knew I had found my mentor, my "rabbi," my confidant ... and we were barely past the pleasantries!

We talked for over an hour, interrupted from time to time by another lawyer in the office or a paralegal or his secretary, each of whom he waved into his office affably, introducing me to each. His door literally open, it also remained figuratively open to all who wanted to speak with him.

About seventy minutes into our conversation, Norman asked with a smile, "When can you start?"

My mind stammered—this came as a gigantic surprise—but my mouth managed to work perfectly.

"Well, Mr. Sheresky, thank you so much for the opportunity."

"Norman. Please call me Norman," he interrupted.

"Norman," I restarted. "Thank you. I'm honored to be able to work with you. When would you like me to start?"

"How about tomorrow?" he replied instantly. "I'll show you your office."

He got up from behind his giant desk, the one I would sit opposite from him for the next thirteen years, and I said in a rush of words, "But I'm getting married in a month and then I'm supposed to go on my honeymoon. I was thinking something like October 17."

"Congratulations. Lucky guy," he said. "You'll start tomorrow. Take the Friday off before the wedding, have a terrific honeymoon, and when you come back, you'll hit the ground running."

This first "argument" that he won would not be the last. It went exactly how he said it would go. I worked for about a month, got comfortable with my fellow lawyers, the paralegals, the staff, and the office procedures, and as I got ready to leave on the Thursday before the wedding, he called me into the conference room at 4 p.m.

Champagne, balloons, gifts, and lots of hugs from Norman and my new colleagues. This surprise bridal shower, lorded over by a beaming Norman, filled me with such warmth. Although they had only known me for a month, I got bear hugs and kisses from every person in the room.

Heading down in the elevator, a tiny bit tipsy from the champagne, the excitement, and sheer exhaustion—I had billed about eighty hours a week each week since I'd started—I looked up at the fluorescent dropped ceiling and said aloud, "Thanks, Dad."

From 1984 to 1996, my bonds with my law firm family ran deep. With Norman the bonds felt unbreakable. He took me under his legal and paternal wing, and if his wife, Elaine, and daughter, Brooke, felt anything but supportive of our relationship, they never showed it.

For Norman, the sun rose and set on Elaine, a beautiful, vivacious, and talented professional meteorologist, amateur dancer, and later, professional witness coach. As for Brooke, she was the light of his life. Her photo was prominently displayed in his office—her head thrown back, a broad smile on her face, her hair a mass of dark curls, her eyes aglow with the same mischievous twinkle as her father's.

He said to me early on that he wanted me to be his shadow, that he wanted to teach me everything he could to be "the best"—in some category that didn't include him, of course!

After a few meetings together with clients, Norman quickly decided that he had seen enough and could trust me to meet with them one-on-one.

The first time I met alone with a client, who had a truly nasty husband, she asked my advice about an issue she and he had during one of their typical tugs-of-war involving their five-year-old son. I offered what I thought was rock-solid advice, at which she scoffed derisively, "What would you know? You look like a kid yourself."

Ouch.

After she left, I just sat in my office, offended, feeling ineffectual and frustrated.

About ten minutes into my pity party, my door opened and in walked Norman.

He flopped into the chair that the client had vacated shortly before and put his perfectly shined wing-tipped feet up on my desk.

"So, Leeser. How'd it go?"

For some inexplicable reason, he always pronounced my name as if it had an "er" at the end instead of an "a."

"Not that great," I confessed.

"She stopped by on her way out. Said she thought you were smart but too young," he said, laughing. "Then she asked my input on the weekend handoff, and when I told her what I thought, she said, 'That's exactly what Lisa suggested!'"

"So, what's the deal? She made me feel like an idiot."

"You're no idiot. You just need some gray hairs," he said, laughing again and pulling at a few strands of his own silver locks.

I felt reassured for the moment, but my self-confidence was still fragile. Norman knew this and had a cure for it: he gave me even more responsibility. He asked me to sit in on every client meeting and go with him to every court appearance. And yes, that meant I got to *schlep* around his handsome, but very heavy, monogrammed litigation bag. His phenomenal legal assistant, Judy, taught me how to create deposition notebooks and organize trial files and witness testimony outlines exactly the way Norman liked them to be organized. We were together practically every working moment of every day. One morning in court, he turned to ask me for a document that I already had in my hand. He winked at me just then and I knew we had reached a new place in our relationship. My career progressed at a satisfying clip, and as the only woman in nearly every room, sometimes I got ignored, but more often my opinion got actively solicited. Those were strange, schizophrenic times.

The small pool I swam in with Norman had the words "Men's Club" hanging on the fence. Breaking into the Men's Club became an obsession.

My father had always told me that I could be anything I wanted to be, and I wanted to be one of the best matrimonial lawyers in New York.

When I mentioned this aspiration to a male colleague, he suggested that I "grow a pair."

I decided that nothing could substitute for hard work. Just as Dad had once said that he would never be "outhustled" on the basketball court, I would never be outhustled in my law firm.

One weekend, after working forty hours straight to prepare for a trial scheduled to begin on Monday morning, I just lay down on the sofa in my office to close my eyes for a few minutes. When I awoke hours later, in the middle of the night—in the early hours of Monday morning—I realized I couldn't get home, shower, change, and get back to the City in time for court. I refreshed as best I could and took the spare suit from the back of my door to change.

The emergency suit had been my secretary's idea. The spilled cup of coffee, the unexpected temporary restraining order—endless reasons could arise when I might need a change of clothes.

I dressed, brushed my hair, and got back to my desk just as Norman arrived in slacks and a shirt.

"What are you wearing?" I asked. "We have to be in court in a half hour."

"No, we don't," he said sheepishly. "I should have called you. Opposing counsel and I settled it on the golf course on Saturday."

I took a deep breath. *Careful. Don't say anything you'll regret,* I warned myself. So instead of berating him for being so thoughtless or whining about having wasted two days in the office for no reason or complaining about having had three hours of sleep since Friday, I said the words that might have had the greatest impact on my legal career.

"Norman," I declared, "I guess I better learn how to play golf."

And I did.

Work life chugged along, married life seemed great, and for a while I felt that the cosmic injustice of having my father die so young earned me an otherwise charmed life.

Then Norman nearly died—not from the heart problem that took him to the emergency room, but from the wound infection he developed from the open-chest surgery they did to save him.

During the weeks after his surgery, I walked around in a daze. The thought of losing Norman terrified me. Leaving aside the business aspect of the firm—Norman was the "rainmaker," the partner who brought in the most business—the excruciating wait to see if my friend and mentor would live or die nearly broke me. It felt like *Groundhog Day.* Life was unspooling in the same way it had before. The thought of Norman dying made it hard for me to sleep or eat, and I felt a pain in my chest every time I walked past his empty office, which was about twenty times a day. Yet I also felt guilty about the intensity of my feelings. I mean, the guy's great, he's taught me tons, but he's just the guy I work for, right? And besides, the rest of the people at the firm had known him for decades.

This guilt kept my fear bottled tightly inside; I felt embarrassed about just how anxious Norman's near-death experience made me feel.

On his first day back in the office, I took my usual spot in the chair opposite him and the dam broke. I just couldn't keep back the torrent.

"Didn't think you'd get rid of me that easily, did ya?" he said with a smile. The heart surgery, and the wound infection and its aftermath, had taken a lot out of him. He'd lost weight and looked as if he had stepped out of the portrait of Dorian Gray.

"Wanna see?"

Mr. Wound, as Norman called it, ran the length of his chest. Flinging aside a colorful Brioni tie and unbuttoning a perfectly starched custom-made shirt, he revealed Mr. Wound. We checked its progress daily thereafter.

The heart scare meant some significant lifestyle changes for him. Norman had an enormous appetite and truly reveled in good food and great wine. This being the '80s in New York City, elaborate lunches happened many days of the week. We frequented an Italian place that he adored. Exchanging the pasta special for a piece of fish didn't come easily.

The staff at the four-star restaurant several blocks from the office knew Norman well. Post–heart surgery, they fussed and fretted over him the first day we returned there for lunch. Norman loved their Dover sole, a signature dish of which the chef was rightfully proud. Norman ordered it and promptly proceeded to cut his portion in half the instant it arrived at the table. He pushed one half off onto the bread plate, where it lay mournfully alongside the roll he'd left untouched.

As we always did, we chatted amiably during lunch about sports, a case we had in court the next day, and how soon his doctor said he could return to playing golf.

We were interrupted by the appearance of the chef himself, distinctive toque perfectly straight on his head.

"Monsieur," he addressed Norman, "is there something wrong with the fish?"

Norman let out his wonderful, full-throated laugh and explained to the concerned French genius that he was under "doctor's orders" to cut back on his calories.

"Perhaps Monsieur could do that in another restaurant?" suggested the chef.

"And miss your cheese course, Chef? Never!" responded Norman and the two men erupted with laughter.

Norman was back. I felt like I had dodged a bullet.

BOOK FOUR
NICU REDUX

37

T-Minus Not Counting

Exhibit D—This Woman's Right to Choose

January 1992

"You're pregnant!" beamed the nurse at my OB-GYN's office.

"You're pregnant," flatly stated a shocked Dr. Sheldon Cherry.

"You're pregnant?" asked my stunned husband.

"You're pregnant?" huffed my mother, adding an epithet directed at my husband.

"You're pregnant!" shrieked our nanny, Joanie, delightedly as she cradled our twenty-five-week-old son in her arms.

"You're PREGNANT?" thundered Norman, undoubtedly because I shared the news while still on maternity leave with Harrison.

In the ensuing weeks I heard wry comments about my sanity, praise for the swimming prowess of Leon's sperm, and one very corny but sweet remark from my favorite aunt, who proclaimed that I was a "regular Fertile Myrtle."

According to the sonogram, I conceived in mid-December 1991, when Harrison was barely seventeen *weeks* old. But the real attention-grabber was how quickly I became pregnant following an incredibly stressful eighty-five days in the Neonatal Intensive Care Unit with him. Since we had just endured the roller coaster of a baby born thirteen weeks prematurely, our friends and family thought we were crazy getting pregnant so soon.

We hadn't meant to get pregnant so soon. I have no idea why I thought that if I hadn't gotten my period yet, I couldn't get pregnant. Didn't the whole ovulation/menstrual cycle thing we learned in high school biology mean I couldn't get pregnant?

Well, according to the line on the pee stick—yes, I took a pregnancy test as soon as I got home, just in case someone in Dr. Cherry's VERY busy office mixed up my urine with some other woman's—I was indeed pregnant.

To say I felt overjoyed would be lying. To say I felt terrified and overwhelmed would be an understatement.

While Dr. Cherry had repeatedly assured me that Harrison's early arrival had nothing to do with the pregnancy and everything to do with a bacteria-laden piece of French cheese, I couldn't help but wonder if this new pregnancy would be the smooth sailing Dr. Cherry anticipated.

And then one morning I got my answer. Enjoying the early spring sun with a fresh cup of coffee, Harrison in a baby swing beside me and the *New York Times* resting against my little belly, I felt something weird. Not the good kind of weird when the baby makes its first noticeable kick. Nope, this was the bad kind of weird, the kind that I had failed to understand as labor pains just months before.

I was eighteen weeks pregnant.

An hour later, my heart beating so fast that the nurse took my blood pressure three times, I lay frantic on a gurney in the ER, clutching Leon's hand as if I could somehow transfer some of the pain to him. After a short wait, the on-call doctor administered a harrowing pelvic exam. He stood up, pulled off his gloves with a self-satisfied snap, and said to Leon, "Her cervical membranes have partially ruptured. She needs a D&C right away."

My otherwise brilliant husband, clueless about the alphabet soup of medical jargon, nodded, not understanding the significance of the dilation and curettage this doctor was proposing—a fancy way of describing a medical procedure designed to empty my uterus of its contents.

"I'll schedule it," said the doctor, starting to pull the privacy curtain away.

"Wait!" I yelled, as forcefully as I could. Four eyes looked at me. "What about our baby?"

"There isn't going to be a baby," said the doctor matter-of-factly. "It's not viable and your membranes have already ruptured. There's a significant risk of infection if we don't do a D&C right away."

Leon's expression went from confusion to understanding in a matter of seconds.

"Hang on, Doc. Let me get this straight... you're saying you want to give her an abortion?"

"Well," the doctor started dryly, "she's obviously fertile. If she were my wife, I'd say, 'Have an abortion.' You can start over when she's recovered."

Have an abortion? Start over? This was our *child* he was so glibly suggesting we vacuum out of my uterus and send down the medical waste drain.

"There must be another option," I stated firmly.

Clearly annoyed, the doctor said, "Well, we could stitch her up, give her drugs to stop her labor, hang her upside down, and hope for the best." This again directed at Leon.

Leon took a fleeting glance at me before he said to the doctor, "We need a minute."

"She doesn't have a minute," the doctor retorted.

"We NEED a minute," my husband insisted.

Fuming, the doctor drew back the curtain and with a forceful yank, pulled it closed behind him, the beads on the headrail jangling loudly.

We were as alone as we could be in a crowded ER with a flimsy blue piece of nylon curtain our only source of privacy.

My husband gently asked, "What do you want to do?"

I emphatically said, "I want to try everything."

"Agreed," he said, squeezing my hand reassuringly. I'm sure I didn't understand the practical consequences of this decision, but giving up on this baby was not an option.

"I'll go find Dr. Sweetness and Light," Leon quipped, ducking around the curtain.

Waiting anxiously for a risky surgical procedure that only *might* work to save my baby, I thought about choice, and for the first time realized that my right to choose meant I got to pick what I wanted to do. For so long I had thought of "choice" only as my right to terminate a pregnancy. But choice also included my right to choose to keep one.

Thirteen years after choosing to end a pregnancy, I found myself coming down on the other side. Against medical advice and without hesitation, I sent Leon off to find the doctor who would help me exercise my choice to fight to keep my baby.

Lying there alone, I felt scared and suddenly filled with guilt. How could this be happening again? I hadn't touched a piece of French cheese since finding out I was pregnant, I was following every rule, I was reading every word of *What to Expect When You're Expecting*. I mean, c'mon, man, I just did this.

38

Mama Bear's Mama Bear

April 1992

With Leon and me united against the abortion suggested by the ER doctor, my gurney started rolling down the hallway, heading for a risky surgery with a murky prognosis. But I was determined to fight for my baby and would try anything to make sure it stayed right where it was.

"Tie her up nice and tight," I remember Leon calling from behind me as we sped through the "Medical Personnel Only" double doorway. He was referring to the cervical cerclage about to be performed on my already partially ruptured cervical membranes, a procedure that involved sewing my cervix closed.

It's not surprising that once we decided to try to keep our impatient baby from being born early enough for certain death, my mind is blank for the surgery I'm told lasted about three hours.

After that, my first clear memory was waking up in a semi-private hospital room with my feet elevated above my head. I had an awesome view of the acoustic ceiling tiles, but not much else.

Being tilted upside down, my eye level about ten inches lower than normal, felt very disorienting. Even my hearing seemed different—muffled—since the sound was above me.

I turned my head to the left and could see only the sky through the big window. I turned to the right and could see my neighbor's bed, but not the face of the patient in it. The IV pole beside me dripped what felt like ice water into my veins. I shivered against the weight of multiple blankets that clearly couldn't keep the chill at bay.

Seconds later I heard my mother's voice. It sounded agitated and uncharacteristically angry. Given the volume, her voice was likely what had roused me from my anesthetic slumber.

My mother has a well-deserved reputation as the nicest person on the planet Earth. What could possibly have made her mad enough to shout—in public?

"Get the charge nurse in here," she demanded, and I watched the lower half of what I imagined to be a nurse walking quickly out of the room.

"Can you believe this?" my mother asked. While I wondered if the question was meant for me, I heard Leon's voice saying not quite calmly, "It's okay. She's fine. We'll figure it out."

"Figure it out?" my mother shrieked. "There's nothing to figure out. Either they go or we go," she huffed with finality.

I still felt foggy from the anesthesia and the emotional drain of the day. Trying to follow the conversation, especially from my upside-down vantage point, was impossible.

"Are we ready to try again, Mommy?" cooed a soft singsong voice on the other side of the room.

"Are you kidding me?" This rhetorical question came from my mother.

"As I was saying earlier," said the singsong singer coming closer, "sometimes it takes a few tries for both of you to get the hang of latching on, but don't you worry, soon she'll be eating like a champ."

At that, I saw the scrubs-clad lower back, butt, and thighs of the voice's owner come between me and my neighbor's bed, pulling the privacy curtain between us.

"Excuse me," I heard my mother say, in a supersweet voice. "I wondered if you had asked the charge nurse to come by."

"Yes, ma'am. But she's with a patient right now. She'll be here as soon as she can," replied the singsong singer, and then cooing again, "Okay, Mommy, are you ready?"

I heard a soft cry. So that's why my mother sounded so twisted! My roommates were a new mother and her breastfeeding newborn.

"Nurse, you had me paged?" came a new, authoritative voice.

"Yes, ma'am," the singsong voice replied. "Mrs. Roday's mother asked to see you. She's just on the other side of the curtain."

I watched a set of Dansko-shod feet—the go-to footwear for many nurses I knew—cross over to my side of the flimsy cotton.

My mother, sounding charming, introduced herself, finishing with, "And are you the nurse in charge of this floor?"

"I am. Nice to meet you. How can I help?"

"Well, it seems that my daughter has been assigned to the wrong room," my mother began.

"That's hardly likely," responded the nurse, giving my mother the opening she needed to raise the volume.

"I'm sorry, Nurse, but do you know *why* my daughter is here?" my mother asked, all the sweetness disappearing from her voice.

"She's here because she's in labor and this is the Labor and Delivery Unit," volleyed back the head nurse.

"Then put her in a room with another patient in labor," backhanded my mother.

"Your daughter is the only laboring patient in the unit," lobbed back the nurse.

"Then put her in her own room," cross-handed Mom.

"The unit is full," shot back the nurse.

"Then put her in a different unit," responded my mother.

Silence.

This was not a great strategy for the nurse to use. In the vacuum of her quiet, the baby next to me began to whimper. My mother, whom I couldn't see but could hear, took a deep breath.

"How can you put my daughter in a room with a mother and baby?" she demanded. Without pausing for a response, she continued her barrage with, "How is she supposed to feel lying upside down like that, trying to save her baby, with a newborn right next to her? How do you expect her to get any rest?"

These all seemed like reasonable questions to me. I couldn't help but admire her ferocity and wondered if I would ever be as articulate and passionate a voice for my kids.

My mama bear proved to be immediately effective. Within an hour, I moved from the delivery unit to the surgery unit. My new roommate had her gallbladder removed, and it felt far less soul-crushing to hear her *kvetching* to her visitors than to listen to a whimpering baby.

I didn't give her the credit she deserved at the time, but my mother's insistence that I be moved to another room saved my sanity during those worrisome early days of waiting to see if the stitch would hold.

Filled with antibiotics and tocolytics (anti-contraction drugs) and armed with a bunch of prescriptions and a remote uterine contraction monitor, I was discharged a few days later—with strict instructions for continued complete bed rest, bathroom privileges only, absolutely no stairs, and a stern warning that I avoid stress.

39

Worse Than Getting Picked Last for Dodgeball?

April–June 1992

During my literally upside-down days in the hospital, Leon had arranged for the delivery of a king-size bed that he had put in the den of our home, my mother had bought a stunning and cheerful English cabbage rose–patterned set of sheets with a matching reversible comforter, and my law firm had sent over four bankers boxes of my current files, a fax/scanner/copier machine, and a cheery plant.

On the ride back home from the hospital, my excitement at seeing Harrison eclipsed my fear about the coming weeks of bed rest. I had spent as much time with Harrison as humanly possible every day since his premature birth thirty-six weeks earlier, and I missed him with an aching that physically and emotionally exhausted me.

Leon arranged for our nanny, Joanie, to be out walking with Harrison when we got home. We thought that if I could get settled into bed before he saw me, it might minimize any possibility of frightening him.

I heard the front door and the simultaneous beep-beep of the alarm panel. I could hear Joanie telling Harrison he was "coming to see Mommy," her soothing voice accompanied by the long beep that meant the front door had closed.

Joanie padded across the hardwood floors (she always took her shoes off), and I imagined her walking thirty feet from the front door to the den, where I was eagerly waiting, her soft voice murmuring soothingly, "We're going to see Mommy."

And suddenly there they were! My beautiful boy was dressed in one of the dozens of adorable outfits that my mother had bought for him: a dark turtleneck and a pair of baggy pants with snap-up legs and matching striped socks.

My heart skipped as I held my arms out in the universal "come to me" gesture. Joanie dutifully brought him close and leaned down for the handoff. But in a diss I will never forget, Harrison whipped his head around, buried his face in Joanie's neck, and clung tight to her.

Avoid stress, I thought as my tears started falling. Who knows if it was the drugs, my hormones, or the unvarnished truth, but in that moment I felt like Harrison loved the nanny more than he loved me. Not only did he refuse to come to me, but I wasn't even sure he remembered I was his mother.

"He's just tired," Joanie assured me. "I'll put him down for a nap."

I put my hand reflexively to my stomach and said aloud to the baby inside, "This is your mother speaking," like an airline pilot doing the preflight announcement. "You just stay right where you are. You gotta keep cooking. And don't ever forget I'm your mother," I added for good measure.

This was going to be much harder than I thought, and it was only Day 1.

My law partners said all the right words when they called, but they weren't happy.

When I try to think about it from their perspective, the timeline helps me realize how difficult it must have been for them to carry their caseload and mine. From August 16 through November 8, 1991, I spent four to five hours a day in the office and the rest of the day and evening at the hospital. From November 11, 1991, through February 14, 1992, I took my maternity leave, which I mostly considered sacrosanct. There was the occasional emergency phone call about one of my cases, but everyone in the office treated my maternity leave respectfully.

I returned to the office full-time plus (which really was the only way I knew how to work), immediately jumping back into sixty-hour weeks. My promise to be home every night to kiss Harrison goodnight was broken before the end of my first week back at the office.

Between my mother and our nanny, I knew he was loved and very well cared for in my absence, but I felt haunted by the conflict between wanting to be with Harrison and putting in the hours I needed to put in to do my best work for my clients. I had reconnected with all my cases, and the associates and partners who had shared my load were all too happy to transition my clients back to me. That push-me-pull-you world had little upside and the schedule began to take its toll on me. From February 17, 1992, to that April morning when my premature labor started, there I was, back at the office, full steam ahead.

Eight weeks. I made it eight weeks before my membranes ruptured, putting me on bed rest for the duration of my pregnancy.

So yes, I guess my partners were less than pleased. As the only woman at the partnership table, I appreciate that they all tried their best to navigate this unfamiliar territory.

But I had clients who rightly demanded the attention of the lawyer they had hired, and while they were empathetic about my forced bed-rest incarceration, they had their own dramas that needed to be addressed.

In the meantime, I had a precocious six-month-old whom I adored and who was used to spending most of every day with me since the day he was born.

Once my maternity leave ended, the struggle to leave Harrison every morning was physically painful.

There were days I sat on the Long Island Railroad train and just cried about how unfair it all seemed. Like many other women in my generation (and beyond, sadly), I had been fed an advertising tagline my whole life. We were sold a bill of goods.

The phrase "You can have it all," penned by some Madison Avenue whiz kid, wasn't an implication. It was a promise. If you do x, y, and z, you can get all the marbles, have the whole shooting match, hold all the cards.

The problem is that many of us got duped into believing that we *could* have it all—the great education, the nice house, the perfect job, the wonderful kids, the happy marriage. But as many of us found out the hard way by trying to keep all the plates spinning, until one by one they came crashing down, the saying is only partly true.

You *can* have it all, just not all at the same time.

My life from February to April seemed proof positive to me that I was working it. I had it all under control. That is until the baby in my uterus had a different idea.

While the first few days at home didn't go as smoothly as we had hoped, eventually we settled into a routine. The permanent bed rest started to feel almost normal.

Five times a day, my uterine monitor screeched and squawked over the phone line to a calm, patient "monitor buddy" cheerleading me with each transmission, and I started to think I could really do this. Inspired by these supportive conversations, I found myself telling my baby that we were a team, that together we could do whatever it took to stay pregnant.

In the meantime, the fax machine also screeched and squawked, but with unnerving unpredictability. At least the uterine monitor had a fixed schedule, so I could plan for it. But the fax machine seemed to transmit some urgent messages right when I had fallen asleep for a nap, or just as Harrison had warmed up to me enough to come into the bed with me.

Sandra Leslie, patron saint of new moms and assistant extraordinaire, did her best to weed out the more trivial messages, but nothing could stop my partners or their assistants from sending me faxes whenever they needed something or felt disinclined to look for the answer themselves.

My favorite fax was from one of my younger male partners. It was handwritten in block letters—name changed for privacy reasons—WHERE IS THE SMITH FILE?

I sent him back an irritated fax. HAVE YOU CHECKED THE FILE ROOM UNDER "S"?

The days were a mix of various activities and work. I worked some part of every day during my entire bed rest. (Yes, I think that was the stress the nurse had warned me to avoid.) Playing with Harrison was the highlight of each day. Trying to eat and drink "plenty of water," ugh, enough with the water. And, of course, I had my five times a day with my monitor buddy.

I don't count the time I spent just staring at the ceiling and worrying. How could this be happening to me again? Hadn't we paid our dues with Harrison? I occasionally looked heavenward and asked Dad to take care of this little critter, to make sure we were all right.

I had read that it was motivating to have a giant calendar and to make a nightly ritual out of crossing off each day—one day closer to the goal of having a full-term baby. So we added that to our nightly routine of Harrison spending "mommy time" cuddling with me in bed while I read *Goodnight Moon* to him. He could barely hold the magic marker even with Leon's help, but there was so much clapping and whooping each night as we crossed off the day that he couldn't help but clap for himself. It was heart-meltingly adorable.

This routine continued, day after day, week after week as April turned to May and May melted into June and June was about to cross over to July.

Leon had encircled the date coinciding with the start of my twenty-seventh week, the week I had delivered Harrison, with a red marker. There was extra fanfare that night in June as the thick black marker crossed off the day in our second baby's journey to maturity.

40

Baby Boy Roday

June 28, 1992

Ten weeks after my preterm labor started, I woke up in the dawn hours one June morning and knew there was no stopping the train. Within minutes, my uterine contraction monitor buddy confirmed that I needed to get to the hospital immediately.

The day was a whirl of choreographed chaos. There was the hunger—they wouldn't let me eat in case they needed to knock me out. There was the unrelenting cold—it seemed like the magnesium sulfate to stop my contractions had replaced my blood and every millimeter of my body was freezing. And there was the all-consuming fear—twenty-eight weeks was better than twenty-seven, but it was still a preemie, and the risks were huge. Hours into this strategy came the 180-degree shift in treatment plan and medications. An amniocentesis had confirmed an infection (and also precipitated my water breaking), and it now became emergent to reverse course. Instead of trying to stop the contractions, the medical staff decided they needed to speed them up. Along with this about-face came hopeful news. In the few short months since Harrison was born, the FDA had approved the use of a drug called surfactant, which clinical trials had proven to boost critical lung development if administered immediately at birth. Surfactant would give this baby's lungs essential respiratory support.

No matter which part of the script it was—stop the contractions or speed up the contractions—it was more agonizing because I had seen the movie before. I had already spent eighty-five days in the NICU, riding the roller coaster one step forward and three steps back. Would I have been less nervous if this had been my firstborn and I didn't know what I was in for? Or would I have been flat-out terrified if this baby had been first because the unknown of the NICU simply couldn't be understood until it had been experienced?

While Leon and I seemed preternaturally calm to the nurses in Labor and Delivery, we weren't calm as much as we were seasoned. We knew what lay in store for us if this baby wouldn't wait.

At 9:39 p.m., exactly ten months, thirteen days, thirteen hours, and two minutes younger than his brother, Ethan Royce Roday arrived weighing a whopping 1,380 grams ... a little over three pounds.

Rather than the silence I heard when Harrison was born, this time I heard a lusty cry. I also heard Dr. Cherry mutter something that I couldn't quite catch, something that triggered a very peculiar expression on Leon's face. But I was too preoccupied with craning my neck to get a quick glimpse of Ethan and his full head of golden hair before they whisked him off to the NICU.

It wasn't until a few days later that Leon shared what Dr. Cherry had said: Ethan's umbilical cord was "putrid yellow and infectious green." Dr. Cherry commented that he had never seen anything quite like it.

Pichel, a member of the famed law school Group and still one of our dearest friends, waited for me in the recovery room. He had been waiting for hours. As with many of us who feel helpless in a situation spinning out of control, he was desperate for something to do.

I sent him to Jackson Hole, my favorite burger place in New York City, to get me a burger and fries. When he returned with burgers and milkshakes for all, nothing ever tasted so great. I was giddy from the sugar, the meds, the adrenaline, all of it. I felt over-the-moon happy.

Then a nurse appeared with a wheelchair and asked me if I was ready to meet my son. Leon visibly paled. He looked like I felt. I could feel the food sloshing uncomfortably in my stomach and suddenly became terrified at the prospect of going back to the NICU, a place we never thought we would see again when we left there only seven months earlier.

As I gingerly transferred from the bed to the wheel-chair—whoopie cushion already in place to make sitting more comfortable for me—the nurse gently and efficiently covered me with blankets, tucking them in so nothing could get caught in the wheels.

She started to move behind the chair, but Leon stopped her. In a barely audible voice he said, "We know the way."

Coming off the elevator and making a right turn to head toward the locked metal doors that say "STOP. Neonatal Intensive Care Unit. Authorized Personnel Only" is intimidating—the first time.

But the second time, well, it felt as if all the air had been forced from my body. I felt dizzy, nauseous, and absolutely petrified. When we got to the intercom and Leon said, "We're here to see Baby Roday," I was on the verge of collapse right there in the chair.

There was the familiar "click" that I had heard hundreds of times during the eighty-five days Harrison had been in the Unit, the noise that signaled permission to enter. I gripped the arms of the wheelchair. Leon touched my shoulder, and I could hear him stifling a sob.

We had barely made it through the doors when my wheelchair was surrounded by familiar faces. I recognized the doctors and nurses and orderlies and respiratory therapists, all these people who knew our family so well.

Karen, one of Harrison's frequent caregivers, exclaimed, "I saw them write Baby Roday up on the board and I couldn't believe it. I feel like you were just here!"

Thanks for stating the obvious, I thought darkly, as my husband pushed the wheelchair to a small room on our left. We knew the routine. First stop—the scrub sink. Next—the gown closet. Last—the shoe covers.

"Do you want to come and meet your handsome man?" Karen asked. "He's just on a little nasal cannula!" She beamed with genuine joy.

Nasal cannula? Just a bit of tubing with two tiny prongs providing supplemental oxygen. I turned this news over in my head. Harrison had been on a ventilator for weeks.

I nodded to the nurse, and a phalanx of people walked with Leon and me to an isolette on the "outside" of the hub-and-spoke-style intensively intensive care unit. They were leading us to the "step down" unit where Ethan lay, naked but for his full head of golden hair.

"Do you want to hold him?"

My breath caught in my throat. Leon and I both started to cry. Ten excruciatingly long weeks had passed before we could hold Harrison. Being offered the chance to hold this newborn on his first day in the world felt momentous.

The blurry Polaroid that captured that moment shows an elated but tired-looking woman, smiling broadly while holding a tightly swaddled tiny baby. Fleetingly, holding Ethan for the first time, I thought of the doctor on call that night ten weeks earlier. If I had listened to him, let him talk me out of the decision I had made, this miracle who is Ethan would not be here at all. *It's unimaginable*, I thought, gazing down at Ethan, my brave and ferocious partner in this adventure. I had decided that I needed to try to save this beautiful boy, but I couldn't have done it without him. He couldn't have done it without me. We had been to the brink and back *together*, and as I held him and kissed his forehead, I knew our shared commitment to getting him safely born would forever connect us. I risked my health to give Ethan a chance to live. And if I had to do it all over again, knowing everything I then knew about what it meant to have an infant in the NICU with an uncertain future, I'd do it again in a heartbeat. I looked at him with wonder and thought, "*he is here because of a choice I made, a choice to give him a shot. I am here because he needed me to be the vessel that carried him. Our lives depended on each other.*"

41

The Crucible

July 1992

Early in our first NICU stay, Dr. Andrea told us that she had watched so many couples during her years in the Unit that she could tell which ones would make it through and which ones wouldn't.

We had lots of chances to talk more about it during the eighty-five days we were there. As a divorce lawyer, I knew well the main stressors in a marriage, the ones often debated in articles in *Cosmopolitan* and *Vogue*.

As I observed in my legal practice, among the many reasons why couples get divorced are money; poor intimacy; infidelity; physical, emotional, or mental abuse; incompatibility; addiction or serious illness; poor communication; perception of inequality; and loss of identity.

The NICU tests couples (often young marrieds) in ways they likely haven't been previously tested.

And once I knew what Dr. Andrea looked for, I could easily spot it too.

She would start by observing an extremely basic communication form—body language. For most couples, standing opposite each other with the incubator between them, rather than standing together on the same side, turned out to be an early "tell."

Time stretches awkwardly and unexpectedly in the NICU. Sitting in that crazy, uncomfortable tall chair hour after hour, day after day, night after night, gave me plenty of time to watch couples uncoupling right in front of my eyes.

I had a little notebook where I kept my running list of seemingly endless medical questions for Dr. Andrea and her colleagues. My years of keeping score at baseball games—something Dad insisted on teaching me as an essential component of fandom—proved invaluable. I created a relationship scorecard to pass the time.

The scorecard included points for standing apart, coming to the NICU alone or separately, speaking in voices loud enough to be heard by others, meetings with the doctors (alone or together), and lack of public displays of affection.

Watching couples navigate their child's NICU experience turned out to be a reliable indicator of how they did as a couple by the end.

In an actual crucible, objects are subjected to extraordinarily high heat. The result is one of two things. The objects either calcinate—quite literally undergo thermal decomposition—ceasing to exist, or they fuse, melding together to form a single new object.

The NICU did much the same thing. The severe test of having a critically ill child resulted in one of two outcomes. I watched marriages unravel right in front of me, and I could see marriages cementing, including my own.

I know Leon and I would never have gotten through it unscathed had we not found a way to forgive each other after our deep freeze. That fissure would have grown into an unnavigable chasm during the months in the NICU the first time around.

Instead, we drew closer together and leaned heavily on each other for support. But the fear of the unknown, the worry about what crisis would greet us that day, wore on both of us. And the seemingly capricious way that things went well or very, very poorly meant our guard was up all the time. We were physically exhausted and emotionally spent.

There had been so many perils along the way: the suspected meningitis, the NEC scare, the multiple failed attempts to wean Harrison off the ventilator, his inability to hold down food and, of course, the Brain Bleed.

We had learned about the hard knocks that either bruise and batter you until you can't get up when the bell rings, or toughen you up enough to go the distance.

But could we do it again? How many couples had Dr. Andrea seen who were two-time NICU offenders, like us? What new surprises would this second NICU internment bring?

42

Shoebox Babies

July/August 1992

My grandmother, Hannah, had a brother named Lou. Uncle Lou was a diminutive man with bushy eyebrows and startlingly sparkling blue eyes. He looked like an elf who had stepped out of a Grimm's fairy tale. He smiled warmly and was easy to love.

Grandma Hannah once told me that Uncle Lou was born very prematurely. Apparently, my great-grandmother put the tiny Uncle Lou in a shoebox next to the wood stove and fed him drops she squeezed from a cloth she had moistened with milk.

He eventually outgrew the shoebox and my great-grandmother moved him to her bed, where she let him sleep next to her warm body, a practice that would make modern physicians cringe. But in the late 1800's, her intuition and ingenuity likely saved Uncle Lou, her feisty shoebox baby.

Right from that first day, when we got to hold our precious boy, I knew that Ethan's journey would be more like Uncle Lou's than like Harrison's. Ethan was a "feeder/grower", the colloquial description of a premature baby who is medically stable; an infant who needs to eat and gain weight until he reaches his gestational age of roughly forty weeks.

I felt the stress of having an infant in the NICU very differently the second time around. I didn't experience the terror that comes with the mystery of the NICU, the fear that came with not even knowing what I didn't know I needed to be afraid of. No, I was a NICU veteran. I knew the routine, the staff, the protocol. I didn't fumble with the paper booties or wonder what all the jargon meant or get bewildered and disoriented by all the blinking lights and sounds coming from the various monitors. My months in the NICU with Harrison had "shown me the ropes". But they had also made me wary as I settled in for the many weeks I knew I'd be there with Ethan. I knew how capricious things could be in the NICU, how quickly things could change, how NEC could inexplicably find even a relatively healthy infant in the unit. Now that I knew what I needed to fear, I feared it.

Although Ethan's progress, measured daily in grams gained and ounces consumed, moved along smoothly, each day as I waited for the familiar click that unlocked the doors to the NICU, I felt a surge of adrenaline. It was irrational, I knew. If anything changed in Ethan's condition overnight, the night nurse would have called us. But the intellectual reality bore no resemblance to the visceral reaction I felt.

Day after day, I entered the NICU, scrubbed and gowned, and after getting the nod from the nurse, picked up my beautiful boy for a morning cuddle and I would feel my heart rate slow. *"He's fine. Everything's fine,"* I told myself. "We're fine. We're going to be fine," I'd whisper into his golden hair.

The only bumps along the way were actual bumps—two tiny knots Dr. Andrea felt one morning during her exam. Ethan had an inguinal hernia on each side that would need to be removed before he could go home.

43

"Minor" Surgery

August 1992

Leon and I racewalked anxiously behind the medical team whisking fifty-seven-day-old Ethan toward his "routine" bilateral hernia surgery, as his surgeon called it.

Routine? Really? You say that to a mother who has spent months in the NICU? With two different children?

When the doctor stopped us with a stern shake of his head, Leon and I practically collided with the closing elevator doors as the team took our beautiful fair-haired boy to surgery.

I clutched Harrison so tightly that he began to cry. I felt so scared that I started to cry. Leon took me by the hand, and we walked to the family lounge just beyond the elevator doors.

We sat down on the amazingly uncomfortable pleather loveseat side by side, a squirming and unhappy Harrison half-straddling us both. He looked up at us with his enormous blue eyes and his disproportionately gigantic forehead.

For a few joyous minutes, I forgot how nervous I felt about Ethan's surgery.

Ethan's hernia surgery went perfectly, just as the surgeon had assured us it would and the countdown to bringing him home officially started.

That night I allowed myself to believe we had made it through. We had successfully eluded all of the dangers I knew lurked in every NICU stay. As I rocked beside my sleeping son,

I started to cry. I could never explain to Ethan what the miracle of his birth meant to me. The sheer grit and determination I needed to get him to twenty-eight weeks took a strength I didn't know I had. But he returned the favor by showing the same grit and determination to live and thrive once he'd been born. I might have been a NICU veteran, but he was the true NICU champ.

44

Homegoing

September 1992

A week later, released from the NICU a bit earlier than expected, we settled Ethan in at home with his brother, Harrison. Our two sons were now three months and thirteen months old, respectively.

It's true that by the time you bring your second child home, you're a pro at the whole parenting thing. You know babies don't implode, shatter, or spontaneously combust under normal circumstances.

We had Harrison in a Moses basket next to my bedside for weeks and weeks after he came home. Ethan famously lasted a single night.

Turns out, Ethan snored. The diagnosis was more complex than that, but the practical outcome of having him in the same room with us meant that only one of us slept—and it wasn't me or Leon.

By morning, Leon looked down less than lovingly at our second son and decreed, "That's it. Tonight he sleeps in his own room."

That night, having dutifully rearranged my night table to fit two baby monitors on it, we lay awake for hours listening to the snoring coming through loud and clear from the receiver in the nursery down the hall.

On night #3, Leon said, somewhat menacingly, "Don't you dare put on that monitor."

That night I walked the long hall toward Ethan's room every hour. I never once made it all the way. His snoring greeted me long before I got there.

And modern technology being what it was in 1992, when Ethan woke up for his middle-of-the night feeding, his lusty cry got picked up by the receiver across the hall in Harrison's room!

I padded down the hall, bottle of breast milk in hand, and picked up my hungry, towheaded squawker. I thought back to that night in the emergency room and felt an involuntary chill.

I have reflected on that moment from time to time throughout the past thirty-two years. I cannot imagine my life without our extraordinary Ethan, the baby the ER doctor wanted to abort, and whom I wanted to keep.

He was born twelve weeks early but was a feisty "feeder-grower"—in other words, he had no significant medical problems and just needed some extra time to get big enough to come home.

In June 2022, when the Supreme Court ruled in the *Dobbs* case to overturn *Roe v. Wade*, I couldn't help but think about my uniquely wonderful Ethan. When given the opportunity to have a safe and legal abortion, I chose life.

But I never take it for granted that I got to *choose*. It is unthinkable to me that for so many women, *that* freedom is a history lesson.

45

A Womb Surrenders Its Secrets

1992

My official postpartum checkup with Dr. Cherry didn't feel as joyful as I had expected.

He sat across his desk from me, mindlessly twirling a pencil between the fingers of one hand, his chair tilted back.

"We got lucky," he said. "Really, really lucky." I knew he referred to the happy outcome of delivering a healthy baby after having had my membranes rupture at eighteen weeks. Ethan and I had defied the odds, and I knew it. "But we may not be so lucky the next time. I think you should seriously consider there not being a 'next time,'" he said solemnly.

I protested. "What about the whole Harrison/listeria thing? You said I should 'go forth and multiply.'"

"I know I did," he allowed, "but I think you've proven with a second preemie that the listeria masked some fundamental problem."

I saw a vision of our large family suddenly evaporating somewhere over Dr. Cherry's left ear. Leon had always wanted lots of kids, and reluctant as I had been about having children at all, now I felt "all in."

"What kind of fundamental problem?" I probed, unwilling to give up this easily.

Dr. Cherry sat forward in his chair, dropped the pencil on his desk, and looked me straight in the eyes.

"Aren't two miracle babies enough? Can't we just call it a day?" he asked wearily.

"Look," I said. "If there's a fundamental problem, maybe we can fix it. Shouldn't we at least try to figure out what it is?" I had no clue what my question meant, practically speaking. It just seemed to me that to close the baby factory without fully checking the machinery smacked of fanatic conservatism.

"Well, there are some tests we can run. But honestly, Lisa, I must tell you that they aren't pleasant and I'm not sure I see the point. You have two beautiful sons when you could just as easily have none. You, of all people, know how quickly things go sideways in the NICU. Especially with boys. Especially with extremely low birth weight boys … " His voice trailed off.

I knew the statistics. Too well. I knew that Harrison's birth weight and gestational age had a 50 percent risk of morbidity. He slept soundly in his crib at home thanks to Herculean medical interventions. And Ethan, at twenty-nine weeks, still carried the "very preterm" designation. Despite his gestational age, he practically sailed through his NICU stay with very few bumps along the way. There remained the repressed but terrifying concern about Harrison's developmental progress. Would the Brain Bleed cause some damage we hadn't yet seen?

I knew that a third roll of the dice didn't improve the odds against us. Still, shouldn't we at least find out?

"I need to know. If there's something wrong with me, I need to know. And if there's nothing wrong with me, then we can discuss the next steps. But right now, we are just speculating. If there's a way to know for sure, let's do it."

Dr. Cherry didn't seem happy with this. But he buzzed the intercom on his phone and asked his nurse to bring me the patient education information on HSG.

He stood up, walked around his desk, and in a complete lapse of professional decorum gave me a warm hug.

"If you were my daughter, I'd be giving you the same advice."

I felt touched by his concern. I took the envelope his nurse brought in, shoved it in my briefcase for later review, and walked through the overflowing waiting room into a warm summer day.

Hours later, when I had a few minutes to myself, I opened the envelope to find an extremely detailed description of a hysterosalpingogram. No wonder they shortened it to HSG.

I read the information with a mixture of eagerness and dread. It certainly seemed that if I suffered from an illness or a structural problem, the HSG would find it. It also seemed like the test wouldn't exactly be a walk in the park.

But, heck, I figured I had wandered around the basement of a hospital in active labor, I had hung upside down and stayed confined to bed for ten weeks, and I had delivered two children without an epidural. I could do anything.

By the day of my procedure, I had read everything I could find about what to expect. I felt physically and mentally ready for the moderate to severe uterine cramping I had learned would occur for about ten minutes but might last for hours in some women.

I knew I would be lying down on a table underneath a fluoroscope (an X-ray imager that would take pictures during the study). I knew that the radiologist would do a physical exam of my uterus and then put a speculum in my vagina. So far, so good. Not so different from a routine pelvic exam.

But as much as I had read, I wasn't prepared for what happened next. My cervix got cleaned with some freezing-cold Betadine, and the doctor inserted a cannula into the opening of my cervix. The cramping started immediately.

He then filled my uterus with a liquid containing iodine. The cramping got worse. He told me what a great job I was doing. I felt like taking one leg out of a stirrup and kicking him in the face. I didn't.

The contrast would show up as white on the pictures he took, highlighting the contour of my uterus as the liquid traveled from the cannula into the uterus and through the fallopian tubes.

HSG is often used to diagnose blocked fallopian tubes for women who are having trouble getting pregnant. The contrast is tracked up the tubes to find blockages or abnormalities.

In my case, the radiologist peering at the images of my insides looked for abnormalities inside the uterine cavity.

Thanks to the copious amounts of literature I had consumed, I wasn't surprised when the radiologist had me move around on the table so that he could get side views of my uterus.

I heard a distinct "Aahh." I immediately asked, "What? Did you find something?"

He didn't answer me, but rather snapped off his gloves and told me to get dressed.

I nervously pulled on my jeans (I had taken the day off just in case the cramping felt too distracting to work) and waited in a tiny, cheerless room to be summoned.

Instead of a nurse coming to tell me the doctor would see me, a head popped around the door. Just the radiologist's hand around the doorframe and his head and one shoulder fit into the few inches that he had swung the door open. He seemed unwilling to commit any additional part of his body to coming into the room.

"The good news is that you don't have any masses. What you do have is cervical insufficiency," stated the radiologist matter-of-factly.

"Which means what, exactly?" I asked, relieved that I didn't have cancer, but upset that I had *some*thing.

"I read in your chart that you've terminated a pregnancy, have had at least one miscarriage that you're aware of, and had two preterm births. This is entirely consistent with the HSG findings," he said, not answering my question, not telling me anything I didn't already know, and still awkwardly just leaning into the room. "I'll send my full report to Dr. Cherry."

And with that he was gone.

Remember this was 1992. Whipping out my phone and asking Siri what cervical insufficiency meant was still years away. I felt so frustrated by the doctor's abruptness that I just sat in the changing room for a while, hot tears in my eyes, to collect myself.

It would take a few days and a few sleepless nights for the call from Dr. Cherry.

"You have an incompetent cervix. Your cervix is shortened and makes it incompatible with carrying a baby to term. Now that we know what it is, if you got pregnant again, you would need a cervical cerclage early on and you might be able to carry a baby into a third trimester. But," he hastily added, "if you get pregnant again, you'll need to find another doctor to stitch you up. With your history, I wouldn't recommend it, let alone do it. We should talk about getting you back on the Pill."

His little speech left me with nothing to say. I thanked him for calling and mused on the exact wording of my diagnosis. An incompetent cervix.

Having tried to overcome the feelings of guilt that plagued me and dispel the idea that my premature births were my fault, now I got labeled with a word that meant "useless, inept, incapable." Yes, sirree, that really boosted my self-esteem.

My womb and Mars—uninhabitable.

I later learned that one of the primary causes of an incompetent cervix is a history of cervical surgery. Cervical surgery? Who, me?

Well, only if I don't count the abortion, the D&C following my miscarriage, the two laser surgeries for HPV, and the cervical cerclage I had with Ethan. I finally had my answer. For months, instead of accepting the news and moving on, I berated myself for all the ways I had been unknowingly complicit in my cervix becoming incompetent.

It took someone else's tragedy to finally put me at peace. About a year after the HSG, I ran into a colleague coming down the subway steps as I was rushing up them. In that awkward moment of indecision, when I couldn't make up my mind whether to just smile and keep on running up the stairs or stop to talk to her, something about the dark shadows beneath her eyes made me stop.

About three minutes into our conversation, she began to cry. She had been trying to conceive for many years apparently. She had finally gotten pregnant, but her baby was born at twenty-six weeks gestation. He was in the NICU for fifteen days before he died.

I gave her a warm hug, expressed my condolences, and with heartfelt apologies that I was late for a court appearance, I pulled away and left, haunted by her pain. By the time I reached the main entrance of the New York County Courthouse at 60 Centre Street, I had decided that my two miracle babies were more than enough.

46

A Doctor in the House

1966/1994

I had a rough third grade. I got scarlet fever, chicken pox, and mononucleosis all in the same school year.

Getting mono was great fun. During a class trip to a New York Mets baseball game, several of us took a drink from the same water fountain and all got sick.

Having mono, not that much fun. I remember spending long stretches in my parents' bedroom watching television but mostly napping.

One evening was a fevered blur. I remember hearing my mother say my fever was 105°F. I recall the crisp white hankie being pulled from the top right-hand drawer of the highboy dresser, the smell of a rubbing alcohol–soaked cool compress, the sound of dripping water as the cloth was dipped into a bowl of cool liquid and then gently squeezed, and the instant of shock and relief as the cool cloth made contact with my burning forehead.

My mother's ministrations notwithstanding, the fever wore on for hours. I remember my mother exclaiming, "Look who's here!" with such enthusiasm that I thought it must be Cleon Jones, my favorite New York Mets player.

Alas, instead of my baseball hero, it was Dr. Zarchay, my pediatrician. I recall seeing the black medical bag, just like the one I'd seen a million times watching a hospital soap opera on television. I loved Dr. Zarchay. He was kind, always smiled, and offered several flavor choices for the post-visit lollipop. What's not to love?

He wore "regular" clothes instead of the white coat I had always seen him wear at the office. In fact, I had never seen him *outside* the office; this first-ever house call made me feel even sicker than I already felt.

Although my mother had already taken my temperature a hundred times, the first thing he did was ask me to roll over on my side. I can still remember him telling my mother that "rectal was the most reliable." While he waited for the thermometer to do its thing, he took out his stethoscope. Although he thoughtfully rubbed it on his shirt to warm it up, it still felt icy cold against the burning skin on my back.

"Deep breath. Hold it. Breathe out. And again. Deep breath. Hold it. Breathe out." Now he moved to the front. "Breathe normally. That's it. Just breathe."

He withdrew the thermometer and as I rolled over, I could see him frowning.

"Still 105," he said to my mother, who hovered somewhere in my peripheral vision. "It's a good thing you called. Run a lukewarm bath," he added, and I saw her rush out of the room.

He asked me how I felt as he touched my throat and all around my neck. I could think of words, but I could not get them out of my dry mouth. I tried to wet my lips with my tongue, but it, too, was parched.

He put a cool hand to my head, assured me I'd be all right, and gently placed his stethoscope back in the dimpled black bag that closed with a snap.

"We need to get her fever down. Let's get her in the tub ..." I heard his voice trail off as he left the room talking to my mother.

The rest of the evening is lost to me; I recall just those few moments of Dr. Zarchay appearing at my bedside like something out of a movie.

Soon thereafter, a young doctor joined the practice and more and more of Dr. Zarchay's patients transitioned over to the new guy, Dr. Steinfeld.

Dr. Steinfeld seemed as different as could be from Dr. Zarchay. Frankly, my brother and I were afraid of him.

So, why, might you ask, when I had a choice of a dozen well-regarded pediatricians in the neighborhood, did I choose Dr. Steinfeld when we finally brought Harrison home?

Why, indeed?

Twenty-five years later and twenty-five years wiser, Dr. Steinfeld seemed to have morphed into Dr. Zarchay! I did my "interviews" with the pediatricians recommended to me by anyone and everyone. Recommendations, solicited or not, always came with the preamble "After what you have been through ..." Hands down, Dr. Steinfeld instantly won my trust.

Within three hours of leaving Mt. Sinai—after a rousing welcome home at Bea's, our favorite luncheonette, and a tearful welcome home from my mother—Harrison, Leon, and I found ourselves in Dr. Steinfeld's otherwise empty office for our first "well-baby" visit.

He had given us an appointment in the middle of a Saturday afternoon, outside of normal office hours, to be sure that Harrison didn't get exposed to any sick kids. How thoughtful was that?

Harrison looked even more miniaturized than usual when Helaine, the nurse, carefully laid him on the rounded white-enamel scale and pronounced him a whopping five pounds, fourteen ounces.

Harrison and Dr. Steinfeld became fast friends. A combination of first-time mommy jitters and legitimate fevers, ear infections, and breathing issues made us frequent visitors to the office.

I joked with Helaine (who had been Drs. Zarchay and Steinfeld's nurse when *I* was a child) that the parking spot right in front should have my name on it; surely, we were the most frequent fliers.

And when we added Ethan to the mix, my trips to Dr. Steinfeld became even more frequent.

In the thirteen months between Harrison's discharge from the hospital and the end of 1992, we visited the doctor an average of once every twelve days. There is a note in my day planner on December 29, 1992, that says, "Dr. S—32nd visit!"

All this brings me to April 1994. Both kids were sick. I took Ethan's temperature, and it was 103. I took Harrison's and the thermometer read 105. Something about that number ... 105 ... I called my mother.

"Harrison has 105," I said. Before I could utter another word, she stated with authority, "You need to call Dr. Steinfeld right away and tell him he must make a house call. That is a very dangerous temperature. You once had 105 and Dr. Zarchay was so worried he came right over."

"Mom, doctors don't make house calls these days," I told her.

"You call him right now and say that he needs to come over immediately. After everything that child has been through."

I sighed. She didn't need to finish her thought. She was super cautious about Harrison's health, and this wasn't the first time she had started or finished a sentence with "after everything that child has been through."

I hung up and called Dr. Steinfeld.

It was 10 p.m. on a Saturday night. Not expecting much, I left a message with the answering service.

Within five minutes, Dr. Steinfeld called me back. I reported that Ethan had 103 and Harrison had 105. He asked me if they were oral readings or rectal readings. I told him they were rectal readings. He said, "It's a good thing you called. Run a lukewarm bath."

Unlike Dr. Zarchay, he didn't offer to come right over; instead, he instructed us to take Harrison to the emergency room if his fever didn't go down "significantly" after the bath.

When I went back to Harrison's room to tell Leon what the doctor had said, the two of them were sitting on the floor and Harrison babbled happily.

It was hilarious in a terrifying sort of way.

Leon volunteered to get into the lukewarm bath with Harrison and Ethan. Leon's teeth were chattering, but the kids thought the whole thing was perfectly delightful.

Harrison's temperature dropped to about 102, a fever but nothing scary.

The next day, with both kids still feverish, Leon and I felt exhausted from too little sleep.

In what I think Leon considers a highlight of his life as a father, he turned on the final round of the Masters golf tournament, lay back in his recliner, with one burning hot son on each side of his chest, and the three of them took a desperately needed nap. By the time they awoke, Leon awash in sweat, both kids' temperatures were normal.

47

Incomparable Grief

1979–Present

Few things have a greater capacity to wreak emotional havoc than a loss. It cuts a swath of destruction inside your heart and your mind, the strewn wreckage caused by whatever storm you've survived—the loss of your home or a loved one—leaving in its wake a scarred landscape that only sometimes recovers fully, but more often bears telltale signs of the disaster.

Feeling emotionally bereft has been famously described by Dr. Kübler-Ross as being accompanied by five distinct stages of grieving: denial, anger, bargaining, depression, and acceptance. When she first published her theory in 1969, she described them as linear stages. This soothing notion of progression, of experiencing one stage, finishing it, and moving on to the next, felt like a salve for my brother, mother, and me after Dad's sudden death. It seemed possible that we could get to the "end," whatever the end looked like.

As the three of us learned, the stages were not linear, and we each repeated one or more stages that we thought we had "finished." My mother had Dr. Kübler-Ross's book on her nightstand for over a year after my father died, and referred to it often, perhaps increasing her despair at what she viewed as backsliding in her grieving process.

The trap of thinking that grief followed a linear path, coupled with the myth that each of us would experience grief in the same way, led the three of us to pinball off each bumper and obstacle that came along, veering off in random directions that rarely resulted in us being available to one another.

Dr. Kübler-Ross updated her writings several times over the ensuing decades to better align the five stages with how people experience them. The *Titanic* had already sailed for us, unfortunately.

But an even more destructive path developed—comparing my grief to everyone else's. Here lies the dragon.

I have lost friends, offended acquaintances, and angered strangers by indulging in this damaging—and thoroughly obnoxious—behavior.

Having my father die when both he and I were so young felt like the greatest tragedy that could ever happen, one that *ipso facto* entitled me to membership in the DPC. I derisively wrote off every other person's loss as somehow "inferior" to mine. Invariably, no matter what the loss was, I held it up against mine to see how it compared.

What I now find so shocking is that despite all objective measures, I knew people who had suffered unimaginable losses, yet I still indulged in the self-destructive process of comparison.

Examples abound.

Leon and I sat at our favorite table at our favorite restaurant, Henry's End. Our table was set against an exposed brick wall directly across from the open kitchen where the chef, Clark, prepared the food. In the early '80s, the open kitchen concept, used for decades in Japanese restaurants, sparked a sense of wonder and cachet that diners today seem to take for granted.

So there we sat, bantering now and again with Clark, while trying to focus on each other, when something set me off (it didn't take much in those days), and I started crying about Dad. I felt then, as I did many times before and after, that I lacked the fortitude to ever get over it.

This was not the first time I had subjected Leon to my drama. He always met my outbursts with empathy and patience. That night, he met my anguish with his own truth—a truth so awful that I immediately felt guilty for burdening him with my repetitive episodes of grief.

I sat transfixed as he told me how his mother, at the age of forty-four, died during a massive fire in their family home in the middle of a winter night, how he barely escaped through a basement half window with his father's help. He was eighteen and his younger brother was only ten at the time.

I know he didn't share the story of that unspeakable loss to distract me from my own grief or to jolt me out of thinking that my own tragedy could somehow compare to the depth of his. No, he told me so that I would understand that he "got it"—that he knew deep in his soul how much pain I felt. I saw on his face that telling me about his private hell came at a great cost to him. There was such love in his gesture.

Yet instead of feeling gratitude, I felt guilt. Instead of focusing on the utter tragedy of his mother's death, I thought of how it made my father's heart attack pale in comparison.

About a year or so later, Leon and I got a call from our dear friend Pichel with dreadful news. His twenty-two-year-old brother had drowned in the Pacific Ocean the night before. I couldn't imagine how this must feel. And his parents! Could there be anything worse than burying a child? In the ensuing days, at the memorial service, at the funeral, at his parents' house during their week of shiva, my mind reeled from this catastrophe. I remember thinking that this young man's death put my father's death in perspective. This death—so young, just a boy—so much worse than my father's.

Once again, indulging in that destructive need to compare.

This happened many times, usually in the opposite direction—the dragon's breath was especially fiery during those times. The friend whose father died peacefully in his eighties sobbing over coffee about her "tragedy." Me getting into my car afterward thinking about how childish and selfish her behavior was. She enjoyed her father in her life into his eighties for heaven's sake ... What made her think she could cry like this was somehow the end of the world? She danced with him at her wedding. He was there for the birth of her daughter, her daughter's birthday parties, her daughter's Bat Mitzvah and graduation from high school. I gripped the steering wheel so tightly that my knuckles turned bluish. By the time I got home, I had worked myself into a rage. Did she honestly think this was "tragic"? Sad, yes. Her father died and that's sad. But how could she think that could be compared to my losing Dad when I was only twenty-one?

Membership in the DPC was exclusive and like most clubs, there were rules. The dead parent had to be younger than fifty, tragic in and of itself. The child left behind had to be no older than twenty-one at the time of the parent's death. If neither of these criteria was met, you couldn't get into the DPC.

This irrational behavior sapped me. It took so much negative energy to be this bitter. Instead of feeling empathy and compassion, I felt envy and anger.

Decades after my father died, I received extensive, high-quality grief counseling training by professionals at the March of Dimes in preparation for a job I started with them in 2007. For the first time, I had an educational foundation that allowed me to understand the emotional roller coaster of grieving. There's nothing linear about it. It's more like ocean waves, ebbing and flowing—horrible moments, better moments, denial edging out anger, then anger overtaking denial.

My training in grief counseling was eye-opening, humbling, and in some ways humiliating for me personally, but it allowed me to do my job—supporting families with a sick or dying baby in the Neonatal Intensive Care Unit—more professionally. It also enabled me to look back on all the hardships in my life—Dad dying so young, the laser surgeries, the miscarriage, my own two terrifying NICU experiences—with a new, more forgiving perspective as well as a deep appreciation for the individuality of grief.

Most importantly, though, it reinforced what I had already learned the hard way: comparing my loss to another person's loss is a recipe for disaster.

Loss is as unique to each person as are their fingerprints. In the five years that I worked in a NICU, I met hundreds of families who grieved in hundreds of different ways. And I always tried to help them avoid the dragon's lair—avoid comparing their loss to anyone else's.

Dad's death, at once the worst and the most consequential thing that ever happened to me, taught me resilience. Without it, I don't know how I would have faced my miscarriage, or the brain bleed, or two NICU stays within a few months of each other. As German philosopher Friedrich Nietzsche pointed out, "What doesn't kill you makes you stronger." Dad's death certainly accomplished that. Not right away, but eventually.

Writing all this down has helped immeasurably. In some ways, it has allowed me to see things that I didn't see or understand before—and to discover some surprises along the way.

That both Leon and I shared membership in the DPC gave us an unspoken bond. We understood things about each other from that shared perspective. And I believe that it was our dead parents who helped us through our toughest tests. I don't mean supernatural help. Our mutual experience of losing a parent tragically, of that parent being so young, of each of us being so young—it gave us a language of understanding that needed no words.

48

The Star Athlete

2020

The eighteen-year-old hoopster staring back at me from below the fold of the college newspaper, all knees, ears, elbows, and rakish grin, bears a startling resemblance to my nephew, also eighteen years old. The headline, "Cagers to Begin 15-Game Season Tonight: Inexperienced Saxons to Clash with Highly Touted Hobart Five," questions the decision to start four first-time varsity ballers anchored by a single returning veteran.

The sportswriter briefly lists each sophomore's previous court credentials. The young man I'm eyeing—the early '50s version of my father—led the intramural league in scoring as a seventeen-year-old freshman while helping take his team to the League Championship.

As I sift through the archived newspapers from his days at Alfred University (in Alfred, New York), I'm impressed with my dad's performance as a young forward. The postgame report does little to quell my enthusiasm. In describing the Saxons' 47–38 win over the Statesmen, the sportswriter gushes, "With Printz controlling both backboards, the Saxons played possession ball and made their shots count."

I continue to comb through the digitized versions of *Fiat Lux*, the school newspaper, marveling at how quickly I can navigate through some easy filters to find everything ever written about Dad's illustrious basketball career.

What's even more remarkable to me is the newness of the information. I knew he had "played some ball" in college, but Dad had never shared with me the extent of his success.

I read the account of the game played five nights after the home opener. The Saxons narrowly lost to the Brockport Golden Eagles. I search for any mention of Dad. I'm rewarded by this account: "It was at this point that Printz collided with [a Golden Eagle] under the Alfred basket and both men fell to the ground. The injured [Golden Eagle] was taken out of the game and Printz made his foul shot."

Scrappy, too. I love reading about this! Not surprisingly, as an athlete he was willing to stand up and take the heat. That's a familiar quality to me.

When the Saxons play the Rochester Rivermen, Dad, still a young sophomore, again graces the front page of the paper. The caption roars his name in all caps scoring the final basket. I flip to the article and scan for his name.

"The second half started with a flurry of action. Printz took the opening tap and [laid] it up to give Alfred a three-point lead."

Dad is a standout in the game against Cortland, scoring the first five points of the game and turning in another solid overall performance under the boards.

I love reading about his confident progress throughout the season. In the game against Clarkson, the postgame reporter effervesces, "The surprise of the game was Harv Printz, who poured 16 points through the net and did yeoman's work under the boards. Printz, who never played with a high school or college team, was plucked by Coach McWilliams from the ranks of the intramural leagues."

Not afraid to take on a challenge, meet it head-on, and exceed expectations. As I read more about him, I'm kvelling, my heart swells with pride.

Dad completes his sophomore season with the third-highest average-per-game scoring percentage and a strong second in rebounds.

In his weekly opinion column, Marv Eisenberg positively gushes, "Saturday night also marked the entrance of another Saxon into the '100' club [scoring 100 points or more per season]. Harvey Printz in his first year of Varsity competition joined the ranks with a total of 105 ... Harv was the Team Captain four times and the [Alfs] were victorious all four times."

Leadership gets added to the list of impressive qualities I'm learning that my dad showed early on. Despite how tired I am reading the small print on my computer screen, I smile when I read that Dad received a varsity letter for the purple-and-gold Saxons.

That purple wool sweater, with a purple-and-gold "A" on it, is familiar to me. My mother used to wear it when she and I were both much younger. I recall what it meant to her—the boyfriend sweater. I have no idea how this works these days, but in the early '50s the lettermen gave their sweaters to their steady girlfriends. That was step one of the very proper dating rituals that included getting pinned (the boyfriend would give the young lady his fraternity pledge pin) and then becoming engaged.

As I think fondly of the sweater and wonder where in the world it could be, I'm eagerly scrolling to the start of Dad's junior year.

In regular season play, he breaks out against McMaster University in the tenth contest of the season. He sets the highest score for an individual in a game with an astounding twenty points. Noting that "Printz startled the exposition and probably himself" with high-scoring honors, the weekly beat writer commends Printz for also being "outstanding" under the boards. Clearly, he had a strong work ethic.

He doesn't make it into the "100" club, though, finishing his junior year with a still impressive ninety-four points. I wonder why his performance dipped that season. It isn't until I read the May issue, which mentions that he pinned a young lady named Sonny Katz, that I put two and two together. He might have been a bit distracted his junior year by the lovely woman who would become my mother and who bore a striking resemblance to a young Katharine Hepburn with a tiny waist and impossibly high cheekbones.

With my mother now in the picture, as I read on, I find myself worrying about Dad's senior year chops. I'm crestfallen when I read that he's the starting quarterback for the intramural football team. I think, *What are you doing risking your senior basketball season messing around with intramural football?*

Coach McWilliams apparently agreed, calling the first basketball practice "ragged" as the Saxons faced a tough twenty-game season. But wait, what's this? Dad, who played forward throughout his college career, is now starting as a guard? I don't understand.

I look again at the stats from last season. A young addition to the team, Millard Evak, seems to be a game changer for my dad's basketball career. Evak can shoot. In fact, he was the season scoring leader during Dad's junior year. Maybe Evak's hot hand and not my mother's charms accounts for the dip in Dad's stats?

Senior season starts. The box scores tell the story. Dad is lucky to score two points a game. And then, as I read in the December newspaper, during halftime of a game at Hofstra, Dad tosses an engagement ring up into the stands toward my mother. According to the reporter, the crowd went wild witnessing this romantic gesture.

Although Dad scored thirteen points in the win against Hobart, he isn't among the starting five for the rest of the season.

My heart sinks for Dad as he loses his starting slot. But when the season ends, Dad "letters" again, joining seven of his teammates to receive the purple "A" trimmed with gold—his third in as many seasons.

His send-off in the college paper includes another photo of him, crouched, basketball in both hands, staring intently back at me. He has my sons' eyes and my brother's and my pointy chin.

Sitting at my computer deep into the night and reading about Dad's exploits, seeing his photos as a teenager, well, it feels somehow like we're visiting each other.

Turns out, my father was a hoops star—something I didn't learn from him, but from reading these wonderful press clippings from the '50s.

He often told me that "actions speak louder than words." This takes on new meaning after the revelations of his basketball achievements. It also adds lustrous color to his advice about the importance of humility and modesty.

But the most important new perspective I have gained about my dad is how his successful basketball career informed his parenting. Throughout his career he showed the traits that would become staples of his advice to me.

His drive, his ability to overcome adversity, his willingness to "leave it all" on the court, his grit to face into the unknown and give it his absolute best and then some, his confidence that he could be excellent at anything he put his mind to, his belief that life is a team sport, his natural tendency to demand more of himself, the tough exterior that protected the heart of a hopeless romantic—all these things make more sense to me now that I understand his basketball career.

Although he might have approved of Woody Allen's observation that 80 percent of success is just showing up, Dad believed that the secret to real success lies in the other 20 percent.

My father strived to dwell in the space that separates the good from the excellent, the competent from the extraordinary. And he expected me to be right there with him.

He was the father who looked down at the "A" on my test and asked, "Why not an A+?"

49

Candy's Room Revisited

March 2023

The global pandemic that killed millions was demoted (graduated) to being endemic. Less of a killer, unless your loved ones happened to succumb to it, it became more of a disrupter with the threat of being lethal.

Leon and I, accidentally dressed alike in black jeans and black shirts, stood in the Wells Fargo Arena in Philadelphia at a Bruce Springsteen concert. The rock idol and the E Street Band had canceled the three concerts immediately preceding this one due to COVID.

My first time in a large, enclosed space without wearing an N95 mask made me feel vulnerable and exposed. Looking around at the capacity crowd though, I figured most folks must have felt that the reward outweighed the risk. Their maskless faces radiated excitement.

Seeing Springsteen for something like the fifteenth time did nothing to dampen my enthusiasm. The set lists were published for each of the shows Springsteen did in the weeks since he had started this tour, and several of his most popular hits had been featured night after night. I felt excited to be doing something so normal after three years of government and then self-imposed captivity.

When the houselights went down, a lone spotlight lit the stage. One by one the members of the band emerged into that white light to thunderous applause. "The Boss" emerged last, to a greeting befitting his stardom. But rather than bask in it, he swung the guitar slung over his shoulder and we were off.

Being at a Springsteen concert feels like hurtling down a ski slope that's just a tiny bit too steep for me. Barely past the crest of the slope, within seconds of pointing my skis downward, I pick up speed, my heart starts to race as I give myself up to the slope and the rush of flying down, in control, but on the edge of it. Time speeds up and slows down simultaneously. I see the path down, know where to turn and when to let gravity take over. I see every bough sticking up through the snow, every tiny patch of ice that I know will catch an edge, every bit of litter that makes me curse the disrespect of people who care little about the pristine beauty of nature. And in what feels like an instant, it's over. I reach the bottom, pulse thrumming in my ears, exhilarated, exhausted, eager to do it again.

Leon and I grin at each other as we join the thousands of other voices committing to the promise of "no retreat, baby, no surrender," and I feel much younger than my sixty-four years.

During "Prove It All Night," Leon and I sing to each other, "I'll prove it all night for your love," exchanging a look that needs no explanation. It's muscle memory that makes me reach for his hand, shout the repeated refrain, and occasionally bump my hips into his as best as the small aisle space allows. When Springsteen belts his warning, "Girl, you want it, you take it, you pay the price," my husband flashes me his best "come-hith-er" smile with a wicked twinkle in his eyes, and I feel that rush, that same surge of excitement that has overcome me the hundreds of times Leon and I have made love to this song.

A subtle change in the lights leaves the stage mostly shrouded in shadows but for the spotlight over Max Weinberg's head as the drummer brushes the opening notes of the one song I have come to hear. Max is bathed in blue light, his drumsticks calling out to me. I wonder how many people in the Wells Fargo Arena can name this tune after hearing just those first few gentle sounds. I don't have to look at Leon. I know he's one of those people.

But I look at him anyway. I look at him for every instant of this song, my throat filling with tears, mostly of gratitude for the hunger I see in my husband's eyes, a hunger that burns with the same intensity that it did that very first time I danced naked for him on the dresser in his apartment, channeling Candy, letting my inhibitions slip away as I twirled, catching a glimpse of that other girl in the mirror, breathlessly leaping across the space between us, and just as I did back in 1980, I now feel his desire as we press against each other, fusing ourselves together as his lips brush my ear and he and Springsteen sing, to me:

She knows that I'd give
All that I got to give
All that I want, all that I live
To make Candy mine
Tonight

I close my eyes as Leon kisses me, I feel the thrill deep in my body that only he can make me feel, the same thrill I felt during that first unforgettable kiss on the subway platform in Borough Hall. I shudder in Leon's arms and gaze into the blue-green eyes of my Rogue Prince.

50

Another Consequential Flag

Fall 1993/2023

About the pesky Brain Bleed. Weeks went by, then months. Eighty-five days passed from Harrison's terrifying birth to the day we got to take him home. The final head sonogram prior to discharge revealed nothing—no bleeding, no swelling. I wanted to relax. I tried to relax. I couldn't relax.

The Saturday morning Harrison left the hospital, we immediately took him to Bea's to celebrate. The cook/owner, the waitstaff, everyone crowded around our booth in the back, as our tiny Harrison, all five pounds of him, lay rocking in his removable car seat in the center of the table.

By the time we got home, my mother, who had been wearing out a spot on the floor waiting for us, seemed unable to decide if she should show righteous anger because we had taken Harrison to Bea's—"God knows what kind of germs he got exposed to"—or joyous relief—"Thank God! I prayed to your father every night for this day!" She settled on speechless tears, gazing adoringly at her first grandchild.

After discharge we were referred to the "preemie clinic," an outpatient follow-up program that regularly monitors developmental progress in premature infants.

Each appointment took on mystical significance. The intense anticipation and stress surrounding them kept my husband and me awake the night before each one. Yes, our son was gaining weight and getting taller right on target with his preemie-adjusted milestones. But we wondered aloud, recalling the covert characteristics of the grade 3 bleed, whether there could still be something.

One morning at the preemie clinic, the doctor did a flash card exercise with our two-year-old son. There were cartoon drawings of common objects arrayed in groups of three in front of him. Since Harrison was still preverbal, the doctor asked him to point to a specific object—a car, a tree, a dog, a house, a chair, a train. He sailed along until one card in one array stumped him. The doctor changed the array three more times and in each of the four arrays, our son couldn't identify that one card.

The doctor looked somber when he delivered his assessment. "I'm concerned that on four attempts he was unable to identify a flag."

"A flag?!?" I exclaimed. "He doesn't even know what a flag is!"

"Still," continued the doctor, "we need to keep an eye on this. Can he follow complex commands?"

Both Leon and I shrugged. Had we ever even given him a complex command?

That weekend, I was folding laundry when Harrison crawled over and pulled on my sweatpants leg. My arms filled with laundry, I turned to put the pile down so I could pick him up. In that split second, I looked down, and there he was, already halfway across the kitchen, pushing his favorite stuffed Thomas the Tank Engine pillow. He stopped, looked back at me, flashed a brilliant smile, and resumed his crawling.

I followed him out of the kitchen, through the dining room, across the foyer, past the living room, and into the sunroom where my husband sat reading the newspaper.

Our son reached Leon and tapped his leg. When my husband looked down, Harrison turned around and pointed at me.

My husband beamed. "Yes," he said in answer to the question posed several days earlier. "He can follow complex commands. I told him to go get Thomas, find Mommy, and bring her here."

I didn't need any more convincing that we could put the Brain Bleed behind us. Not so for Leon. His watchful waiting lasted for years. He blamed every hiccup in our son's development on it.

Our son was about six when Leon got far enough past that fear to joke about it. When Harrison whiffed three times at T-ball, my husband turned to me and said with a smile, "Must be the Brain Bleed."

This all comes flooding back to me as I trudge gratefully up a mountain trail, hiking behind Harrison's broad shoulders and long, confident stride. He is now thirty-three years old, six feet four, and an accomplished professional—and I know that time has rendered its verdict.

Brains bleed.

Sometimes, as Dr. Green told us that morning all those years ago, we can't explain why, but everything turns out fine.

As we climb, the early morning sun blinding us as we negotiate our way up a winding staircase in Sequoia National Park, I'm confidently ascending, knowing that Harrison leads the way and that Ethan has my back.

I'm exactly where I want to be, where I need to be, book-ended by these two extraordinary human beings—Harrison, who tenaciously defied and overcame the challenges of being an extremely preterm, very low birth weight male, and Ethan, who forced his pro-choice mom to choose life, and deliver him safely into the world in spite of the slimmest odds. We've hiked at over forty national parks, Harrison, Ethan, and I. It's an annual tradition we started in 1997, and we'd be much closer to the brass ring of sixty-three had we not gone back to revisit our favorite ones so many times.

It's no secret that this is the highlight of each year, these days alone with my little boys, adolescents, teens, young men, and now, undeniably, adults. We leave Leon behind to hit golf balls to his heart's content, while the three of us venture out into the beauty of America.

Harrison is principled, deeply thoughtful, and has a moral compass that always points true north. He carries himself with quiet dignity, is an empathetic listener, and has a loving and giving heart. He is extremely involved in a nonprofit that provides access to affordable capital for historically marginalized small businesses, chairs the board of a nonprofit that offers low-cost capital to regenerative farmers and food entrepreneurs, and has an abiding love for democracy. The only "tell" that he started his life thirteen weeks too early is that he lacks the fine motor skills to thread a needle. Or he's just using his alleged lack of fine motor skills as an excuse to avoid sewing on that missing shirt button.

Ethan, recently married to a fellow computational linguist, works on the sustainability team at a Fortune 25 company. In addition to his passion for helping make a difference in climate change, he has acted, worked crew, sung in many formal and informal a cappella groups, arranged music, and conducted, and has otherwise led an exemplary life. He is kind, gentle, and staggeringly smart. About the only thing I can point to that ever hinted at his humble beginnings was the time he ate beach sand—for an entire summer.

It surprises me still to see the shock on the faces of people who meet my grown, extraordinary, accomplished sons when they learn they were born thirteen and twelve weeks early.

Where the miracle stops, and medicine starts, is a fuzzy place. All I know for sure is that without the miracle or medicine, Harrison and Ethan might never have lived to see.

Aunt Vi's words are with me still. *Ozmer lebt, derle'bt.* If you live, you live to see.

Epilogue

Some daughters arrive on the planet, and with one loving, wondrous look, instantly become Daddy's Girl. Bible stories, mythology, folklore, books, songs, and movies have all dealt with the phenomenon. In my case, the less glamorized clinical definition is spot-on—girls who have an extremely strong bond with their fathers.

This comes as no surprise to those who knew my father and me. My mother *kvelled* in how close Dad and I were, and one might say, still are.

My parents tragically lost a son before I came along, and I always suspected that while my father was truly ahead of his time as an egalitarian thinker, another factor in our tight connection might have been that he treated me like the boy he had lost as his eldest child.

He taught me to shoot hoops, play Wiffle ball, dig for worms, bait a hook, catch a fish, play two-hand touch, climb trees, and tinker at our basement workbench in a crowded, damp, and overheated space that served triple duty as the boiler room, the tool room, and the laundry room.

He also brought me the first baby doll with eyes that opened and closed, long eyelashes, and a soft, squeezable body I loved cuddling. And I will never forget the afternoon he walked off the jet bridge—those being the days you were allowed to meet passengers at the gate—with a stuffed black-and-white teddy bear that easily outweighed me by twenty pounds.

Dad read voraciously, had a dictionary for a mind, and manifested a penchant for all things World War II. He loved to be outside, especially in the woods, and he appreciated and felt awed by nature. He played basketball, golf, and tennis avidly and well. He smoked Kent 100s—"a dirty, filthy habit" he'd often say before lighting up—put Brylcreem in his comb-over hairdo, kept Harvey's Bristol Cream Sherry in the liquor cabinet for my mother, and wore Canoe aftershave.

Super competitive, but always kind, he turned nearly everything into a game. His fondness for Boggle, Scrabble, the license plate game (which I know he did not invent, but I always thought he did), and crossword puzzles made me a precocious child.

I will not be the last daughter to attempt to explain the complex dynamic that makes my relationship with my father singular. And by no means do I intend to imply that he didn't have a uniquely special bond with my brother, Robert, too. He did. An amazing one.

Part of what made him such an incomparable person lay in his ability to make all of us who shared his air feel that our relationship was exceptional to him.

Of course, relationships are constructed of moments. Often, we recall the spectacular moments with such vivid clarity that we place disproportionate importance on them. Yet, the mundane, daily moments often provide greater meaning than do the outstanding ones.

When I reflect on what made my relationship with my father so special to me, there are indeed many extraordinary experiences we shared. But I think the secret to our bond lies in what happened during the everyday moments. What I learned during those moments as his daughter shaped me in many ways, most profoundly as a mother.

Dad, a regular guy who did nothing famously earth-shattering, had undeniable flaws. He was, however, an exceptional father, who took his job as "mentor in chief" seriously. Unquestionably, he had an outsize impact on my world *and* our family universe. There are thousands of examples, just a few of them recounted here, but they cannot do justice to my memory of him and all the many gifts he gave me.

His legacy lies in how I live his values and pass them along to my children—and hopefully how they pass them on to their children. I certainly didn't get what I wanted when I became a member of the Dead Parent Club, but to paraphrase the Rolling Stones, when I try sometimes, (most of the time) I find I got what I need.

And the Rogue Prince and me? We just had our fortieth wedding anniversary, a milestone that neither of our parents got to celebrate. We each acknowledged our birthdays with reverence and humility in the years we turned the ages that his mother and my father had been when they died.

I can't speak for Leon, but I think of my father every day, usually more than once. Sometimes wistfully, other times angrily, but all the time with love.

As for me, my life is the epitome of the amended version of the Big Lie. I'll call it the Bigger Truth. You can have it all, just not all at the same time.

I had the huge career. After practicing my craft at the top of my profession, it felt like such a relief to step off that constantly turning hamster wheel, even though it was housed in a gilded cage.

Harrison and Ethan were five and four when I left my practice, the trailing spouse when Leon took a job across the country. I discovered that despite the cases I had won, the well-known people I had represented, the opposing counsels who were household names, I no longer wanted to be a part of hostile legal battles that left the children trapped in the middle. It was only after having my own children, knowing that I would do anything to spare them from pain, feeling so much raw love for them, that I started questioning my chosen profession.

I simply couldn't understand how any parent could put their children through the knock-down, drag-out fights that many of my clients did. I mean the petty arguments about sending the kids for "Dad's weekend" without the soccer shoes the mother knew the children needed for their games on Saturday.

Or the father who deliberately removed the permission slip for a class trip from his son's backpack just so he could embarrass the poor kid's mother. Or the couple who got divorced, sold the house and everything in it while their daughter was away at camp, then sent a driver to pick her up and bring her to her new "home" without ever telling her what they had done or where she was being taken.

Becoming a mother made all that meanness seem meaningless and destructive. Becoming a mother made being a divorce lawyer feel like I was a paid accomplice to psychological warfare.

Yes, there was glamor when our firm was featured in a popular glossy magazine, or when I won a case that headlined in the *New York Law Journal*, or when an article I wrote was published in the *Family Lawyer Magazine*. But all of that was flash compared to the next job I had.

Of all the many hats I've worn, "Mom" is by far my favorite and the most rewarding.

That's not to say that it was all smooth sailing. I've made mistakes along the way. For years it was a running joke that the kids were having a necklace made for me with the initials MM for "Meanest Mom."

I am incredibly fortunate. I have lived a life of privilege that is not available to everyone. I don't ever take for granted that I got to have it all (just not at the same time). I know there are women who will never get the opportunity to have even *some* of that, but who deserve the opportunity to have it *all*.

I learned many things from the man whose death earned me membership in the DPC. These are some of the most important:

Be a confident and passionate voice for the voiceless, whether it's for battered wives, abused children, or dangerously tiny infants.

Be your own advocate, to live to see, and to speak the truth of what you see.

Always do the right thing.

Never get "outhustled."

Be a leader—or as Leon would say, "Never be ashamed to be first on the buffet line."

Acknowledgments

I didn't set out to write a deeply personal memoir. Initially, my sole intent was to write every day for a year, an aspirational goal born out of a four-week course designed for adults who want to figure out what they want to be when they grow up.

I am grateful to Professor Jon Pineda, at William & Mary, who provided me with early encouragement to keep writing and suggested that I consider turning my attempts at essay writing into a full-length book.

My "professional" readers were candid and inspiring. The quality of this book was enhanced by the thoughtful initial readings and reviews I received from Ellen Bonbright, Debra Morgenstern Katz, Amy Jaffe Barzach, Suzanne Raitt, Jay B. Gissen and Loren Chodosh Harkin.

My wonderful family and friends, whether they read bits and pieces or multiple drafts, provided invaluable insights, helped me see my blind spots, and pushed me to dig deeper. Rick Shapiro, Ronna Brown, Sandy Wright, John Anelli, and Sara Long each helped improve this work.

Kiper Prince, a truly singular person, helped me consider death from a completely different perspective. During his regular and ritualistic cataloging of birth dates and ages of people and pets I love, he quite simply describes the dead as having gone "back to nature." Such a lovely way to think about it.

Joan Parchment, a constantly sunny person who was part parent, part magician, and part Mary Poppins, taught me not only how to be a mother, but how to be a better mother.

The men her "handsome boys" grew into is in large measure because of her loving care of them.

My brother, Robert, was wildly enthusiastic about this book. As an eyewitness to most of what happened during my life, that he never told me I had my facts wrong is a testament to his loyalty.

My father, Harvey Printz, physically present for my first twenty-one years, but with me always, gives me inspiration, guidance, and curiosity. As the first man to capture my heart and the first man to truly break it, I love him for everything he gave me and mourn for everything we missed by his way-too-early exit.

My ninety-two-year-old mother, Sonny Printz née Katz, has given me everything else. A widow for almost twice as long as she was a wife, she has an inspiring and indomitable spirit. She gives me unconditional love and kindness, shows the strength of character to always do the right thing (especially when nobody is watching), and is unfailingly nice to everyone. By her example, she has taught me perseverance, independence, gratitude, and the perpetuation of her unshakable belief that there is nothing more important than family and having a warm winter coat.

Ethan and Harrison shared their advice, their love, their support, and their generous consent to allow me to tell our stories. They were honest with their feedback and never let me get away with anything less than my best effort. Each of them, fighters from the start, taught me to respect the fact that the will to live can often be stronger than the best medicine.

And, of course, my Rogue Prince, Leon, who once thought of me as one of his many "wham, bam, thank you, ma'am" playthings, became my life's partner and one true love. After littering Brooklyn Heights with the tatters of my broken heart, he picked up all the pieces and fitted them lovingly and carefully back together. Forty years, two cats, four dogs, one miscarriage, two preemies, too many funerals, plenty of weddings, some tears, more laughter, and several careers later,

I don't think I'm premature in predicting that we're in it for the long haul.

Last, but certainly not least, the medical team at Mt. Sinai Hospital in New York City are the heroes of this story. Without their dedication, skilled care, and vigilance, Harrison, Ethan, and this book would have had a vastly different outcome. Of all the places we could have landed, I am grateful every day that it was in their collective capable hands.

Endnotes

Snippets of lyrics of several songs (and one poem) are referenced in this book for solely illustrative purposes. The titles of these works and their authors are listed below.

Chapter 10

"The Future's So Bright, I Gotta Wear Shades"
Words and Music by Pat McDonald
© 1986

"The Road Not Taken" by Robert Frost
@ 1915

Chapter 18

"Love Is Blue"
Words and Music by Pierre Lemaire [Pierre Cour]/André
    Popp/Bryan Blackburn
© 1964 Copyright Renewed

"Love Story (Theme)"
Words and Music by Francis Lai and Carl Sigman
© 1970 Copyright Renewed

"As Time Goes By"
Words and Music by Herman Hupfeld
© 1931 Copyright Renewed

"Sunny"
Words and Music by Bobby Hebb
© 1966 Copyright Renewed

"Leave Me Alone (Ruby Red Dress)"
Words and Music by Linda Laurie
© 1973 Copyright Renewed

"Raindrops Keep Falling On My Head"
Words and Music by Burt Bachrach and Hal David
© 1969 Copyright Renewed

Chapter 29

"Alice's Restaurant Massacree"
Words and Music by Arlo Guthrie
© 1967 Copyright Renewed

Chapter 49

"No Surrender"
Words and Music by Bruce Springsteen
© 1983 Sony Music Publishing (US) LLC and Eldridge Publishing Co.
All Rights Administered by Sony Music Publishing (US) LLC, 424 Church Street, Suite 1200, Nashville, TN 37219
International Copyright Secured All Rights Reserved

"Prove It All Night"
Words and Music by Bruce Springsteen
Copyright © 1978 Sony Music Publishing (US) LLC and El-
    dridge Publishing Co.
Copyright Renewed
All Rights Administered by Sony Music Publishing (US) LLC,
    424 Church Street, Suite 1200, Nashville, TN 37219
International Copyright Secured All Rights Reserved

Acknowledgments

"Suffragette City"
Words and Music by David Bowie
© 1972 Copyright Renewed

About the Author

Lisa Printz Roday is a former matrimonial lawyer who practiced in New York City for nearly 15 years. After relocating to Virginia in 1997, she created the March of Dimes NICU Family Support Program at one of the busiest neonatal intensive care units in Central Virginia. As its first Specialist, for over five years Ms. Printz brought her personal experiences as a NICU parent to the role and became an invaluable bridge between parents and the medical team. Her work earned her recognition as the Virginia March of Dimes Employee of the Year. Her data-driven efforts to enhance the use of skin-to-skin contact between new parents and their tiny infants, also known as kangaroo care, resulted in an award-winning, published abstract and became the standard of care in hospitals nationwide. Ms. Printz has been an entrepreneur and business owner since 2011. In addition, she has nearly four decades of non-profit board experience. She lives in Henrico, Virginia with her husband.

www.lisaprintzroday.com